It's No Sin
to Make a Profit

It's No Sin
to Make a Profit

JOHN BLOOM

W. H. Allen
London & New York
1971

First published, January 1971
Printed in Great Britain by
Northumberland Press Ltd., Gateshead
for the publishers W. H. Allen & Co. Ltd.,
Essex Street, London WC2R 3JG
Bound at Bungay by
Richard Clay (The Chaucer Press) Ltd.

ISBN 0 491 00076 6

For Anne

Illustrations appear following
pages 96 and 192

1

THE DAY WAS FRIDAY JULY 17TH 1964. THE PLACE WAS THE holiday resort of Sunny Beach, Bulgaria. The time was five past seven. I was standing on a jetty in the warm evening sunshine waiting for a speed-boat to take me out to my £330,000 yacht anchored in the bay.

As the boat arrived a messenger rushed up to me and pushed a piece of paper into my hands. It contained two Telex messages which the appalling Bulgarian communications system had delayed for several hours.

The first message was from my fellow directors on the board of Rolls Razor, the washing machine company which I had made into a household name and which, in turn, had made me a multi-millionaire. It read: 'We have been trying to send this message for ages. Urgent urgent urgent you phone at once. If you cannot phone by 3.39 British Summer Time this afternoon, irrevocable decisions will have been taken.'

The information had reached me hours too late. In London, 1,200 miles from the Black Sea coast, those irrevocable decisions would already have been taken. As the speed-boat waited, my eye travelled down the piece of paper. It half took in a comic-opera exchange between Telex operators: 'Can we have the message in English?' the Bulgarians had asked. 'We are waiting.'

'We have sent you the message in English,' was the laconic reply.

At the bottom of the sheet was a message which had been sent later by my assistant, Harvey Langer. It read simply:

'Press and Stock Exchange have been advised that the company has been put into voluntary liquidation.'

The information was blindingly simple. Rolls had collapsed. Nine months earlier the company was valued at £13 million and the shares had been changing hands at 47s 10½d. That afternoon, after the board's announcement, those same shares could be bought for a shilling.

As I stepped into the speed-boat, I was in a sort of coma. I knew, of course, that the company had been unable to keep its sales target of 8,000 washing machines a week. I knew that the free gifts and the enormous amount of advertising had been gobbling up the profit margins. I knew that we had become short of cash for meeting our bills. But I also knew, or thought I did, that this was being remedied.

I had hoped, before I left for Bulgaria to check up on the operation of my package deal holidays, that Sir Isaac Wolfson would put over a million pounds into Rolls and that I would take over as chairman—a position which had been vacant since the resignation of Richard Reader Harris, M.P. a few weeks earlier. I had agreed to do this in a phone conversation on Monday night with Malcolm Cass, my brother-in-law and a Rolls director. We had discussed the whole reorganisation of finances and of the board. On the Wednesday—only two days before the collapse of Rolls—I had received a message from Malcolm which said: 'Everything proceeding as discussed Monday evening.' And the next day he Telexed to say that the question could not be finally settled until the following Monday when I was to attend a board meeting. Yet within 24 hours of this last message the board had decided to wrap up the entire Rolls empire. They had obviously acted hastily and under great pressure. What had been going on?

When I reached my yacht I found my wife Anne as confused and distressed as I was. She had heard the news from the yacht's captain, Don Christie. He had been listening to the BBC's overseas service on his Japanese transistor earlier in the afternoon and had gone to her cabin to say: 'I think they've just said Rolls shares have dropped to 1s 3d.' Anne had said: 'Oh no, that can't be right. They've probably fallen a bit because the postal strike

8

has been stopping inquiries from customers.' She told me she had not thought any more about it until Christie arrived again at seven o'clock to say: 'It's right. The company's crashed.'

Anne said she instinctively rushed to the window to see if I was on my way back to the yacht. She was just in time to see the messenger deliver the fateful Telex messages. The news had reached her through the radio about a minute before it reached me on the so-called Telex hot line.

I was so bewildered that I hardly knew what I was doing. I decided to go to bed and I just lay there for the next day and a half, wondering if anything could be done to save the situation, thinking about the fate of my other inter-dependent company, English and Overseas Investments, which ran enterprises such as the package holidays and TV rentals. Its shares had been 52s at their zenith and had, I later learned, plummeted to about 4s on the news of the Rolls crash.

Ironically the yacht was decked out with drinks and food for a cocktail party we were due to give that evening for hotel managers, head waiters and officials from the government Balkantourist organisation. My trip ashore that day had been to see if anyone on my tours was dissatisfied, and the party had been planned so that I could tell the Bulgarians how to handle English people and to deal with any grievances of which I had been notified. But now, there could be no question of 'the show must go on'. There no longer appeared to be any show. And there was no time to be nice to people and let them know that the party was cancelled. I simply ordered all the food and drink to be swept away and told Christie that I had to sail along the coast to the resort of Golden Sands at once. Sunny Beach had no direct communications with London, whereas there was a government telecommunications office at Golden Sands. And it was imperative that I should talk to somebody in London as quickly as possible.

We set sail even though the seas were rough and reached our destination a few hours later. I was still in bed so Anne had to become my messenger, and for the rest of our time in Bulgaria she put in a fantastic amount of work in trying to hold everything and everybody together. Although it was dark

9

by the time we anchored off Golden Sands and the sea was still rough she went ashore, with the mate, in the speed-boat. The Balkantourist people were just as shattered as we were by the crash but they were extremely helpful. If they had severed connections with us, as so many fair-weather friends did in the next few days, we would almost literally have been stranded.

Anne booked several calls to people in London but she was told that, as usual, there was a delay of several hours so she came back to the yacht. Later, she and the mate went back ashore, with the seas getting rougher all the time, and waited into the early hours for one of her calls to come through. Eventually she managed to speak to her brother Malcolm. We learnt that he had not been at the board meeting which had put Rolls into voluntary liquidation but, as my accountant, he said that if I could get back to London by Monday as planned the firm might still be rescued.

It turned out that the next plane I could get was on the Sunday—an ordinary tourist flight to Ostend. We told the government tourist officials that we would like to be on it. However I felt sure that the Press would descend on Bulgaria in vast numbers and I did not want to speak to anyone until I had contacted people at Rolls to find out exactly what was going on and what we could do next. So I was left with the problem of what to do with myself during the next 24 hours. The Bulgarians advised me to pull the yacht out of Golden Sands and hop along the coast to a tiny secluded bay where no tourist ever set foot and where I would be completely hidden. And so, at the height of the crisis, I was in the totally unreal situation of being in bed aboard a yacht hidden along the Black Sea coast and unable to contact the rest of the world.

However it seemed as if the rest of the world was trying to contact me; my fears about the Press had been well-founded. Hundreds of journalists had traced me to Bulgaria and were working hard to narrow the field. I was again grateful that the Bulgarian government were batting on my side. They were telling the journalists that they believed I was in Sophia, or Sunny Beach or anywhere that would waste vital time. Anne again went to the Golden Sands telecommunications centre to try and raise people in London and to organise our trip home. While she was there she found herself in the bizarre position of helping local officials to fob off the Press. She took several incoming telephone calls and, putting on a thick pseudo-Bulgarian accent, she told them she was sorry but Mr Bloom was certainly not in Golden Sands.

Although I managed to dodge the Press all that day it did not help much in the long run. Instead of the garbled interviews I was trying to avoid for the sake of the company's future, the British Sunday papers were full of 'Where is Bloom?' stories—making a meal of speculation about my whereabouts and exhorting me to return at once. These tales were extremely damaging to me and the company and undoubtedly killed any remaining chance of saving Rolls.

On the Sunday the Bulgarians laid on one of their huge black Zim limousines with curtained windows to take Anne and me to Golden Sands airport. We were driven right on to the tarmac and we climbed into a part of the plane which had been specially sealed off from the home-going tourists. With all this secret service stuff in the best Iron Curtain manner, they must have wondered who they had aboard.

When we reached Ostend Anne and I were met by Harvey Langer and the Rolls accountant Toby Hoffman. Langer said he thought we had managed to throw everyone off the scent except for Tom Mangold—then of the *Daily Express*, now of the BBC—who was at the airport. I knew that once Mangold found out where I was he would stick with me. He was up to all the dodges and would probably have on hand everything from a charter aircraft to a spare toothbrush. Langer had arranged to take us across the Channel in a private charter plane which stood a few hundred yards away down the tarmac. He had also arranged to dispense with customs. But it was still going to be a problem for Anne and me to swop planes with Mangold on the lookout. Then I thought of a way out. I told Langer to make a telephone call to the airport pretending to be the *Daily Express* and to ask them to put out a Tannhoy call for Mangold. We watched Langer disappear, heard the sweet sound of the Tannhoy call and then, giving Mangold time to get to the phone, Anne and I nipped smartly across the tarmac on to our second plane.

During the flight I picked up more details about the company's collapse and discussed with Toby Hoffman the possible escape routes that were still open. But there was more desperation than optimism. We landed at Stanstead in Essex to clear customs and then did a short flip over to Elstree for a final landing. Ronnie Pressman, another of my assistants, was standing by with a car—but there was not a sign of any newspaper or TV men, then or later as we reached and drove into the West End. If my mind had not been concentrating on other things it would have been a satisfying thought: the might of the British Press was scouring Europe for us and there we were, driving along Park Lane. When we got to Aldford House, of course, the story was different. There seemed to be a hundred or more reporters, photographers, TV cameramen and technical crews waiting in a desultory manner on the pavement. When Anne and I drew up they suddenly surged into frenzied action. There was a tumult of shouts as we pushed through the mob and raced down the hallway to the sanctuary of the lift at the bottom end. And as the lift gate closed, our last sight was of commissionaires struggling to keep back a tide of newsmen.

That night in my flat I had endless hours of talks with accountants, lawyers and financiers, but no convincing solution emerged. The phone was ringing continuously but I refused to speak to anybody. Then at about two o'clock on Monday morning, after everyone had left, it rang once more and I picked it up to find I was talking to William Davis, City editor of the *Evening Standard* and now editor of *Punch*. He asked me if he could put some questions to me and I said: 'All right.' He must have fallen off his chair. Because he happened to telephone at what must have been the right psychological moment he had got exclusively the interview which his rivals had been trying to get for almost three days.

Looking back at his story it is interesting to note my attitude at that moment. I was, as he described me, 'weary and subdued' and I did say that although I wanted to do my best for the public, 'I don't see what can be done now to save Rolls Razor.' On the other hand I told him I still thought that the public had confidence in me. 'I have always given them value for money,' I said. 'They know that.'

Unfortunately no such confidence extended to the City or to the Rolls creditors. Following the board's announcement on Friday the banks and everyone else were clamouring for their money. The damage had been done. The token attempts to save the company had virtually been doomed from their frenzied beginnings.

The next day—Monday July 20th—I attended an Extraordinary Meeting of the Rolls board. At 2.39 in the afternoon a statement was issued. It read: 'At the meeting this morning Mr Bloom and all the other directors expressed their agreement with the action taken by the board at its meeting on Friday and confirmed that steps should be taken as soon as possible to place the company in a creditor's voluntary winding-up.'

It was a bald epitaph.

2

I NEVER SET OUT TO MAKE MILLIONS. I NEVER THOUGHT IT WAS possible until the washing machine idea turned into a winner overnight. But, even as a boy in the East End of London, I was always on the lookout for ways of making a few shillings.

I was born in 1931 when my parents were living in a tiny terraced house in Nelson Street, not far from the docks. My father Sam, who was born in Poland, was working as a jobbing tailor in one of the streets behind the busy Commercial Road. There was not a lot of money coming in, but by the time war broke out we had somehow saved enough to move a few miles north to a semi-detached in St Kilda's Road, Stoke Newington.

However, it was hardly the last word in luxury and we were still pretty cramped. My mother and father had one bedroom, my younger sister Noreen had another and in the third bedroom we had my uncle Sam and aunt Eva. I lived in the combined dining room and bedroom downstairs.

While I was at the local primary school I used to sell marbles, which helped to eke out my pocket money, but after I started going to Hackney Downs Grammar School I hit on one or two rather more profitable schemes.

The first was selling fireworks—which at that time, the end of the war, were very scarce. When Guy Fawkes day came round, only a few shops had them, and you had to queue for hours after school to get any. Most boys were not prepared to do this, but I was—if I was going to make money out of it. So I stood in the cold, bought the fireworks for 1d each and sold them next day for 3d. Then one morning, for a joke, someone dropped a match in the satchel in which I was carrying my fireworks and blew the whole lot sky high. Very colourful, but not very funny.

I never sold fireworks after that. Instead, I concentrated on another enterprise. I had built up quite a posse of American pen friends and I found that there was a ready market for all the things they used to send me in return for English magazines and souvenirs. I sold chewing gum and bars of chocolate—which were still rationed in England—comics, and more exotic items such as ties which glowed at night with the command, 'Kiss Me'. This little business thrived right up to the time that I left school.

My departure from Hackney Downs was rather inglorious. I was quite bright at maths and English but, on the whole, my academic career had been less than brilliant. My reports always used to say things like: 'Could do better if he tried harder' and 'Should apply himself more'. I am sure some of the teachers wondered how I had ever passed the entrance exam.

The headmaster, however, certainly did not wonder whether I would pass my Matriculation exams. He was convinced that I would fail—and he called my father to the school to tell him so. He then asked him to remove me as I would only be wasting my time by staying on. My father took his word for it and at the age of 16 I was knocking on the counter of the local Labour Exchange.

They had no jobs in the area, so I wrote a few letters myself and managed to land a junior salesman's job at Selfridges. It was in the domestic appliances and hardware department in the basement. I was getting £2-odd a week. Among the things I was selling were refrigerators and washing machines, both of which were luxuries in those days. After a few months, I decided to get a small rise by becoming a clerk in the Press office at the Board of Deputies of British Jews, where I stayed until my national service in the RAF in 1950.

By a strange coincidence, these first jobs turned out to be grass-roots experience in the fields in which I was to specialise —washing machines and publicity.

Shortly before I went into the RAF I managed to scrape through my driving test, and, to celebrate, I bought a 1929 Austin Seven for £29. I always remember the number, HX 2104. I decided to go round Europe in it with a friend of mine called Leslie Goldbart.

We dropped another friend off in France, then drove into Switzerland and down the St Gotthard pass into Italy. My knowledge of driving was still so poor that, instead of going down the pass in low gear, I put the Austin into neutral and used the brake all the way down. The next time I tried to stop, the car just kept going. The brakes were almost completely burned out.

I learned to live with this slight inconvenience and we continued our travels in comparative safety until our last night in Europe when we were driving to Ostend. Somehow, my concentration failed and I found myself on the wrong side of the road with a pair of huge headlights rushing towards me. At the last minute, I swerved and felt a tremendous crunch. I kept going. I knew that, at £29, I could afford to write off the Austin completely if necessary. But I felt I must have cut up the other car considerably and did not relish facing the wrath of the driver.

After a few hundred yards I turned off into a natural lay-by in a dip and switched my lights off. I was just in time. Down the road we saw a huge American saloon swing round in the road and start to give chase. We crossed our fingers and the car roared straight past us into the darkness.

Soon after this I was hauled into the RAF and sent to West Kirby, near Liverpool, for my square-bashing. It was bitterly cold the day that a trainload of us arrived at the local station, and we were delighted to find a batch of lorries waiting. This delight was short-lived, however. After we had all sprinted across to them we were told that they were only for carrying our kit. We were supposed to reach the camp by marching. Unfortunately everybody seemed as bad at marching as I was, and by the time we had shambled the three miles to the camp, the corporal in charge of us had been reduced to babbling hysteria. It was an inauspicious start to service life, and, as far as I was concerned, things only got worse.

The trouble started over my car. They were not allowed in the camp and hardly anyone had one. But, after a few weeks, I decided that I would like to use the 1935 Singer which I bought after the accident in Belgium. I drove it up from home and hid it in a farm at the back of the camp, along with a complete change of civilian clothes.

I used the Singer on weekend leave, when I would drive into Liverpool or up to Blackpool with a couple of friends from my billet. Then one weekend, by a piece of bad luck, the corporal in charge of our billet spotted us driving past Lime Street station and his eyes nearly popped out of his head.

Not long before my squadron was due to pass out I was tackling the assault course when I fell into the water. But since I did not want to antagonise the corporal I clambered out and finished the course. That night, which was the night for bulling up our hut, I felt rather hot and told the corporal that I felt ill. He said: 'There's nothing the matter with you. You're just skiving.' So I carried on, although I felt terrible by the end of the evening.

Next day I told him I just could not tackle the assault course again, but he said that if I refused he would put me on a charge. I took a chance. I did refuse, and insisted that I would have to report sick the day after. But the next morning I was still not allowed to see the medical officer and, although I was not put on a charge, I found myself on fatigues in the bread shop, handing out bread rations to every man. I did this all day, although I felt I had a ludicrously high temperature, and by the evening even the corporal thought I looked ill.

He said: 'All right, you can go for a medical in the morning. But if there's nothing the matter with you I'll definitely put you on a charge.'

There was no danger of that; the medical officer said I had a very bad attack of scarlet fever and rushed me to the sick bay. When he discovered I had been handling everyone's bread he nearly had a fit. For days, every man in the camp lived in fear of a scarlet fever epidemic although no-one seemed to catch it in the end.

I was in the sick bay for three weeks. By the time I emerged, my squadron had passed out and I was assigned to another squadron. I was made NAAFI orderly for a period and discovered that it was a very cushy number, just clearing away a few teacups. I also found that once you were NAAFI orderly everyone seemed to forget that you existed and I simply re-allocated myself the job every day. It was a great improvement on all that marching and I dodged all the hard grind for weeks, until my warrant officer came into the NAAFI, asked me who I was, and discovered that I should have been square bashing.

He dragged me in front of my squadron commander, who was horrified to learn how far behind I was with my drill. He decided, quite correctly, that I would never get through the parade on passing-out day, so when that day came he insisted that I should spend my time in the latrines and, at all costs, stay clear of his squadron. I did stay in the latrines, the squadron passed out and the commander's reputation was saved.

After this I took the RAF aptitude test. From this, they deduced that I would make an excellent teleprinter operator, and I was sent to the training school at Compton Basset in Wiltshire. I found that the camp was a remote place which I wanted to get away from as frequently as possible. The trouble was that firms running the official camp coaches were charging 26s for the trip home to London. Since our total weekly pay was 28s, nobody could afford to go regularly.

One weekend, when I was in London, it struck me that I might be able to organise trips more cheaply and I asked a fellow called Bob Smith, who I knew had a couple of coaches, how much it would cost me for a day's hire. It worked out that if I managed to get together a full coach I would have to charge only 17s 6d a seat and would still have a free seat for myself.

During the next week I easily assembled a coachload at the cut price from the men in my billet and billets nearby. Bob Smith himself drove the coach up from London to collect us and on the way home he had a race with about ten official coaches.

Early the week after, a corporal came to me from a billet I had not previously approached and asked if I could arrange a coach for his men. I immediately hired Bob Smith's second vehicle, but it soon became obvious that my idea was going to snowball. I would have to hire yet more coaches. That weekend I spent my leave getting quotations from several London coach companies and within weeks I had seven coaches running, with the fare down to 12s 6d a seat. I was making a small profit, there were free seats for the corporals helping me to organise the operation and everyone was happy except the firms running the official camp service, who had lost about half their business.

On one trip home I went to the Nuffield Centre, a club for servicemen, where I met some of the boys who had been with me in West Kirby and who were now stationed in various places. They agreed to help me and I soon had cut-price coaches running from RAF camps all over the country, while a friend was operating a similar scheme for me among soldiers at Salisbury.

When I became a fully-fledged teleprinter operator I was assigned to RAF Stanbury, at Leighton Buzzard in Bedfordshire, I left someone else in charge of the coaches at Compton Basset and gave up the day-to-day organising altogether. Instead, every weekend I visited some of the many corners of my coach empire in a Hudson Terraplane car which I had bought out of the proceeds.

By this time, of course, I was treading on the toes of quite a few coach operators and, to eliminate my competition, one of them tipped off the police who took me to court for breaking a couple of laws that I did not know even existed.

The magistrate, Mr Frank Powell at Clerkenwell, was very sympathetic and he told me that he wished there had been someone like me in his unit to get him home more cheaply. But he said there was nothing he could do. I was guilty on two counts: I did not have a licence to operate a commercial coach service, and, if I was supposed to be running a purely self-help venture I was not allowed to make a profit.

However, Mr Powell added: 'It's no sin to make a profit' and

19

for that reason he gave me a conditional discharge. Unfortunately, though, I had to promise to stop running coaches. So that was the end of the scheme.

The next day I was reading the papers when I saw the headline 'He took his pals home—at a profit'. I thought: 'What a swine'. Then I realised it was me.

While people might have stopped short of calling me a swine, there were several at Leighton Buzzard who strongly disapproved of Leading Aircraftman Bloom's money-making pasttimes. There were the adjutant and the commanding officer to name but two—and their opinions were certainly not softened by the Hudson parked ostentatiously outside the camp gates.

Even after the end of the coach venture, however, the car was a necessity. I often used it to nip home in the evenings to see my mother whose health was not good. On one visit I suddenly went down with flu and my mother called the doctor who said I had to stay in bed even though I was due to report next morning. He gave me a medical certificate which I sent back to the camp.

Two days later my mother came into my bedroom and said: 'John, two friends of yours from the Air Force are here to see you.'

'Oh good,' I said, 'I could do with cheering up.'

When they walked in, they turned out to be SPs—members of the RAF police—in full uniform, hats and everything. They bundled me into a jeep and said they had been ordered to take me to the medical centre at West Drayton because the adjutant did not think I was really sick. I was furious and when we reached the centre I insisted on seeing the medical officer that night. He found, of course, that I still had a raving temperature and I was immediately sent home—only this time I was driven in an RAF Austin saloon. It had all been a mistake, they said later, and the whole thing was hushed up.

Soon after this my mother became very ill. She had disseminated sclerosis. The Soldiers, Sailors and Air Force Association talked to the RAF authorities and got me a posting to the Air Ministry so that I could live at home.

I became a teleprinter operator at the Communications

Centre which was in the BBC's Bush House building. This was a different sort of RAF altogether—you forgot you were in the forces at all. Hardly anybody wore uniform and there was no discipline at all as long as the work was done. We worked in shifts round the clock, but when I was on the night shift, from 10 pm to 8 am, I had plenty of time to wander out to Covent Garden for a drink, or to have meals in the BBC canteen. I also saved quite a bit of cash from the fantastic allowance that the RAF gave to men living out of camp.

One weekend I decided to use some of this to visit Ireland. I sailed from Holyhead to Dun Laoghaire and ended up in Dublin where I found that there were lots of English people buying second-hand vans and lorries, taking them over to England and selling them.

I investigated this operation and found that there was a tremendous shortage of commercial vehicles in England. There was also a regulation which said that provided a vehicle had been made in England in the first place it could be re-imported without having to pay Purchase Tax or duty. There was obviously a big profit to be made on such vehicles—and Ireland was full of them.

I persuaded a second cousin of mine, Julius Granatt, to put up £1,000, and we started importing second-hand 5 cwt, 10 cwt and 12 cwt vans. I was still in the RAF but I went over to Ireland most weekends to buy the vans, ship them to Liverpool and drive them to London. Julius used to come with me at the beginning, but the thought of that 200-mile drive soon put him off and I started hiring drivers to help me.

We reckoned we were making about £50 profit on each van, and this sudden wealth made me feel less like a National Service man than ever. Which made things very difficult when I had to go back to Leighton Buzzard for the farce of the three-day demob. I had not worn my uniform for months and it was in a diabolical state. I had lost my boots and other bits of kit. Everyone was horrified when they saw me and when it came to the pay parade I had forgotten you had to say: 'Sir, 856790,' and salute. The officer in charge bellowed: 'Don't you realise you're in the Air Force? You'll never get demobbed.'

In the end I did get demobbed. I had to have a new kit and I had to have an Air Force haircut. But I did get demobbed.

I then went into the van business in a big way. I was determined to work the situation for all it was worth and I set out to become a tycoon at the age of 20, making two or three trips to Ireland every week, to search for vehicles. After nine months we had a couple of Austins and three Bedfords, each worth about £500, in a yard at Willesden. We had put all our money into these vans—they comprised our total profits on the whole enterprise.

Then came a shattering blow. Overnight, Australia and New Zealand stopped importing British vehicles and all the new models which should have gone there flooded the home market instead. Second-hand prices slumped by about 60 per cent which meant that the total value of our five vans was now only £1,000. We sold them off and Julius just about got his money back. I was back where I started.

I went along to the Labour Exchange again and came out as a wages clerk with a firm called Robert Legg in Clerkenwell, who made machinery for the cigarette industry. I started at £6 a week and was getting £7 after a year, but I was then offered a job at £8 with Eastwoods, a London firm of brick manufacturers, and I took it.

I was assistant to the transport manager and soon learned enough to be able to move on to a £10-a-week manager's job with London Bridge Transport. When I got there I found that they were a transport firm without any lorries of their own; they had delivery contracts with several manufacturers, paid haulage firms to do the jobs, and pocketed the difference. It was simplicity itself, and I decided to form my own company and do the same.

I advertised for partners in 'Motor Transport' and eventually set up a firm called Payne & Bloom with two fellows called Freddie Payne and Major Fred Warwick. Freddie Payne had some lorries and, more important, some money to finance everything. The Major, who had been running the British Road Services depot at Brentford before joining me, brought with him contracts for delivering Pears Soap products and Claygate fireplaces. On paper we had a good business.

In fact, there were two flaws. First, Freddie Payne had too little money and second, we found that, unlike BRS, we did not have enough business to be able to absorb some of the losses involved in contract work. We found, for instance, that we would be sending a lorry all the way to the north of Scotland with one fireplace.

I became involved in several other transport firms—one with the ambitious-sounding name of Haulall. But by 1958 these and Payne & Bloom had all flopped and I later paid most of their debts myself. All I had left after five years in the transport game was a six-ton lorry which I kept outside the house in St Kilda's Road.

3

ALTHOUGH I DID NOT KNOW IT AT THE TIME, IT WAS A MEETING with a young Irishman called Mick Cosgrave, in January 1958, which started me on the road to washing machines. I was a keen table tennis player in those days and some friends suggested that I should ask Mick for a game as he was a good player. Perhaps it was their idea of a joke; I found that he could give me 18 points start and still win.

One day I was talking about ways of making money and he said: 'Why don't you go into the paraffin business? Lots of people are selling it door-to-door and making £40 or £50 a week easily.'

I told Mick that I had a lorry and was willing to give the idea a try. He agreed to join me. We bought a big tank to put on the lorry, filled it with Fina Green paraffin and we were in business.

We concentrated on the areas of East London where there was a big West Indian population. The West Indians feel the cold in England and as several families were often sharing a house, many of them were living in rooms without fireplaces and were relying on paraffin stoves for their heat. Although we had a more-or-less captive market I decided to help sales by presenting gifts such as ballpoint pens and little dolls to new customers. This was an idea which I later used on a grand scale with Rolls washing machines.

After a few months we had built up a good regular round. But we were having to work from eight in the morning until

eight at night to keep it going and it was very arduous physic-
ally, lugging paraffin up to people at the top of four flights of
stairs. I worked out that, in theory, we were making £20 to
£25 a week each, but then we were spending astronomical sums
on cleaning our clothes because the paraffin got splashed everywhere. The smell was everywhere too; it used to cling to me
24 hours a day. It was worse than having the worst BO. Eventually I decided I had had enough and told Mick that we were
wasting our time.

Mick, who was a former washing machine salesman, then
came up with another idea. A friend of his was buying cheap
washing machines from Holland, selling them door-to-door for
about £50, and making huge profits. Mick thought we could do
the same. So we went to see this friend, who was called Jim
Elvins, and bought two of his machines for £29 each.

I took them home and parked them in the tiny hall. My
mother was not too happy about this because the machines—
which looked like big round boilers—practically filled the
place. However, I persuaded her that there was room for people
to squeeze past, and when my father and sister came home for
their tea they managed it without too much difficulty.

As washing machines were knew to me, I decided to practise
my demonstration technique on the mother of a girl-friend. I
went round one evening, put in three or four towels and the
machine performed admirably. I was confident that I was on
to a winner and, also, on top of the job.

But when Mick and I did our first real demonstration things
did not go quite so smoothly. It took us quite a time, knocking
on doors round Highbury, until we found a couple who wanted
to see the machine; they were called Mr and Mrs Michael Ward,
I remember. When we got in the house they produced a pile of
clothes for us to wash—much more than three or four towels
—but I put them all in the machine very confidently while
Mick talked to them in the living room. When I opened the
lid after a couple of minutes to see how things were going I got
a nasty surprise, however. All I could see was a huge knot of
tangled clothes.

I put my head round the door and said: 'I'll just have to

make a slight adjustment here. I don't think your washing powder is very suitable.' Mick took the hint and kept the couple talking while I hauled out the clothes and untangled them. I then discovered that if I put them in one at a time they stayed separate. In the end they were remarkably white, the Wards were delighted and they agreed to buy the machine for £50.

They bought it through what is known as a credit sale. This means that customers only have to pay a low deposit—which Mick and I thought was vital to attract business—although they have to pay off the balance in nine months. The alternative is a hire purchase sale which gives customers several years to pay off the balance but which requires a much larger, off-putting, deposit.

In our case we got a £4 deposit from the Wards who then agreed to pay the rest to a company that Jim Elvins was dealing with, called the Belmont Finance Corporation. This company immediately paid Mick and me the balance, less 10 per cent, which meant that we got £42 from them, bringing our total to £46—a profit of £17. I thought that if we could sell five of these machines a week we would make over £40 a week, which would be fantastic.

We set ourselves up in a tiny office over a shop in Black-stock Road and called ourselves the North London Advertising and Distributing Co. When sales lived up to my hopes we hired a couple of salesmen on a commission-only basis, with someone to supervise them, and sent them out in a rented Dormobile. In the first week they sold five machines. Their commission came to £6 a machine but that still left £11 for Mick and me, plus the bigger profits on the machines we were selling ourselves, so we were still doing nicely.

We advertised the machine by pushing reply cards through people's doors. Quite a number of the cards that were sent back directed us to addresses which did not exist or to friends of the sender who were not expecting us. Then there were comedians who invited us to contact Mr Kruschev or the Queen. But despite all this it was not long before we had four salesmen who were running three vans and selling 30 machines a week between them.

26

The only real problem we had at that time was with the vans. They kept being stolen and relieved of their contents. The first time it happened was one day while I was sitting in my office. I was surprised to see our Dormobile being driven off down the road and I said to Mick: 'Have any of the salesmen taken the van?' He said: 'No.' And I said: 'Well, who's got the keys?' Mick said: 'I have,' and threw them down on the desk. We realised the Dormobile must have been stolen and called the police. They found it half an hour later—with all the washing machines unloaded, of course.

We were plagued by these thefts for some time until I had burglar alarms and special locks fitted to all our vehicles. Eventually the vans had a complete security system fitted, and I kept this on throughout the history of Rolls.

At this point came a major tragedy in my life: the death of my mother. Mick and I were in the living room at St Kilda's Road when we heard a cry in the hall. My mother had fallen over and somehow broken her leg. She was taken to hospital and was recovering well when septicaemia set in and she was transferred to the Prince of Wales hospital in Tottenham.

One day my father phoned me from the hospital and said: 'You've got to come right away.' The doctors there told me there was no hope for my mother. I was amazed. I thought she was improving, but they said she would not last more than 48 hours. They were right, and my mother died next day.

During the seven-day traditional Jewish mourning which followed I did not shave and at the end of the week I had quite a healthy stubble. When I looked at myself in the mirror, I decided that if I grew a proper beard I would look a few years older, and that this might be a help in business dealings. That was the start of what became my personal trademark virtually throughout the rest of the washing machine venture.

I had been very close to my mother and was naturally very miserable after her death. I stayed at home for some days and, to keep my mind occupied, I started going through all the accounts of our business which had become rather neglected.

To my horror, I discovered a considerable number of notices from the Belmont Finance Corporation telling us that our cus-

27

tomers had failed to keep up their payments, and that, under the terms of the agreement Mick and I had to pay the money instead.

This meant that a lot of our past profit turned out not to be profit at all. It seemed it was one thing persuading people to put £4 down, but quite another thing to get them to pay the hefty balance over nine months. Often with the best will in the world, our customers had signed for something they just could not afford.

It was obvious that in order to cut the number of bad debts we would have to go over to hire purchase sales with their far smaller monthly repayments. Also, the bigger deposit would mean that customers would have to think more carefully about whether they could afford the machine.

On the other hand I did not want the deposit to be so big that no-one could afford it all. I therefore needed an even cheaper machine. And I believed I knew where to get one.

I had discovered that Jim Elvins was not importing his machines direct but was getting them through a fellow called Danny Ginsberg who was running Universal Distributors in Charlotte Street. I decided to go direct to Ginsberg. He was keen to supply me and he showed me his latest line which was a twin-tub—a washer and spin dryer combined—that he was importing from Holland. This was obviously the market of the future. The drawback was that Ginsberg's twin-tubs did not seem to me to carry a good enough profit margin and I asked him if he could offer any cheaper models.

He said: 'No, I've nothing cheaper. And there's no point in your going over to Holland. I've got the Dutch manufacturers completely tied up.'

I said I would think about it. And the more I thought about it, the less I believed that Ginsberg could possibly be the sole British importer of Dutch machines. So I rang up the Anglo-Dutch Chamber of Commerce and they sent me a list of every washing machine manufacturer in Holland. There were well over a hundred. Surely one of them would do business? I decided to call Ginsberg's bluff.

I took the boat train to the Hook of Holland and drove to

Utrecht where most of the manufacturers were. Optimistically, I started with a couple of the big boys who had enormous sky-scraper buildings and who looked down at a small-time English-man from an appropriate height. Although they did not want to deal with me, however, they were perfectly free to do so. This knocked Ginsberg's claim on the head and gave me heart to continue my search.

After a few more misses I hit on a place just outside Utrecht that was making twin-tubs called Klean at the rate of 1,000 a week and they agreed to supply me. I arranged to have the machines flown in through a private company called Channel Air Bridge, which operated from Southend.

By this time, which was only a matter of months after I had met Mick Cosgrave, we had changed our firm's name to the Continental Washing Machine Co., and moved into bigger offices in Old Street. As part of this new look and in an attempt to eliminate bad debts further, I decided to stop our door-to-door selling and to advertise in the Press, giving our phone number. This way, I argued, we would be following up only genuine enquiries—which would be much better for the sales-men than knocking on doors and spending time trying to win over people who were never really interested in the first place.

I placed my first advert in the *London Evening News*. The Klean, which cost me about £52, I offered at £108 with an allowance of up to £35 in part exchange for old boilers or washing machines. This allowance was my way round the com-pulsory hire purchase deposit which at that time was very nearly 40 per cent. On a £108 machine this meant that the housewife was supposed to put down £40, but if she got £35 in part exchange she only had to find another £5. On our side of the deal, it meant that we were actually selling the Klean for £73—a profit of £21.

We started off by giving a guaranteed £10 for anything offered in part exchange—we took bird-cages, wringers, and even a pair of rabbits—and by giving £35 only for an actual second-hand washing machine. But when things went so well that we got sales up to about 20 machines a week we eventually gave £35 on everything.

Then, suddenly, things stopped going very well. I was visited by an inspector from the Board of Trade. He was not amused at the way I was getting round the 40 per cent deposit restriction. It was against regulations, he said. I was not allowed to give false allowances.

I was not amused either, but there was nothing for it. I would have to abandon my £35 offer. Instead, if I wanted to keep up our level of sales, I would have to find a machine so cheap that the customer could afford the real deposit.

I estimated that people could possibly put down £15 to £20 which meant that I would have to advertise a machine for between £40 and £50—less than half the price of most washing machines then on the market. And to make a decent profit, I, in turn, would have to buy the twin-tub for about £30. Which left one question unanswered: where was I going to find a twin-tub at that price?

The answer was obviously to be found in Holland—somewhere. I started with the Klean people. I argued with them for hours but they said it was absolutely impossible to make a cheaper version just for me. I either took it or left it. They had a standard production line and I was far from being their most important customer.

I did have one stroke of luck while I was at their factory, however. I was standing around waiting to meet one of their executives when I overheard somebody talking about a firm which had brought out a very cheap machine which might provide stiff competition for the Klean. I caught the name Schrouten and as soon as I had finished lunch I drove into Utrecht to try and trace a firm of washing machine manufacturers by that name.

Nobody seemed to have heard of them and I was about to give up the search when I went into a small washing machine shop and asked the man there. Somehow he seemed to know all about the firm and told me exactly how to reach their factory.

I got into the Chevrolet which I had hired to give the impression that I was a man of some substance and followed the shopkeeper's directions. Eventually I found myself down by the side of a canal and I pulled up outside a sort of prefabricated building which was really hardly more than a shed. I wondered if I had the right place but I went in and found that I had.

It was run by three brothers, Tom, Anton and Martin Schrouten, who showed me a very good-looking twin-tub which they had just started making. I asked them how much they were selling it for and they said £23. I was staggered. 'Right,' I said, when I recovered, 'I'll have one.'

The Schroutens then asked me what name I would like on the machine, and I said, half-jokingly, 'What have you got?' To my surprise they produced a long list of names which they had ready-made. Most of them were German-sounding, as they had intended making Germany their main market, but I spotted one name which sounded English and also modern and efficient. So I chose that. The name was Electromatic and it was with these Electromatic twin-tubs that I turned the washing machine world upside down. Later, in 1959, I changed the name of our company to the Eelectromatic Washing Machine Company.

I could hardly wait to get the machine home to show Mick and I insisted that the Schroutens should put it in the boot of the Chevrolet there and then. I drove straight to Rotterdam airport and put it on a plane which would arrive at Southend next day. I caught the night ferry and when I arrived home in the morning I anxiously rang Southend to see that my prize possession had arrived safely. They said that it had and that they would clear it through customs at once and send it on to me in a lorry.

As soon as it arrived I started to work out all the costs and decided that I could sell two versions—one for 49 gns and one for 59 gns. The 59 gn model would be a de luxe model with a heater, which I knew the Schroutens were also making. The attraction of this was that the housewife could fill it with cold water and heat it in the machine instead of having to drain off her household hot water supply.

It then occurred to me that the deposits required for these machines would be about £20 and £25—in other words, for only an extra £5 deposit the customer could have a heater and a few trimmings thrown in. I was sure that most people would opt for the dearer model, which was more profitable, and they did. I continued to offer this choice between standard and de luxe models throughout the history of Rolls.

Having done my calculations I was convinced that my Electromatic was such a good buy—and so much cheaper than the models then being sold by people such as Hoover—that I should advertise it in a national newspaper. I got all the details from an advertising agency called Gordon and Gotch, and I found that the space I wanted on the back page of the *Daily Mirror* would cost £424.

Just before this, to give me some working capital, I had borrowed £1,000 from my mother's brother, Alfred De Lara. But these were virtually his life's savings and £424 would make a very large hole in them if the advert failed. So I talked to Mick about it. He was dead against it; he thought I was off my head risking half our capital. But Uncle Alf said: 'I'll leave it to you, John. I've lent you the money, now you must do what you like with it.'

I over-ruled Mick and decided to take a chance. I also decided to include in the advert, along with our phone number, a cut-out coupon which readers could return if they wanted more details and a demonstration. The advert appeared on the nation's breakfast tables on September 24th. It was the first big turning point in my fortunes.

As it happened, the next day was the Jewish New Year and I was spending the day's holiday at home with my girl-friend Ruth Laren who was also working in the business. At five o'clock, the phone rang. It was Mick, sounding alarmed. He said that the *Mirror* readers had been ringing him all day, and that the GPO had delivered three sacks of mail in reply to our coupon advert. When I got into Old Street the day after, there were eleven more sacks of mail, and in the end the one advert drew in over 8,000 inquiries. This was it. This was the big time.

It was obvious that when people saw how cheap the Electromatic was they suddenly realised that a washing machine was no longer a luxury. It was something that many working mothers and newly-wed couples could now afford. This, then, was where our market lay. And we had reached it by national advertising in the popular Press, using coupons which my salesmen could follow up with demonstrations in the home.

With one advert I had started two revolutions—the first, in the kitchen; the second, in my method of selling directly to the public on a large scale and eliminating the shopkeepers.

I had found the formula for making a fortune. But first, I faced a few rather pressing problems. The response to the advert had been much greater than I had envisaged (for instance, we only had 1,000 leaflets printed) and I simply had not got enough machines.

I telephoned the Schroutens and arranged to visit them at once. After a lot of heart-searching, they decided that they could just about manage to make 100 machines a week, but that since they were short of cash I would have to pay for half of them on delivery, and for the other half within a fortnight. The trouble was, of course, that I was short of cash as well. The remains of Uncle Alf's £1,000 would not go very far playing in this league; in effect, I would need £2,300 a week to pay the Schroutens, plus another £1,000 for air transport and various Government dues.

It was then that I started to scrutinise the whole financial situation, and made a remarkable discovery when I examined my bank statement: the cheques that I had been paying to the Channel Air Bridge for flying in the Klean machines had been taking three or four weeks to clear. I therefore calculated that I could keep afloat by selling the Electromatics quickly and using the money from the hire purchase companies to pay back the Schroutens—provided that I could stave off the air freight bills for a few weeks until the business got going.

I decided to take a chance and it paid off. It seemed that the more machines I imported the more confusion arose in the accounts department at Southend and the longer credit I seemed to be getting.

Through national advertising, the demand for machines became so widespread that I could no longer run everything economically from London and I had to set up four regional depots each serving area salesmen. Also, the Schroutens' 100 machines a week were just not enough and I toured all over Europe looking for additional manufacturers.

Eventually I discovered an Italian firm who were making revolutionary washing machines called the Jetmatic which worked through water power by some strange system I did not pretend to understand. However they were mechanically reliable and they looked fantastic. The only trouble was that they did not get people's clothes very clean, so I had to stop selling them. As I had bought a hundred or two, they were a financial disaster I could well have done without.

At the same time I was having terrible trouble handling our greatly increased turnover at Old Street, where we were on the top floor of a building owned by an umbrella manufacturer. The only way of getting our machines on to our floor was by using the solitary lift, which was quite reasonable for things like people and umbrellas but ludicrous for washing machines.

This had not mattered too much when we were handling only 20 or 30 machines a week. But we were now getting 50 machines twice a week and it was taking us from 6 pm until well after midnight to get each batch to the top floor. And this was achieved only by cramming two machines at a time into the lift through turning them on their side and putting one on top of the other—which was bad for both the mechanism and the finish. Obviously we had to move and I soon found much better premises just down the road in Great Eastern Street.

Not long after the transfer, I received a phone call from the Channel Air Bridge accountant—which sounded ominous—and after an uninformative preamble he put me on to the proprietor, Mr Freddy Laker. It was indeed ominous. Mr Laker said they had been checking their accounts and had discovered that we owed his company quite a lot of money.

He and his accountant came round to see me and we went through the figures together. Whichever way you looked at it we owed his firm £11,300. Although I had realised that we owed them money, the actual figure gave me quite a shock. Poor Mick Cosgrave practically collapsed and left the office, probably to nip round the corner for a few brandies in the pub.

I explained the situation to Freddy Laker. 'Look,' I said, 'I just haven't got the money. The business is on its feet but your £11,000 is tied up. If we stop selling now it will be the end of everything and you won't get your money.'

Then I said: 'But, if you agree, I will promise to pay you £1,000 a fortnight until we clear off the money. I will personally guarantee it with everything I've got. It isn't much, but at least you'll have some assurance that if I don't pay, you can make me bankrupt.'

Freddy was quite happy to accept this, and in so doing saved my firm. But when I told Mick of the arrangement, on his return, he did not think it was possible and asked me to buy him out.

I said: 'You know the position, Mick. We just haven't any money.' But he said: 'You could pay me off the same as you pay them.' So we agreed that I should pay him £2,000 in all and he got it within about four months.

Basically, Mick had never been happy once I began talking in terms of tens of thousands of pounds. When we started out to 'make a fortune', what he had in mind was £50 to £60 a week. This had been my idea too. The difference was that, when I saw there was a chance that we could move into a much bigger league, I worked all-out to get promotion while Mick wanted to stay where he was, dealing with sums of money he felt he could handle. And so, after going through all the ups and downs of our early ventures, he quit just as we were making the big breakthrough.

After surviving the Freddy Laker shock, the business really took off with people sending in our coupons and having demonstrations in their homes. But as usual, I was having trouble finding enough ready cash—a problem that stayed with me all along and finally caused the downfall of Rolls six years later.

I had very little in the bank, probably only about £2,000, and was desperately trying to find another source of credit to replace that of the Channel Air Bridge. I therefore seized on a clause in the purchase tax regulations which meant that if washing machines were assembled or even part-assembled in England I would only have to pay purchase tax on them every four months, instead of having to pay it as soon as I received them from Holland. For example, it would be the end of April before I had to pay the tax for machines bought—and sold—since January 1st. I worked out that if I was selling an average of 200 machines a week, with purchase tax standing at £10 on each machine, I would be getting credit of £2,000 a week. In this way, over the four months, I could use more than £30,000 of purchase tax money to finance the whole Electromatic operation.

All I had to do to qualify was to assemble the machines in some way at Great Eastern Street. I decided that the simplest thing would be to put motors in an otherwise complete machine. And to do this I started buying motors from Hoover —a deal which was to cause great complications when the business grew to the point where I became one of Hoover's main rivals.

The motors also marked the small beginning of my career as a manufacturer, as well as a dealer, of washing machines. Like many other decisions in the early days which were to have far-reaching consequences, the decision to start manufacturing was, curiously, not considered as a strategic move, but was more or less imposed by circumstances.

Another example of this, on a lesser scale, was the company's move to Romford in Essex. The problem which forced us out of Great Eastern Street—but which started by seeming merely stupid and annoying—was the shortage of parking space. Salesmen loading their vans had to park by the kerb and as we were, unfortunately, in a restricted waiting area, they were constantly getting parking tickets.

As business improved the number of vans increased and so did the number of parking tickets. The record was 14 in a week. There seemed to be something of a police campaign against us, but I suppose it was hardly surprising since we almost choked the street from time to time. As with the case of the Old Street lift, the business had outgrown the premises. I would have to move again.

Luckily I soon came across the factory in Romford which was at a bizarre-sounding spot called Gallows Corner. Its rent was very cheap at £60 a week, and although it was a bit out of London, it was good for distribution as it was right on the Southend arterial road. And it had a huge parking area. The buildings were nothing special but they were a big improvement on everything I had had before and I began to think that I really was somebody big in the world of business.

This feeling was enhanced in an amusing way one day soon after the move to Gallows Corner. I was interviewing a few faceless men who had applied for salesmen's jobs when into the room walked someone whose face I knew only too well—a former officer of mine in the RAF. He completely failed to recognise me with my beard and civvy clothes and I solemnly went through the whole interview rigmarole with him. He left me still unemployed. It was a conscript's dream.

Electromatic was by this time achieving a modest renown and I began to get personal write-ups in the Press. The first was in the local paper, the *Romford Times*, as the opening interview of a series called Men of Industry. It referred to me as a 27-year-old meteoric self-made businessman—which was quite a mouthful—and reported that I employed 100 people in the factory and 100 salesmen throughout the British Isles.

The writer concluded: 'Bloom, who works ten to twelve hours a day, including Sundays, did not expect success. It was overwhelming when it came, but no longer surprises him; he is too busy keeping pace.' I thought it was a fair assessment.

This interview appeared on March 4th, 1959—the same day that I arranged a stunt which next morning got the name of Electromatic into the national Press for the first time. The plan, which I arranged with Gordon and Gotch, my advertising and publicity agents, was to produce a story which every woman would want to read—the story of a housewife getting one of our brand new 53 gns washing machines for next to nothing.

In order to rig the story, we first advertised locally that we were having a sale of second-hand washing machines, all for 12s 6d. On March 4th the machines were lined up in the factory forecourt and a good number of housewives arrived to take their pick. Then a lorry pulled up and the driver added the new machine to the line of beaten-up old tubs 'by mistake'.

The salesman in charge was, strangely, looking the other way and failed to notice the new addition. But, sure enough, there was one eagle-eyed lady who spotted the bargain immediately—Mrs Peggy Ketley a 40-year-old farmer's wife from Essex. She rushed up to the salesman, 12s 6d in her eager hand, and asked for the new machine. The salesman was most surprised. He could not understand it. He was terribly sorry but there must have been some sort of mistake. He could not possibly sell the smart new machine for 12s 6d.

Luckily for our stunt, Mrs Ketley turned out to be a lady not easily dissuaded. She demanded to see the manager and in a matter of moments she was shown in to my office by a salesman whose worried face deserved an Oscar. I made a suitably feeble attempt to explain the 'error' but Mrs Ketley was not to be placated. 'It's just not good enough,' she insisted. 'Do I have to call the police?' At this point I conceded the game and Mrs Ketley got her machine.

When the Press boys came on to me I explained: 'It was a mistake by a van driver, and rather than have any unpleasantness we let Mrs Ketley have the machine.' To make the story even better I added that we would deliver the machine to her farm 'for her perseverance and cheek.'

Mrs K was delighted and gave me some very useful sales publicity apart from getting Electromatic's name in the papers. Apparently she used to take all her washing 17 miles to a launderette in Chelmsford but now it was 'good riddance to all of that', as she told the *Daily Sketch*. This was a perfect example, which every housewife could understand at once, of the advantages of owning a washing machine.

Publicity stunts have a way of outliving their usefulness and this one became a menace. For weeks we were swamped by requests for new washing machines for only 12s 6d. People kept arriving at the factory, the telephone never stopped ringing with calls from all over the country and letters poured in— some addressed simply to 'Mr Bloom, washing machine factory'.

There were so many tearful heart-rending requests that I eventually decided that genuinely deserving cases should be sold reconditioned machines for a few shillings.

Partly because of the stunt and partly because of the *Romford Times* write-up the *London Evening News* soon afterwards did a half-page feature on me, called 'The extraordinary story of Mr Bloom'. But the thing which pleased me most was the phone call I received on April 7th from *The Financial Times*, a paper which I had never heard of until a couple of years before. They wanted me to comment on Heathcoat Amory's Budget and its meagre purchase tax reduction on household goods. 'It will be a small help—but nothing like we expected,' I obliged. 'It is a man's Budget—not one for a housewife.'

My comments only made a few lines but the fact they were in *The Financial Times* made me feel that I was achieving some prominence as a business figure.

Ironically, the publicity that I was courting became, in a few short years, a monster which I could not control. By the end of 1963 my every action was reported in gossip columns or news pages. Any deal I was considering became the subject of widespread speculation. Many of my new ventures were hauled into the spotlight and criticised before they had a chance to get off the ground and prove themselves.

I learned many lessons over the next six years, but the dangers of the personality cult in business was one lesson which I learned too late.

4

THE PUBLIC IMAGE THAT GORDON AND GOTCH AND I WERE TRYING to establish in 1959 was of Bloom the Tycoon. I did not have the right sort of money to be a tycoon but we decided that did not matter as long as I had the right trappings.

One of these—and one which always seemed to catch the imagination of the newspapers and magazines—was the fact that I had a chauffeur-driven Chevrolet with a telephone in it. On paper this always sounded the ultimate in luxurious living. In fact it was nothing of the sort.

For a start, although the Chevvy looked opulent, it only cost about £2,500—about a third of the price of a Bentley. And, in any case, I was buying it on hire purchase. Secondly, I had moved out of St Kilda's Road after the death of my mother and into a flat in Dolphin Square, which is down by the river in Pimlico—and a long way from Romford. It used to take me about an hour driving through east London and down the Southend road every morning. I decided that if I had a chauffeur I could use the time spent in the car to get through an extra twelve or more hours work every week which, on an efficiency basis, more than paid for his wages. The telephone—which even today is still regarded by most people as a bit of gim-mickry—was quite simply a necessity for my mobile office. The much-glamourised Chevrolet set-up was, therefore, just plain commonsense.

My furnished flat in Dolphin Square which was costing me twenty guineas a week in rent, was very comfortable but it had one drawback as far as the new image was concerned: it was not in the West End. To remedy this shortcoming I moved into a flat I had found in Park Lane—a very imposing address even by West End standards. In fact, like the Chevrolet, the impression that it gave bore no relation to the facts; the flat was minute and cost only £11 a week—or half that of the one in Dolphin Square. This, of course, did not matter for the Press build-up. The clichés came flowing out, 'budding tycoon, chauffeur-driven Chevrolet, Park Lane flat' and everyone was happy.

At this same time, the early months of 1959, I became engaged to Ruth Laren who was helping with the administration at Romford, and my publicity people, Gordon and Gotch, were quick to seize even on this as an opportunity for a spot of image-building. They announced that I was giving Ruth a Jaguar as an engagement present.

The papers pounced on the story, liberally sprinkled it with 'budding Tycoonery', and Ruth and her Jaguar became known from Land's End to John o' Groats. The story behind the story was that the Jaguar had been bought as a company car a few weeks before the engagement to be used by all and sundry. So it was Ruth's car in a way—but, equally, it belonged to a host of other people.

The effect of all this publicity was exactly as planned. I acquired the image without having to lay out very much money—a cut-price tycoon in more ways than one.

Ruth was not the only friend or relation working for me in those days. My sister and her husband, Herbert Collins—who was trained as a salesman and became a director of Rolls in 1963—were running the East London sales division, my Uncle Alf was in the office in charge of petty cash expenses, and my father was documenting all the coupons which people cut out and sent to us.

As a tailor, my father always used to get up at 6.30 am to be at work for eight o'clock. At Gallows Corner he could only start work at 9.30, when the post arrived, but he was so used to waking up in the morning that he arrived at work on the stroke of eight just the same.

41

Another person working with me then was my former washing machine supplier Jim Elvins. He had seen the light and stopped his door-to-door business and asked for a job in my organisation. I, personally, had so much work on hand—planning adverts, keeping supplies going, visiting our regional branches every week—that I needed someone with experience to take over the general sales administration which was becoming a major headache. So I welcomed Jim Elvins aboard and made him managing director. This did not prove to be the wisest of choices.

My progression from quasi-tycoon to the genuine article began in about May of 1959 when I received a phone call from a fellow called Teddy Smith who was chairman of a lot of public companies, including Knitmaster. He had heard about me through the newspaper stories and invited me to dinner at his flat in Bryanston Square. This was not far from my place in the West End, but it was a different world—a world of maids, butlers and plush furnishings. It was my first glimpse of really big money and it made me realise how far I had to go.

That night I was introduced to the complexities of public companies, that is, companies which are owned by shareholders and have share prices quoted on the Stock Exchange, rather than those owned by a private individual. Teddy Smith offered to take over my company and said I could make a lot of money out of it. Furthermore, with a public company there were great tax advantages, he said. Shortly after this another millionaire, called Michael Lewis, asked me to see him and told me the same thing.

I certainly needed all the tax help I could get because I worked out that at the rate I was going, even if I made £50,000 a year I would still be left with only £5,000 after the tax boys had been at it.

However, although I still knew very little about finance, I decided that if I was going to become a public company I would somehow make sure that I kept a grip on the situation and did not become swamped by the big boys in some sort of take-over.

The way to avoid this, I thought, was to be the originator of the whole scheme, so I put an advert in the *Financial Times*

42

explaining that I was in the washing machine business and wanted to contact backers who had public company connections. Some people, I know, think that this is an incredibly amateur way to go about things, but I reasoned that in my position, with no pals in the city, it was the best way of reaching as many ears as possible. And it paid off.

Through the advert, I met a fellow called Brady who gave me an introduction to Louis Jackson, a financier. I met Jackson in an extremely luxurious office in Hobart Place which impressed me very much. (It was only later that I learned the office was not his—he was working with some other company at the time.) He decided to investigate my business and persuaded me to change my accountant to Gerald Edelman and Co., the firm that he was using.

After making his inquiries he suggested that I should aim at a merger with an old-established public company who were short of money, or looking for something to replace a traditional product that had lost its selling power—or both.

This was in tune with my thinking. I told him that what I would like ideally would be a respected name in the engineering industry which I could take over and use to add prestige to my washing machines.

I agreed that Jackson should find such a company and the first that he came up with was Lea-Francis—the small firm of Coventry car-makers. He and I went up to see members of their board and Jackson then held further discussions. But they could not reach agreement and the deal, in the end, fell through.

Then, later in the year, I was working in my office at Gallows Corner one Thursday when the phone rang and Jackson asked me if I could go straight over to see him in Hobart Place. I arrived to find two other men with him whom he introduced as Colin Kingham and Arthur Sowley, chairman and secretary of Rolls Razor Ltd.

Jackson asked me if I had heard of Rolls Razor. I said: 'Yes,' because I had—vaguely. Years previously somebody had bought me a Rolls razor as a birthday present. I had never used it; I thought it was so old-fashioned. And that turned out to be what was wrong with the company.

They had been going for over 30 years and had become a well-respected name by making an unwieldy but economical everlasting razor—a compromise between the honed blade of Sweeney Todd days and today's expendable safety razor. But they had fallen on stubbly times, especially since the introduction of electric razors, and in 1959 they were making only about 1,000 razors a week. Instead, about 80 per cent of their staff were busy on Government contract work, making rifle magazines and pull-throughs. There was not a lot of money in rifle magazines and pull-throughs. In the four years up to 1960 the firm had accumulated losses of £115,000.

Kingham, himself, had been on the board since 1927 while Arthur Sowley had started with Rolls Razor as a clerk in 1946 and had risen through the ranks until he became company secretary ten years later. It was that sort of firm.

In short, it was just the sort of shell I wanted for putting my firm into—and its name was one of the most exciting things about it. The thought of being able to pin the word 'Rolls' to my washing machines seemed just too good to be true.

I had the same feeling when I went on the following Saturday to look over their factory at Cricklewood in North London. The buildings looked huge from the outside and even bigger from the inside. I found it hard to believe that I could ever become involved in a business of that size.

On the Monday, Jackson and I had a further meeting with the Rolls people and they said that, recently, they had been trying to make a washing machine themselves in an attempt to diversify their business. It was called the Rolls-a-matic and was supposed to operate on a revolutionary vibration system. As far as I could make out, it was a kind of rubber tub which bounced around. It had proved useless.

But Kingham and his technical men did say that they had the equipment and the skilled tool-room men to be able to make any type of washing machine or part that I wanted. A few days later I gave them one of the machines I had imported from the Schroutens and asked them if they could make several of the parts. They said yes they could.

44

The deal was clinched. It was in two parts—there was a manufacturing deal and a financial deal. The manufacturing deal was straightforward; I would become managing director of Rolls Razor and Rolls would start assembling washing machines for Electromatic, still using parts supplied by the Schroutens, who by that time had expanded to keep pace with my sales, but also using several parts made in the tool room at Cricklewood—at a considerable saving.

The financial part of the deal was somewhat more complicated. It started when Jackson introduced me to Gilbert Southall who had become a multi-millionaire largely through take-overs although he was originally a civil engineer. The fruits of his success were obvious—a flat in Belgravia and a beautiful mansion in the country—and I hoped he could put me on the same road.

Southall's plan was that Equity and Share Company (London) in which he had a considerable interest would bid for all three million Rolls shares and that, provided I agreed to sell Electromatic to Rolls at a later date, he would let me have 1,180,000 Rolls shares at the price he paid for them. The hope was, of course, that with me running a new-look Rolls, business would boom, the price of the shares would rise, and that Southall and I would both make money.

All of these negotiations were conducted in great secrecy, with almost every meeting—both with Lea-Francis and Rolls Razor—taking place at weekends in deserted factories or people's homes. All we were short of were trench coats and false noses.

One of the few outsiders to be let in on the secret was an advertising man I had bumped into called Roger Pryer. His was a very small agency, I think he only had two people working for him at that time, but he was like myself—he had lots of ideas. I took my advertising away from Gordon and Gotch and gave it to Roger and from that time until the collapse of Rolls we worked tremendously closely—even when I started employing three other advertising agencies and had them all competing with one another.

I told him of my plan for using the name Rolls to sell Electro-

45

matic washing machines and he started doing dummy advertising layouts. To make sure that news of the planned take-over did not leak out, however, he substituted the word Ajax for Rolls in all the dummies and mystified his colleagues by producing lines such as: 'Electromatic washing machines—now straight from the world-famous Ajax factory.' Project Ajax became our name for the whole take-over.

It slipped into gear on November 19th when Southall's Equity and Share made their bid. Operating through another firm called Harley Street Securities—to disguise where the bid was coming from—they offered 1s for every Rolls share, which, thanks to the fact that Rolls had not declared a dividend for years, were then standing at 4½d each. As planned, the directors accepted immediately, which gave Southall 21 per cent of the shareholding, and people were so glad to get rid of their shares that he soon had more than 60 per cent.

Just after the offer my sister Noreen and I bought 286,500 shares between us for about 1s 2d each and these were the only shares I had at that time. I was so new to the game that I did not have a stockbroker. I bought them through the Westminster Bank branch at Gidea Park, near Romford.

It was obvious that the life I was going to lead would be much different from my life so far. There had already been problems between my fiancée, Ruth, and myself caused by my increasing involvement in business, and these problems were only going to get worse.

Ruth, who had joined Mick Cosgrave and I in the middle of 1958 as a general factotum, was still only 19. She was living at Ilford with her mother and her father, who had a juke box business. I was living in Park Lane and ever since our engagement in May I had been so busy working from 8.30 am till midnight, with all my secret business trips at weekends, that I had been seeing less and less of her—even though she was still working in the business. Any spare time I had I spent with people whom I met round and about in the West End.

Just after Christmas, and only a few weeks before we were due to be married, we decided that it would not work out and so we agreed to end our engagement. It was an upsetting time, but I thought there was no point in getting married and then getting divorced a couple of years later. Ruth continued to work for Electromatic and we stayed the best of friends. Soon I was to need all the friends I had.

Meanwhile, various rumours were flying round as to why a bid had been made for Rolls shares and by the end of the year the price of the shares had shot up dramatically to around 6s each. The Stock Exchange, who like a share price to be a true reflection of a company's prosperity, were very perturbed at this rise since there was no apparent reason for it and when the price continued to go up they suspended dealings in the shares altogether on January 8th. The shares were then standing at 7s after actually hitting 7s 10½d earlier in what *The Financial Times* termed 'an active day'.

For different reasons I personally found it a very active day indeed. To begin with, Louis Jackson called me over to see him. He said he thought it was time that we put into writing the terms of the agreement we had come to when I first discussed my plans with him. He simply gave me a piece of paper to sign and I signed. That signature later caused a great deal of trouble with Jackson's executors and, in 1964, cost me about £330,000 after they started legal action against me.

The trouble with the agreement, although it turned out to be very ambiguous, was that it basically gave Jackson a large proportion of any shares that I received and five per cent of my future earnings. It was the sort of agreement that you are always hearing that pop groups have signed with some fly manager who promises them a demonstration disc. And I was silly enough to put my name to it.

On the same turbulent day, I signed another agreement, this time for the eventual sale of Electromatic to Rolls—for which I would receive three million shares in Rolls. This, of course, was still all being done in secret. It was not until the evening of January 12th that a Press release was issued stating simply: 'The Board of Rolls Razor have pleasure in announcing completion of an agreement for the manufacture and distribution of Electromatic washing machines.'

Shortly afterwards Roger Pryer announced that he had been

appointed to handle the advertising of the Rolls Electromatic washing machine. This was the first time the Rolls name was linked with washing machines and we went on to feature it during the rest of the year in a £200,000 national advertising campaign. The first advert appeared next morning—January 13th. Luckily I am not superstitious.

Gilbert Southall came in as chairman along with his solicitor, Mark Horowitz, to look after the interests of Equity and Share. I became a director in February and was appointed managing director in March. The writing was on the wall for the old guard of Rolls Razor.

Real power had been taken from their grasp even earlier. In the agreement for the eventual sale of Electromatic, a clause was included which said it was agreed that I would have 'sole and absolute control of the production and organisation of the Rolls Razor factory'. And nothing could be clearer than that.

In view of my position, I decided that I would have the office occupied by Colin Kingham the former chairman. He was still a director but it was obvious that he was going to have to go— and I told him so. The only aspect of this news that seemed to upset him was that he would lose his company car, a Rolls-Royce with the number plate ACK 1. So he asked whether he could keep it and since nobody else particularly wanted to drive around with ACK 1 front and rear we agreed to sell it to him at a nominal price. He ceased to be a director very soon afterwards.

His office was styled to look Important with a capital 'I'. It was completely wood-panelled and had an Adam-esque fireplace at one end. In the centre was an enormous table which had always been used—and which I continued to use—for board meetings. The whole place was like something out of a film set.

When I first sat behind the desk I found it hard to believe that in the space of two years I had graduated to this from selling paraffin.

5

TIME AND TIME AGAIN DURING MY WASHING MACHINE YEARS I found myself involved in several major events simultaneously. The start of 1960 was one of these occasions.

After the deal with Rolls was announced, and while I was in the process of transferring the Electromatic business to Cricklewood, I found myself facing a kind of palace revolution within Electromatic which threatened to ruin the company at one stroke.

It all began with one of my bad assessments. When the top-secret negotiations were going on with Rolls in December, I decided to keep the Schrouten brothers informed. This seemed only fair. It was also common sense: if I wanted them to modify their output to suit my new needs I obviously had to give them as much notice as I could.

I explained that we were going to transfer Electromatic to the Rolls factory and that we were going to make some of our own components but that since the aim was to keep the sales graph rising steeply there would still be plenty of business for them. I told them that we were embarking on this huge £200,000 advertising campaign and said that if things went as planned they could come in on our success and even have some shares in Rolls.

I cannot say precisely what happened next, but I have always thought that the Schroutens must simply have got cold feet. Like Mick Cosgrave eighteen months earlier, they probably felt they were getting out of their depth—that the whole project was becoming too vast.

Unlike Mick, however, they did not tell me at the time, they were much more devious—as I learned later from Al Hunt, one of my new publicity agents whom I took on at the same time as I gave the advertising to Roger Pryer.

Al told me that the Schroutens had called Jim Elvins, whom they had got to know quite well, over to Holland one weekend. Behind my back they told him that they planned to set up a company in England called Duomatic which would sell washing machines directly to the public and so become a rival to Electromatic. They wanted Elvins to run this firm.

The Schroutens had an agreement to supply only me with washing machines, but the brothers assured Elvins that they had thought of a way round this and Elvins agreed to take part in the Duomatic venture.

The first that I heard about this *coup* was through a dramatic phone call at two o'clock in the morning one Saturday in January. It was from a fellow called George Brown who was one of our most valued long-distance lorry drivers.

He apologised for ringing me at that hour—although I had, in fact, only just gone to bed—but he had some important information. He said that over the previous week he had heard rumours at various branches that Jim Elvins was leaving to form a rival company. The rumours were fairly consistent and seemed to be increasingly widespread, said George.

I was stunned for I instinctively felt that George's story was true. And fragments of conversation came to mind, a word here and a word there, to confirm this feeling.

I plied George with questions. Did he know anything else about Elvins' plans? When did Elvins intend to start operating?

The answer to this was simply fantastic. He was going to start up on Monday. Only two days later.

'Where does he think he is going to get his staff from?' I asked.

'From Electromatic,' was the reply. Which was even more fantastic.

George explained that Elvins had apparently spent the past fortnight recruiting for Duomatic. George did not, of course, know any precise figures, but it seemed that Elvins had managed to collar a large number of my salesmen and regional sales managers, and about three-quarters of my drivers. And all of this without my knowing.

The most horrifying part of George's news was not so much the double-dealing but the fact that I was about to lose a big slice of my sales staff. These men following up the coupon replies were my lifeline. Without them I had no business. Yet the whole future of Rolls was based on the assumption that Electromatic was a prosperous outfit which would inject life into the moribund public company.

But even while I was on the phone to George I was working out a plan to rescue Electromatic from what could have been annihilation.

I told George to come and see me that afternoon and then worked through the early hours on a contingency plan for Monday morning. The big difficulty was that I did not know quite what contingencies I was planning for, but I looked on the black side and worked out that, if necessary, I could take on responsibility for all the departments as long as I had trust-worthy lieutenants to carry out instructions.

I sat there in my flat, thinking of people who would be suitable and eventually decided to go right back to people I had known in my younger days—such as Leslie Goldbart who was at that time working as a tailor and living in a council flat. Others included Geoffrey Lewis, Barry Manning, and Lew Fearnley. I called them all to a meeting at my flat that afternoon, along with Noreen and her husband Herbie, George Brown, Ruth Laren and Rex Wood, a very large Scotsman who was one of my sales chiefs.

The next thing that I did, in my innocence, was to phone the Schroutens to break what I thought was the news. I said: 'A terrible thing has happened. Elvins is starting a company in competition with us and is taking most of our staff. It's going to be a blow. But don't worry, I'm working on an emergency plan to keep Electromatic going.' The Schroutens heard me out with very straight faces. They seemed most concerned.

On the Sunday I started on the reorganisation task in detail, job by job. Leslie Goldbart and the other old acquaintances all became my personal assistants, Herbie became responsible for both of the London sales divisions instead of just one, and Noreen I made national sales manager.

George Brown, although he was only a lorry driver, had always been interested in the company and had acquired such a good knowledge of how things were run that I made him our area sales manager in Newcastle upon Tyne. He turned out to be every bit as successful as I had hoped. In 1962 he became a director of Electromatic.

During the course of the weekend I discovered a few more details about Elvins' new set-up and discovered some of the areas where I would be hardest hit. I also assessed which of my salesmen were likely to be staying on my side, got in touch with them and used them to plug the gaps in the organisation. Glasgow, for instance, was very badly deserted but I had one very good fellow up there who I asked to hold the fort. Another first-class man called Bill Malone, who was on very friendly terms with me, went from London to run things in Bristol.

There was one good thing to come out of all this: at least I knew the people I could trust.

On the Monday morning, the Duomatic deserters were as many as had been predicted—a good half of our salesmen and managers failed to turn in for work. It was still hard to believe since, in theory, they should all have given in their notice, but it was a fact. They had vanished. And, obviously, to sue them all for breach of contract would have been far more trouble than it was worth.

However, thanks to my 48 hours of non-stop reorganisation, people whom I could rely on slipped into new jobs all over the country. There was a colossal amount of promotion—on Friday they had been salesmen, on Monday they were managers—and we still only had half as many salesmen as we needed. But we managed to keep that lifeline to the customer open and tried to pretend nothing had happened.

The biggest blow of all came two days later, on the Wednesday. That was the day that Al Hunt told me the background to the launch of Duomatic, and how the Schroutens were responsible.

I rang them up at once but they denied that they were in any way responsible. What they did say, though, was that they had decided—by some strange coincidence—that this was the time to start supplying another company with washing machines instead of Electromatic.

I pointed out to them that there was a contract between us but they countered this by saying that the contract merely stated that they undertook to supply us with machines—and this, they now informed me, they interpreted as meaning more than one machine a week. They had therefore decided to keep to the word of their contract by supplying me with two a week.

After an argument about this I changed tack and said that the contract also laid down that I was to be the only person to handle their machines in England. They had an answer for that too. They said that their new buyer was not an English firm. They were selling their machines to some people in Switzerland.

Some time later I proved that this was not true. I hired a firm of private detectives who waited outside the Schroutens' factory watching the machines being loaded and then followed the lorries to Rotterdam airport. Two of the detectives managed to get aboard the Channel Air Bridge planes which flew the machines to Southend, and then jumped into a lorry of their own to trail the lorries of washing machines from Southend to Elvins' Duomatic factory—which, ironically, was at Romford, quite close to Gallows Corner where the Electromatic factory had been.

The invoices accompanying the machines were from the Swiss firm named by the Schroutens. But this was clearly just a ruse; the machines were straight from Holland.

This information, although it satisfied my curiosity, was not of much practical help. I was advised that if I took the matter to court it could take years to settle. And by then I would have been a long time out of business.

This then was the appalling prospect in January 1960, shortly after the Rolls-Electromatic link-up was announced: we were in the process of moving the Electromatic organisation to Cricklewood, where we would have an enormously-improved area for assembling machines; we had started a £200,000 advertising campaign; we still had enough salesmen—and were daily recruiting more—to turn a high percentage of coupon replies into sales. All we were short of were washing machines—our supplies had dried up overnight.

The advertisements, which I dreamed up and which Roger Pryer worked out on paper, only added to our headache. They were too good. They brought in a colossal number of replies and in the two weeks after the start of Duomatic we sold the whole of our small stock. The salesmen then started taking deposits from customers and, to provide us with time to reorganise, they told them that there would be an eight-week delay in delivery.

I decided that the only thing to do was to start making our own twin-tubs at Cricklewood, and I advertised in trade magazines and papers all over the world for people who could supply me with the parts.

Eventually I managed to get these supplies going but this was the first time that we had attempted to manufacture a complete machine and we were tremendously short on know-how.

Rolls Razor had a number of experienced precision engineers, but what they knew about was Rolls Razors. Their only experience of washing machines had been with the Rolls-a-matic monstrosity which had depended on a vibration principle which had not worked. The machines I wanted to make worked off motors in the normal way, but because this was new to the Rolls people our prototypes did not work in the normal way very well.

After a few weeks of trial and error, we did manage to start producing about 40 machines a week but, in all honesty, they were pretty inferior products and our efforts to improve them meant that production could not be speeded up. There were therefore complaints to the Press from the many customers still waiting for machines weeks after paying their deposit.

The effect of all this was to alarm the newspapers who did not like to think they might be carrying adverts from an unreliable organisation. We had a meeting with representatives of the Newspaper Proprietors Association and they told us that if we were to be allowed to carry on advertising in national newspapers they must satisfy themselves that all was right with our world at Cricklewood. It was arranged that advertising directors from the nationals should pay us a visit.

This was a critical situation. If they examined our operation and thought that we could not live up to our adverts then our only line of communication to the customer would be cut off. Somehow I had to convince them that we were producing a fantastic number of machines. And that was not going to be easy.

The main thing, I thought, was to create an atmosphere of incessant and efficient activity. To achieve this I made sure on the Monday of the visit that everyone in the factory was bent over some piece of machinery or metal and was wearing a scientific-looking white coat.

In the assembly section we had plenty of sheets of metal around the place but we were desperately short of mechanical parts, so the factory hands took some second-hand machines apart and busily put them back together again. I made sure that our visitors did not spend too long in this section and on a superficial glance it certainly looked very impressive.

Other parts of the building, where things were going more smoothly, we could afford to linger over. The press shop, for instance, was in full swing, stamping out the washing machine cases, so we made a great production of that part of the tour. The paint shop also had plenty of work since the cases were being turned out rapidly. And we spent a long time, stressing the words 'world-famous' and 'precision engineering' in the razor section—which was still going and occupying about a fifth of the building.

Finally we took the inspection party to the loading section where we appeared to have hundreds of washing machines stacked high. It looked as though we had so many that we could hardly cope with them and to add to this impression of a flourishing production line a large number of vans could be seen waiting outside.

In fact, there could not have been more than 75 machines waiting in the loading area and to get that number we had stacked up every machine we made the previous week, plus about ten which had been made during the visit.

All this eyewash had the desired effect. The advertising managers went away happy that production was in full swing and our adverts were allowed to continue.

But that did not solve my other problem—how to produce Rolls Electromatic washing machines that were reliable. I brought in a couple of people to help on the development side, and if I had simply wanted a copy of the Schroutens' design they may well have produced a perfectly satisfactory machine. But a copy, I thought, was no longer good enough. Since we were having to design our own machine we might as well design one which was an improvement on the Dutch original. And here the problems set in.

The first of these concerned the spin-dryer half of the twin tub. In the version made by the Schroutens the spin-dryer did not stop as soon as it was switched off; it simply spun to a halt in due course and it was possible for a housewife to open the lid while the tub was still going round. This struck me as potentially dangerous if, say, the housewife caught her sleeve in the still spinning tub. I decided to eliminate the risk by incorporating in our Rolls Electromatic a brake which stopped the tub as soon as the lid was lifted. But somehow or other we failed to get it working properly; those early 'safety-first' machines used to wobble all over the place in a very dangerous-looking way.

I also decided to improve the emptying. The Dutch machine simply emptied into a bucket on the floor so I gave my machine a special pump for emptying the dirty water into the sink. It proved a disastrous refinement. When we finally got the Rolls Electromatic into something like production in May—around 400 a week—we were inundated with complaints from housewives saying they had been flooded. It seemed as if half the country was spending its time mopping up kitchen floors after trying to empty our machine.

I thought that the name of Electromatic was getting such bad publicity that it would be politic to change the name—so Roger advertised our next modification as the Starmatic. Unfortunately this machine had a pet problem of its own—the motors.

These were imported from a respected manufacturer in Germany, but in the batch we were using there turned out to be something wrong with the wiring. The result was that they were quite literally blowing up in kitchens, giving housewives hysterics, frightening the cat and filling the whole room with swathes of smoke. The Starmatics were being sent back to the factory more quickly than they were going out.

All this time, remembering our uneasy moment over newspaper advertising, I was worried about keeping up our rate of production—so much so that I had a device put in my office which kept me bang up-to-date with the number of machines we were making. It was a little grey box, like a miniature electricity meter with a four-figure dial, fixed on the wall by my desk. Every time the last woman on the production line put a dust cover over a finished machine she used to press a small button which registered with a loud click in my office and increased the number on the dial by one. I used to reset the dial at oooo every Monday morning.

Strangers who used to come into my office could not understand this click-click the whole time and this used to amuse me a little—especially when they were too polite to ask what on earth that peculiar noise was. To my ears those clicks were like music.

Although the machines were being produced at the rate of about 500 a week in June it was still not enough to keep up with the demand and we were still getting many complaints about late deliveries. I therefore indulged in a spot of public relations with the idea of showing people how busy we were on their behalf. I simply installed a closed circuit TV camera at the end of the assembly line and a linked TV set in the Rolls showrooms. In this way anybody passing by could see with their own eyes that machines were rolling non-stop off the assembly line.

All the trouble we were having rebounded on us later when various opponents were looking for ammunition with which to attack our business methods and the quality of our machines.

But also, in a paradoxical way, it was to our advantage.

Throughout this period I kept up my policy that the house-wife was always right. So any woman who had a machine which broke down—and some, I'm sorry to say, had more than one—always received a replacement. And if any clothing was damaged we paid the bills. Whatever happened I made sure that the customer was always happy in the end. And this established a confidence that spread throughout the country and was one of the main reasons for our colossal build-up of sales later on.

Meanwhile, although our output was improving, the quality was not. Not, that is, until I was suddenly given the technical help I needed. And that help came through the very unexpected medium of Mick Cosgrave.

After he had asked me to buy his 30 per cent of our business in 1958, I had more or less lost trace of him until, one day in April 1960, I answered the door bell at my Park Lane flat and found him standing outside with two men.

Mick introduced them as Jack and Irving Jacobs, two brothers who were selling washing machines from door-to-door and for whom he was working. They had a proposition to put to me, said Mick.

It turned out that Irving Jacobs, who was a born technician, had learned enough from working with washing machines to be able to design a model of his own. Their proposition was that Rolls should produce this machine, under Irving's direction, at a very low price and that Jack—who, like me, was not technically minded—should be sales executive.

Prototypes of the machine had already been made by a company called Bylock Electric Ltd—which was a firm which Rolls bought later on and which proved a crippling error. And the day after our Park Lane meeting the Jacobs brothers brought one of the prototypes for us to examine at Cricklewood.

It was certainly an improvement on the ones which Rolls were producing at that time, but, even so, I thought their proposal was pitching its value a bit too high.

After several further discussions I suggested that we should forget about their invention but that, instead, Irving could join

58

Rolls as works manager and make our problem machines work. He agreed to this and Jack came in to help with administration —as part of the deal to get Irving.

Two years later they both became directors of Rolls—and also became very large thorns in my side. But in 1960 Irving did what I expected of him and, with his help, the exploding Starmatic was succeeded in October by the Rolls 66 which had one giant motor operating both the washer and the dryer and which was the first of our successful models.

After the take-over the razor-making side of the business continued losing a considerable amount of money and I came to the conclusion that, since the company had a long-standing trade with chemists, we could inject some new products into the razor side and use the shops to sell it.

I was constantly on the look-out for something suitable— but finding something that would be a big-seller in chemists' shops was not the easiest of tasks.

I found what I was looking for while flipping through an American magazine. I spotted an advert for an artificial sun-tan for men and thought it was a fantastic idea. I immediately phoned the makers, the Drug Research Corporation of America and Canada, and talked with them for over an hour—at a cost, according to the telephone bill, of £104. A few days later, my contact, John André, flew to England and we arranged that I should have the British concession for this bottled sun-tan, known as Man-Tan, and all his company's other products.

As soon as the first consignment of Man-Tan reached Crickle-wood in June several secretaries and I gave it an office test. We put the liquid on our faces one morning and, as instructed, waited six hours for it to develop into a golden sun-tan as long-lasting as the real thing.

By afternoon we looked as though we had spent a month in the Bahamas. There was just one drawback; because Man-Tan was colourless it was difficult, when putting it on, to see which parts had been covered and which had been missed.

Newspapers were quick to point out this disadvantage and despite our gimmicky publicity photos of two twin girls ('Which twin has the Man-Tan?') and despite the fact that it was easily obtained at Boots and Timothy Whites, Man-Tan did not sell too well.

I therefore suggested to John André that Man-Tan might be more practical and sell better as a cream, and the company eventually did this. But it took time and several imitations came on to the market in the meantime. The whole cosmetic field we found to be ferociously competitive and British males we found to be less eager than Americans to use such products. In the end Man-Tan lost us money. And I was left still wondering how to sharpen up the razor section.

During the autumn of 1960 I came to an agreement with Rolls giving them an option to buy Electromatic. I then bought the 1,180,000 shares that I had been promised by Gilbert Southall. Naturally I did not have anything like enough spare cash of my own; I bought the shares by borrowing the money from Leadenhall Sterling Investments.

It was a strange deal which started when I decided that Rolls was in need of a cash transfusion. I first arranged that Leadenhall should lend the company £165,000. But before they would do this they wanted to hold as security the shares I had agreed to buy from Southall. And in order to buy them, Leadenhall lent me £60,000 at a hefty rate of interest which I paid back in 1961.

Although Leadenhall were holding them, these shares made me the largest shareholder—but not the majority shareholder—in Rolls, with 48 per cent.

However, at the end of the year, although I had anticipated that Rolls would make a profit of £30,000, the accountants said that because of our disastrous machines we had made a loss of over £200,000.

After fighting to get into the big time the net result, after the first twelve months, was that I had become the largest shareholder in a company making a resounding loss.

6

ALTHOUGH I WAS ON THE RIGHT TACK IN MY BUSINESS DEALINGS
from 1958 onwards I certainly went off course for a spell in my
private life.

It started, indirectly, through an old friend of mine called
Barry Huntman who ran the El Toro club—one of London's
first discotheques—in Finchley Road. I saw quite a bit of Barry,
and he always seemed to be surrounded by Rank starlets—who
were very thick on the ground in those days. Among those
whom I met were Ann Scott, Marian Collins and Claire Gordon
and I was fascinated by them; they were so much more viva-
cious than any girls I had known before.

Oddly enough, I never actually went to the El Toro at that
time, but when I moved to Cricklewood and found that the club
was only a stone's throw away from the factory I started using
it regularly after work for informal talks with my assistants.
In fact, we attracted such a lot of publicity and business became so brisk that I decided to buy a half share in the place and
Barry put a big sign outside saying: 'John Bloom and Barry
Huntman proudly present the new El Toro club.' It was my first
venture into night clubs, which are now my bread and butter.

Back in 1958, however, night clubs were all very new to me.
So, too, was the starlet syndrome but, basically, it seemed that
the girls were hoping for a big part by being 'noticed', so they
led a hectic life trying to get their photographs in the papers
and going to the right show business parties.

The king of this whirlwind world was Dennis Hamilton, the

first husband of Diana Dors, who burnt himself out with his wild living and died suddenly in January 1959 at the age of 34. He was a big tough man with an apparently insatiable desire for girls and parties. And although I was only on the fringe of his world the day inevitably came when I was invited to one of the parties at his house in Maidenhead. There was no special welcome for me, of course. There were so many people there, and so many famous names, that one more modestly well-known person was neither here nor there.

As Hamilton's appetite for pleasure had become more and more blunted over the years, his parties had become more and more extravagant and bizarre. The whole concept of them—100 per cent sex—and people's behaviour at them came as a complete shock to me, although perhaps most people would not find them so shocking today. For good or ill, society has moved a long way in the past decade. However, at that time, I never realised such things went on.

It seemed that at every party the first order of the night was that everyone should go swimming in Hamilton's large indoor pool. In the nude, naturally. I was a non-swimmer so I was only a spectator sitting around the edge of the pool or talking with other people who opted out of the water ballet. There was always an incredible mixture of people involved: would-be actresses, men claiming to be film producers, men who actually were film producers, members of Parliament, film stars, chauffeurs, singers, managers, agents and, of course, the irrepressible Dennis Hamilton.

One of his favourite party pieces involved two-way mirrors —mirrors which reflected normally on one side but which could be seen through like a window from the other. Dennis had them in a couple of the bedrooms and even in one of the toilets. His idea of a joke was to wait until a couple were becoming very friendly and then to announce a pub crawl, at which point he and his cronies would leave the couple alone and pretend to leave the house. In fact, they would be hiding in another room waiting for the couple to drift up to the bedroom. They would then gather in the next room and watch the activities through the two-way mirror.

I never saw these mirrors but at one party I met someone who installed them for a living. He offered to fix them up throughout my flat and insisted that his modest fee would afford hours of pleasure but I was not enamoured of the idea and turned him down.

Dennis seemed to fancy himself as a photographer. At every party I went to he would be rushing around taking pictures with a polaroid camera. His aim was to photograph everybody and I saw him pop up in the most unlikely places—sometimes with two spare cameras slung round his neck—to take a quick photograph of some unsuspecting couple. It was like an amateur photographer's benefit.

Some time after Dennis died there were several rumours circulating about MP's and actors being blackmailed as a result of these photographs but there was no danger of this happening. Dennis always used polaroid cameras which do not have negatives. And at the end of each party he presented the prints, the sole record, to the person photographed.

Although the parties started as a great novelty to me I soon tired of them. It took only a few weeks before they all seemed boringly similar and I left the Hamilton circus as rapidly as I had joined it.

Shortly after Barry Huntman and I went into partnership at the El Toro in 1960 it looked as though the venture would be brought to an untimely end. One evening that summer Barry was visited at the club by James (Scots Jack) Buggy. Buggy at that time was a not-so-well known London thug; seven years later he became a rather better known murder victim when his body, bound with wire and ventilated with five bullet holes, was fished in a rather offensive condition from the sea off the Sussex coast. His killer or killers were never traced.

When he next called on Barry in Brighton he was rather insistent that he and I should put fruit machines into the club. Barry said something like: 'I can't do it. My partner John Bloom doesn't want them.' This statement had two results; one was that Buggy threatened to mark all the Rolls company cars, the other was that I was visited as well.

I did not see Buggy himself. I was sitting in the Café de la

Paix in Hanover Square having a quick coffee when two heavy-weights sat down on either side of me. 'We hear you don't want our machines in your club,' they said. 'Club?' I said. 'Club? I have nothing to do with any club.' They were not convinced that I was telling the truth, but they were not sure that I was lying either. So they contented themselves with murmured threats. My mind was far from peaceful as I left the Café de la Paix.

Barry and I told Scotland Yard and several friends about our visitors. They all said: 'It's happening all the time. They're just con men. Take no notice.' I thought this was taking a risk, but the extent of the risk only came home to me a couple of months later when I heard that Buggy had been thrown out of the Pigalle Club in Piccadilly—after trying to persuade Shirley Bassey to go and entertain some friends at a party—and, in a brawl outside, had shot a man in the stomach. He got nine years in Wormwood Scrubs for shooting with intent to do grievous bodily harm. He served six years and it was only five months after his release that his body was found.

It was in the summer of 1960, at the ripe old age of 28, that I made my first visit to the South of France. I was looking for a holiday site suitable for the winners of a competition we were running to promote Man-Tan.

I took the opportunity of visiting a casino for a small gamble at the roulette table. I had no notion of any system, I simply put bets of about £3 on the 8 or 11, which is the date of my birthday—the 8th of November. When I had won a few times I doubled up some of the bets and by beginner's fluke I eventually amassed over £100—which is peanuts on the Riviera but which delighted me as a complete amateur.

Then a very strange thing happened. An extremely lovely girl walked round the table, helped herself to a handful of my chips and put them on some other numbers. Before I could protest, the croupier had shouted: 'Rien ne va plus.' The girl's number failed to come up and she gave me a brief smile as my chips were raked back into the casino's grasp.

I later learned that a crowd of these girls invades the Riviera every summer, often from London. They never have any money; they just sponge off men who are winning at the tables. I was just small fry, of course, there are people gambling every day in much larger units. And a few of their chips can give the girls a very luxurious life for quite a time. Nobody, however famous, ever seems to object to these beautiful parasites. And whether you are with your wife or not they come up and gamble with your money. It is just an accepted part of Riviera life.

It was in the spring of that year, and in a somewhat less glamorous setting, that I met my future wife, Anne Cass. She was sitting with a girl-friend in a coffee bar in Baker Street and I was just leaving with another fellow when he spotted her. It turned out that he was an old boy-friend of hers. He introduced me and told Anne about a committee to help handicapped children which I was starting. Then he asked her if she would like to go to a meeting at my flat a few days later and she said yes, she would.

I was still very shy and hardly spoke to her on the evening of the meeting although I gave her a lift afterwards—so that she would not be late for a date with some other fellow. But we had coffee together soon after and then started going out on a few dates.

She knew nothing about me, my washing machines or my recent move to Rolls; I was obviously not so well-known as I imagined. I always remember that when we first had a real conversation she kept telling me about a boy she used to know, called David Lewis, who had got his name in the papers once or twice and was, she said, very well-known. In fact he was one of the people who had been supplying me with parts for my machines.

In those days the publicity and the money were going to my head, but Anne was not very impressed by either. For example, she could never understand my fascination with ostentatious cars. She proved a steadying influence at just the right time. I was really still running quite wild until I met her.

She was 20, eight years younger than me, and worked as a secretary with a small features agency in Fleet Street. She lived with her parents in Ealing and when we began going out regularly—or as regularly as my flooding and exploding washing machines would allow—I went round to her home for dinner quite often.

That summer she had arranged to spend her holidays with another girl in Majorca and after she had gone I found to my surprise that although I was very busy I still had time to feel a bit miserable. Eventually I rang her parents to find out where she was staying and then, starting at about ten pm, I kept ringing her hotel. It was two o'clock in the morning when she finally answered and I asked her if she would please come home at once. She flew back the next day.

We got engaged one night in September. We had been having an argument about something but we made it up and ended by deciding there and then to get married. We drove straight over to Carberry Avenue to tell Anne's parents the news, despite the fact that it had got to 1.30 in the morning. When we burst in and woke up her mother and father they were naturally a bit dazed and taken aback at the lateness of the hour, but they gave us their blessing and we arranged to get married on Sunday, February 12th, 1961.

The wedding was stage-managed down to the smallest detail by my publicity people, Derek Agnew and Michael Mordaunt-Smith, who looked on it as a unique public relations and advertising opportunity. To Anne and me it was the marriage which was the important thing; we let everyone else get on with organising the ballyhoo.

The gimmick that they came up with was to have two giant wedding cakes—one a replica of the Rolls Starmatic washing machine and the other a replica of a dishwasher we were planning to launch. The cakes were made by Mavis Welch, the wife of Leslie Welch, one of my designers. He gave her the actual technical blueprints to help her to get everything absolutely accurate and the cakes took her 150 hours to finish. The publicity material said they weighed a ton between them and the headlines 'A ton of love' inevitably appeared. To be strictly accurate they did not quite weigh a ton—but it still took four men to carry them into the Savoy Hotel where the reception was held.

I was too busy to have a party the night before the wedding; I was working up till 10 o'clock. But I did take the morning of the wedding off, and was at the Central Synagogue in Great Portland Street in good time for the 3 o'clock ceremony. Anne decided to be a traditional bride in every sense—it was 3.15 when she arrived. But the sight of her in her white satin gown was worth the wait.

The reception was in the Savoy's huge ballroom and Anne and I had to make a grand entrance with the toastmaster leading the way. It was a very unnerving moment as we walked through the big double doors to see about 500 guests waiting for us and applauding our entrance. The ballroom was an impressive sight, the rows of tables were decked out with bouquets of flowers and the candles on the tables were reflected in the enormous mirrors that lined the pale pink and grey walls. High overhead, the light sparkled from the crystal chandeliers.

Although we enjoyed all this grandeur, Anne and I would have preferred a smaller wedding, but it just could not be done. There were so many business contacts and colleagues to invite, and there could be no question of making a selection. There were an enormous number of suppliers of Rolls parts alone. One could not invite the supplier of washtubs without inviting the motor supplier. Then their wives had to come. And their children. And so it went on. To make matters worse I invited the whole of the Arsenal team since I was a great fan of theirs.

The oddest thing about the dinner was that I felt shy about making the bridegroom's speech. I usually speak very fluently and without notes but on this occasion I decided to write the speech out beforehand and learn it. It was very brief and straightforward—starting off, 'Unaccustomed as I am to getting married' and ending with thanks to all the right people. Yet when I heard it on a tape recording later, I was amazed to find what a mess I had made of it. It must have been the worst speech I ever made. Another part of my ordeal by reception was having to take the first waltz alone with Anne on the ballroom floor watched by 500 people. However I told myself they were all watching Anne so I did not feel too bad.

During the dancing that evening many of the guests tape-recorded their good wishes but the person who summed up my own feelings was my brother-in-law Herbie when he proposed the toast to Anne and myself. He said: 'While John has had many successful ventures, in choosing Anne to be his wife he has embarked upon his most successful venture of all'. He was 100 per cent correct.

After the reception ended at midnight, Anne and I stayed at the Savoy. But first thing next morning I was back at work at Cricklewood. The Press made a big feature out of this, but to me it was just common sense. With all my problems at Rolls I could scarcely afford time off even for our three-day honeymoon in Switzerland. Since the train did not leave until the afternoon there was certainly no point in wasting the morning.

We stayed at the Sweitzerhopf hotel in Lucerne which was virtually empty at that time of year. There were the makings of an international incident when they were reluctant to let us in because Anne's passport was still in her maiden name, but they were duly apologetic when I rummaged in our bags and waved under their noses our wedding picture on the front page of the *Daily Mirror*. A young messenger at the hotel, unsuspectingly, made up for this bureaucracy the next day. He had not seen my *Daily Mirror* so when the papers arrived from England he was amazed that we and our wedding cakes were all over the front pages. He could not get over the fact that we were there in the flesh and he made Anne feel as though she were the Queen.

Jenkins, my chauffeur, had driven the Rolls out to Switzerland earlier and took us on mountain sight-seeing tours during our stay. But in the back of my mind I knew that there was terrible trouble over keeping supplies of wash tubs flowing to Rolls. As a result I kept stopping the car in remote villages to hunt for a telephone and put in calls to Cricklewood to find out what was hapening. Anne appreciated that in my position this was something I just had to do. But it was enough to take the edge off the most romantic Alpine idyll.

When we arrived back at Victoria station we were pleasantly surprised to find Mick Cosgrave waiting to greet us. In his arms he had a poodle which he gave us as a wedding present. In return I asked him if he would like to rejoin the business which he had helped to start and he eventually became a general assistant at Rolls. But he was ill for a considerable time so did not play any real part in the events of the next four years.

I had, by now, left my little place in Park Lane and had moved into a much larger flat in Aldford House, Park Street, which gained the reputation of being an unbelievably luxurious place. In fact it was nothing out of the ordinary and cost only £1,000 a year to rent. It was basically a set of rooms off one corridor. There was a large living room at one end, a kitchen and maid's room at the other and, leading off the length of the corridor were two bedrooms, a dining room, a small bar and the bathroom.

There were no incredible gadgets in the kitchen, no astonishing pieces of ceramic art in the bathroom, and the central heating never worked efficiently from the day I moved in. It is true that I had a few television sets—but I did not have one in every room as was always being stated. I think there were four. The only real luxury was an enormous double bed, incorporating many gimmicky electric gadgets, which cost me £1,000 from the Ideal Home Exhibition.

The bed, which was really twin beds side by side, had two television sets at the bottom, one for each person in case they wanted to watch different channels. At either side there were two compartments extending from the bed head. In each top compartment was a radio and identical sets of control buttons which could close the curtains, switch off the room light and raise the top end of the bed into a reading or TV-watching position. In the bottom compartment at one side there was a teamaker and in the other a tape recorder. A heater was built in to the mattress.

The only thing wrong with this wonder bed was that its electronic marvels were very rarely all working at the same time. And when they were, there was a steady hum which was not conducive to sleep. Anne and I put our thousand pounds-worth in the guest room. We ourselves had a good old-fashioned four-poster.

Very soon after our honeymoon I had an idea for boosting sales which radically altered my private life by making me into a weekend commuter to the blue seas of the Riviera. The idea was born, however, on the rather less glamorous sluggish grey waters of the Thames.

I always believed in keeping staff in touch with the company through lots of questions and answers face-to-face with me, and in the spring of 1961 I decided to hold one of these off-the-cuff sessions—sales conferences they were officially called—aboard a boat which Electromatic had owned for some time. The vessel, a 77ft ex-naval job called Lalage, was down in Bristol and in need of care and attention but I arranged that Rex Wood should go down and help sail her round the south coast to the Thames. He contrived to run her aground on the Goodwin Sands but by this time I was learning to live with such unexpected complications to apparently simple plans and I waited patiently for Lalage to reach the Thames. When she arrived a group of 20 London salesmen gave her an overhaul and face-lift and she was looking very smart as I and about 80 London salesmen boarded her at Putney some weeks later.

As we sailed past the Houses of Parliament at Westminster I grabbed a large megaphone and bellowed: 'Why not help the poor washing machine manufacturers? Cut the purchase tax on washing machines. Help the washing machine manufacturers and help the housewife.' But apart from this piece of showmanship we spent the time discussing Rolls.

During the discussion I told the salesmen that I had thought of a new idea to step up sales—not by giving the housewife more incentive to buy but by giving the salesman more incentive to sell. This statement was really made just to whet their appetites. I could not go into details because I had not worked any details out. But I did have the basic idea at the back of my mind—to hire a villa in the south of France and to let men who sold a certain number of machines spend a holiday there. This, I was sure, would be an attractive bonus and one which the taxmen could not make less attractive by demanding his cut.

The way it worked out in the end was that if every salesman

at any one branch sold seven machines a week for four successive weeks then they and their wives and the whole of the branch office staff had a week's holiday on the Riviera entirely at the company's expense.

I was particularly pleased that this gave the salesmen's wives an incentive too. Since my policy was that a machine should never be sold to the housewife alone—as the small-time door-to-door sharks were doing—the salesmen used to do most of their work in the evening when the husbands were at home. And although my best salesmen were making £3,000 a year many salesmen's wives resented the fact that they were out in the evenings. The chance of the holiday of a lifetime was one way of proving that these evenings were worthwhile and that Rolls was not such a monster after all.

If I wanted the villa incentive scheme to get under way that year I had to move fast in search of a suitable villa. The fastest way of moving was by air, and although I had always avoided flying before—even on my brief honeymoon—I decided that as the business grew bigger I would have to fly sometime and this seemed as good a time to start as any. Somehow I had managed to make everyone else at Rolls worried about my flying and they kept saying: 'What would happen to Rolls if John wasn't here?' However, when we inquired about insurance we found it would only cost the company £700 to insure me for a million pounds for a year. At these odds I suddenly started feeling much safer. The flight itself was perfect and my whole attitude to air travel changed completely.

Before leaving, Anne and I visited several top London estate agents who gave us details of what seemed perfect villas with luxurious fittings and beautiful settings. Neither of us had any house-hunting experience but I realised later that the trouble we faced with the villas was the trouble people have with any other house—they fall far short of the agent's description. Although villas do not look their best out of season and we had to make allowances, many of them were incredibly dilapidated. One place in particular needed repainting from top to bottom, its much vaunted swimming pool was a dirty hole in the ground the size of a duck pond and the 'five acres of beautiful park-

71

land' was about as cultivated as the furthest reaches of the Amazon jungle. But at least that villa was large; most of the ones we visited were like ordinary houses—so much so that Anne and I renamed the South of France *Costa Suburbia*.

In desperation we then went to some French estate agents. We told them what we were looking for—a villa about the size of a small hotel in order to accommodate our big parties of salesmen, one that was near an airport as I wanted the travelling time cut to a minimum, and one which had a large swimming pool if it was not actually on the Mediterranean.

The place belonging to Garfield Weston, the biscuit king, was ruled out because it had no pool. But we were then shown a villa called La Serena at Cap Ferrat which, although not beautiful, was very comfortable. We rented it for April and September for £500 a week from Viscount Bearsted. Just after this we were shown probably the best-known and most opulent villa on the Riviera—La Fiorentina, which Elizabeth Taylor and Mike Todd had for their honeymoon. It was one of about five villas owned by Lady Kenmare, the third and last wife of Viscount Furness the shipping millionaire. I only saw her once. I was looking round the villa on one occasion when I saw a woman perched on some ladders painting a bedroom. I hardly noticed her but I later discovered that it was Lady Kenmare; she enjoyed decorating and had done a lot of her house herself. We were lucky enough to be able to hire La Fiorentina for May, June, July and August at £1,000 a week.

It was a huge white colonnaded building situated in eleven acres of cypress trees on a peninsula of its own, again at Cap Ferrat. The huge hall had a marble floor with a staircase sweeping up from it in best story-book tradition. There was a priceless 18th century fresco from Turin in the dining room, a hand by Rodin lying on a table and the library was solid with valuable first editions. The villa also had an orangery, a private port, a swimming pool down by the sea and a tennis court. Although the style was in the grand manner all the fittings were new since it had been rebuilt after being occupied by the Germans during the war and blown up by the Americans. It had therefore the best of both worlds and Anne and I fell in love with it at once.

Apart from providing these fabulous surroundings for my salesmen I also laid on 'fringe benefits' such as a Ford Galaxy convertible, which I bought specially, a speed-boat and a cabin cruiser. I was determined to let my salesmen live for a week like millionaires.

There was an enormous amount of organisation to be done by my assistants, but it also meant a lot of work for me personally. When the first branch, London south-east, qualified for the holiday I flew with them by Caravelle to Nice on the Friday, showed them around La Serena, told them how to drive the boats and so on, then stayed on, acting as host until the Sunday night. Anne and I continued this weekend commuting all summer. Sometimes she would be hostess for the whole of the week, and although the villas had large staffs—including an imposing negro majordomo at La Fiorentina—she was kept busy.

But apart from fulfilling our duties we both had a fantastic time, savouring for the first time the rich international life of the Riviera. We moved in these circles for the next three years and it was in this way that the incentive scheme changed our lives. We became a recognised part of the so-called jet-set population in the South of France and went so far as to buy a huge yacht which, in the final year of Rolls' life, was a frequently-quoted symbol of opulence that I may well have been better off without.

During that first summer, in 1961, I invited many well-known names of the business and show business worlds to stay at the villas. They made the week memorable for the salesmen and their wives, and the fact that there was always someone different made each weekend trip more enjoyable for me.

One person who was something of a regular was Adam Faith, whom I had met at a party. He also visited me often at Cricklewood where, being a car addict, I had a miniature racing track complete with pits rigged up on the top floor. After I finished work at perhaps nine or ten in the evening he and I and one or two other people would race cars very intently into the early hours. He was also very interested in business and

73

would sit in at conferences or go with me on visits to Europe to see suppliers. He was at the peak of his success in the early 60s.

Among other visitors at the start of the villa incentive scheme were Sabrina, Bernard Braden and Barbara Kelly, with whom we became very friendly, and the Beverley sisters. Sir Joseph Lockwood, chairman of EMI, with whom I was having negotiations, also stayed with us and so did Dickie Valentine whom I had known years before in Camden Town. His wife Liz became very friendly with Anne.

As I was about to set off on one trip from Heathrow I met Jack Hylton, the impresario, who was to become an important figure in my life and a wonderful friend. He recognised me and came up to speak to me. He explained that he had bought shares in Rolls Razor years before and had hung on to them at the time of our take-over. He now wanted to know whether to keep them or get rid of them so he asked me what plans I had for the company. On the strength of what I told him he decided to hold on to his shares and he later became a very big shareholder.

Jack also had a villa on the Riviera and he used to pop over to see us quite often or we would go to have dinner with him. Through Jack I met many other people including Rosalina Neri, the actress, Keith Miller, the former cricketer, and his fellow impresario Val Parnell.

Peter Ustinov used to play tennis with Reader Harris, and I had met him in London. He had a boat moored at Cannes and he and his wife Suzanne invited Anne and I to dinner. He introduced an unknown actor to us who was then making his first film as the star in Ustinov's film *Billy Budd*. This was Terry Stamp who became an international star through the film— which I later watched being made at Elstree. After the collapse of Rolls, Stamp and I were involved in a night club venture for a short time.

After our meeting on his boat Peter became a very familiar figure at our villa dinner parties. From seven until eleven in the evening he would keep everyone entertained with stories of his varied career in countries all over the globe. He was every bit as brilliant a conversationalist as he appears on television and Anne and I always used to look forward to his visits.

Lionel Bart visited us that summer, along with Larry Parnes, the man who discovered Tommy Steele and with whom I had become very friendly in charity work. I also got to know Joe Loss very well. I met him one night at the Beaulieu casino which everyone seemed to go to. I found him quite an ordinary person—as were most of the celebrities I knew—and he was just as interested to meet me as I was to meet him. He and his wife dropped in on us quite often. On one occasion we all went out in the cabin cruiser and became stranded some miles out of Cannes because we had run out of petrol. Luckily we had the little speed-boat behind us so the crew reversed this order and we chugged slowly back under tow. Actually the mishap made our trip very pleasant; we took two lazy hours to get to the harbour and we all became very sunburned.

I was always slightly apprehensive on these sea trips because I could not swim. When we were at La Fiorentina I had learned how to keep afloat on my back and I could manage just about a length of the pool swimming on my back. But the moment I went on to my face I felt I could not breathe properly. Later on, however, when we were back at La Serena, several people decided they would teach me to swim properly. There was quite a party round the pool as I got into the water and turned on to my front as instructed. All I then had to do to be able to breathe was to keep my chin up, they said. However, just as I was doing this someone said something which made me laugh and as I opened my mouth I seemed to swallow an ocean of water.

The next thing I knew I was at the bottom of the pool looking up at the sky through the rippling water. I remember surfacing once, then sinking again. When I came to the top a second time everyone seemed to be glued to the side of the pool just looking at me. Apparently there was an amazed look on my face which said: 'Why is nobody doing anything?' and it then dawned on people that I was in desperate trouble. Two men, Dave Solomons and Harvey Langer—who was supplying me with table tops for my washing machines—dived in to drag me out. I do

75

not remember anything about the rescue. The next thing I knew I was lying on the side of the pool having water pumped out of me.

I can still only swim on my back.

7

WHILE THE SALESMEN WERE BUSY THAT SUMMER TRYING TO win free holidays and helping to bring the year's sale to 68,000 machines—more than double the 29,000 of 1960—I was busy restructuring Rolls. The aim was straightforward—to get the Rolls shares quoted once more on the Stock Exchange.

Although I had proved I could sell washing machines, I lacked training and experience in matters of finance and I was regarded with caution by the City since by their standards I was still a mere stripling of 29. My policy of employing only people under the age of 40 was also a disadvantage in their eyes. The time had come to surround myself with older and more experienced heads at board level.

I asked Derek Agnew if he had come into contact with any-one who might be a help to me. He said that on the board of Westbourne Press, which was the public relations firm he was running, there were three Members of Parliament whom I could meet: Billy Rees-Davies (Conservative, Isle of Thanet), Mrs Patricia M'Loughlin (Ulster Unionist, Belfast West), and Richard Reader Harris (Conservative, Heston and Isleworth).

I met Reader Harris at a cocktail party given by Agnew and explained that I was aiming to make the directors and the organisation of Rolls more in line with Stock Exchange tradi-tion and that I would like him to be the chairman. After several discussions he became a director of Electromatic—as an interim measure—on March 2nd and Billy Rees-Davies joined the board at the same time.

I was keen to have Reader Harris because of his legal training and his knowledge of business administration. Although he had been an MP for eleven years he was also a barrister and was a director of over a dozen companies—including five in the Livestock Group of Companies which promoted pig schemes. However he resigned all these posts to enable him to concentrate on Rolls and he became chairman in July.

Reader Harris was also useful in introducing me to other figures in the City who were in a position to help me. One of these was Edward du Cann who became chairman of the Conservative Party and with whom I stayed on friendly terms for some years. He introduced me to various City banks, including Rothschilds, and to his stockbrokers, Fenn & Crosthwaite, who agreed to act for Rolls. Edward du Cann had 50 of the 1,000 shares in a firm called EM Central Heating which I started in June of 1961 to sell a cheap electric radiator system that people could take with them when they moved. The firm was in existence for 18 months but did not make any money.

Another person whom I met through Reader Harris was Henry Oppenheim, the dapper 49-year-old Scot who was chairman of City Wall Properties. Reader Harris and he were co-directors of an associated company called Industrial and Investment Services. I met Oppenheim for the first time at Cricklewood, shortly before Reader Harris became chairman. He said he would help Rolls to retain the services of Price Waterhouse as auditors and took me to see John Read a director of Kleinwort Benson, the prominent merchant bankers.

I supplied a lot of information to Kleinworts and they made a detailed investigation into the company's affairs. One of their up-and-coming young assistants, Bobby Brooks, came round all the branches on a fact-finding tour and was very impressed by the enthusiasm of all our salesmen. At the same time Oppenheim wrote to John Read: 'I suppose it is true to say that every generation throws up one or two outstanding individuals and as the gentleman concerned is only 30 years old (I was 29, actually) there may be a chance that he is one of those people.' The result of all this was that Kleinworts agreed to take charge of refloating the company on the Stock Exchange—but I am sure that it was the keenness of the Rolls employees that was the really deciding factor.

Oppenheim also provided me with an introduction to Sir Charles Colston and from this stemmed a deal that caused a sensation. Sir Charles had been the brains behind the success of Hoover in Britain; he joined the company in 1919 and when he left in 1954 after 30 years as managing director—and with an £83,000 golden handshake—Hoover was making more money in Britain than in America where it started. But apart from sharing success we were totally different characters. For a start, he was 69 and I was 40 years younger; he was a traditionalist, a member of the Establishment and the holder of the Military Cross and Distinguished Conduct Medal from the First World War; he was also totally opposed to direct-selling.

When I met him he was head of his own firm, Charles Colston Ltd., which was making dishwashers. His aim was to build up the business to the point where he could leave his son, Michael, a Colston empire as grand as Hoover. The big obstacle that he faced was that his dishwashers cost 90 gns and so were very much in the luxury class—just as washing machines had been before my intervention.

I got on very well with Sir Charles and his close associate Aaron Wright, who was in many ways the brains of the firm, and I was able to convince them that direct selling, with proper after-sales service, could have the same effect on dishwasher sales as they had had on washing machines. Sir Charles therefore agreed that we should set up a joint company to handle the dishwashers—and perhaps later expand into the fields of electric mixers, toasters and so on. On the strength of this agreement he also consented to come on the Rolls board. The advantage to me was that Rolls added a new string to its bow and acquired probably the most respected name in the domestic appliance industry. I was certain that dishwashers offered a great opportunity for repeating my washing machine success if the price was right and the advertising as hard-hitting. We had been unable to perfect the dishwasher promised by our wedding cake—Anne had tested it and had found various faults—but by this deal I got a supply of quality dishwashers immediately and

79

Sir Charles got the direct-selling organisation he needed to cut costs and reach a big market.

The deal was sprung on an astonished world at a Press conference at the Savoy on November 13. We formed a new company called Rolls-Colston Appliances into which we both put £125,000. We bought Sir Charles' factory at High Wycombe, and only a week after the announcement, started selling dishwashers direct to the housewife for 49 gns, with a de luxe model at 66 gns. In the shops, remember, they had been 90 gns. The new board consisted of Sir Charles as chairman and joint managing director, Reader Harris as deputy chairman, myself as the other managing director, plus Oppenheim, Michael Colston and Aaron Wright.

An incidental advantage of this connection was that Sir Charles had another firm, called Tallent Engineering at Aycliffe, Co. Durham. He said they could make washing machines for Rolls very cheaply and in April, 1962, they started making about 500 a week for us. Later on, Tallent saved us from terrible production trouble.

Colston and Oppenheim both became directors of Rolls just before the Rolls-Colston deal was announced and because Oppenheim had introduced me to Colston and to Kleinworts, who were very important to the future of Rolls, I agreed to sell him 50,000 of my own shares in Rolls for 8s 9d each. This was about the price at which Rolls shares were changing hands in unofficial dealings but, obviously, when the shares regained their quotation Openheim's 50,000 would be worth considerably more than he paid me for them.

Shortly afterwards, in December, Rolls finally agreed to buy Electromatic from me. This had basically been agreed during the take-over of January, 1960, when Rolls were going to issue me with three million shares in return for Electromatic—provided that Electromatic's net assets at the end of the year were at least £150,000 and provided that the Stock Exchange restored dealings in Rolls shares. However the Committee on Quotations refused to requote the shares and, since a quotation did not seem on the cards for some time, the Rolls-Electromatic agreement was scrapped.

A later agreement in October, 1960, gave Rolls an option to buy Electromatic whether the quotation was restored or not. This time I would be given two million shares provided Electromatic had net assets of £100,000. It took Gerald Edelman and Price Waterhouse most of 1961 to audit Electromatic's 1960 accounts but they were able to report to Rolls on December 6th that Electromatic had passed the £100,000 barrier with assets of £108,403, and the directors therefore agreed to buy the company on January 1st. At the unofficial price the two million shares I received were worth perhaps £1 million and with the shares that I had from Gilbert Southall I was worth about £2 million—on paper. I also became the majority shareholder in Rolls with 64 per cent, and was therefore happy to hear that Rolls and Electromatic together had made £280,000 in the first nine months of the year.

With Electromatic securely under its belt, with directors like Reader Harris, Oppenheim and Colston on the board and with a promising new dishwasher enterprise under way, Rolls entered 1962 confident that the Stock Exchange must recognise the company as 100 per cent reputable and allow the shares to be quoted once again.

Looking back, this success was symbolised by the dinner party which was held to celebrate my 30th birthday. It was organised by Reader Harris and held in a private room of the House of Commons. The guest of honour was my father, since, as everyone said, without him where would John Bloom be? The other guests included Edward du Cann, several MPs, many friends from the early days—such as Dickie Valentine—and people with whom I sat on various charity committees. These included Gordon Cotton, the son of Jack Cotton, with whom I bought up all the seats for the Sammy Davis Junior show at the Prince of Wales theatre for three days during August. We then sold the tickets at a premium and gave all the money to the Younger Foundation for the Mentally Handicapped.

Though Rolls was set fair for 1962 it had not all been plain sailing. There was House of Commons criticism in early December which came from Philip Goodhart (Conservative, Beckenham) during a debate on a private member's Hire Purchase Bill which was intended to stamp out unscrupulous high-pressure door-to-door salesmen. During the year there had been many attacks on their switch-selling method (showing a house-wife something attractively cheap and then leading her on to something much dearer) and although our salesmen were not door-to-door and were specifically forbidden to switch-sell we had sometimes been tarred with the same brush. Goodhart was attempting to do something similar.

He said he had no desire to indulge in a witchhunt but that he had been asked to draw attention to the Rolls and Colston operations by the Consumers' Advisory Council, who were supported by the director of the Consumers' Association, of which he was a member, and the director of the Retail Trading Standards Association. He told the House that our washing machines had attracted 'a quite unprecedentedly large number of complaints from dissatisfied customers'. He went on to read a letter from the Consumers' Advisory Council which claimed that out of 400 members with Rolls machines as many as 50 had complaints, and he reported that a national newspaper advertising our machines had received 250 complaints.

I was thankful that Rolls had Reader Harris there to represent our interests. He completely demolished the opposition. He pointed out that the Retail Trading Standards Association represented the retailers who were 'angry at our methods, which prevent the retailer getting his normal 30 per cent cut'. And since none of Goodhart's complaints appeared to concern hire purchase he could not understand why he had brought the matter up.

Reader Harris pointed out the difference between the foot-in-door merchants and our salesmen, who followed up coupon replies from people who wished to see them. He also stressed that the husband should always be present to sign an agreement —as was our practice. There was nothing wrong with high-pressure salesmanship, he said—the Government was always urging it on exporters—the real menace was misrepresentation and deception.

Making a mockery of Goodhart's so-called 'unprecedentedly large number of complaints' Reader Harris pointed out that there was no precedent for an organisation like ours. In any case, he said, we had 150,000 HP customers and no retailers to cushion complaints. To attack us because of 50 complaints, therefore, was simply not good enough. In the case of the newspaper complaints he revealed that the paper was the *Daily Mirror* and that the exact number of complaints was 256. But these were irrelevant—they extended over a period of four years and were mainly to do with late deliveries.

The annoying part about this trouble in the Commons was that if it had not been for the Schroutens and the subsequent production nightmare our opponents would have had no statistics to throw at us and it could all have been avoided. However Reader Harris was so adept in handling our case, which we reinforced with a Press statement, that the debate turned out to be a useful piece of publicity for us.

A more deliberate public relations exercise which I had started at that time was an advisory committee for all Rolls customers and potential customers. Anne and I were on it along with Pat M'Loughlin and Barbara Kelly. We were ready to give advice on anything from washing problems to how to make rock cakes. The idea was to make it a purely philanthropic service like those 'Readers Queries' columns in local papers. However the committee never became as well-known as it should have been in order to function properly. There was a complaints department apart from this committee, of course, and Rolls always told customers to send complaints straight to the managing director, so that I was always up-to-date with things which were going wrong.

This was just one of my many jobs, although I was concentrating a lot on preparing advertising and checking the success of each advert. I had started keeping a ledger in which I entered every advert under the appropriate newspaper or magazine, plus its size, selling theme and number of coupons cut out of it and returned. By dividing this number into the cost of the advert I knew the amount of money that each reply had cost. It was vital to win potential customers as cheaply as possible—and I considered this one of my main functions at Rolls. The ledger —which I called my 'leads' book because it recorded the number of people the adverts led us to—was a running commentary on my success.

It was equally vital, of course, to make sure that these leads were converted into sales and to ginger things up I started visiting every branch once a week. Since everything had been plain flying on my weekend trips to the Riviera, I decided to buy a company plane so that I could get around to three branches in a day.

Goldbart, Irving Jacobs and I were given a demonstration flight in a De Havilland Dove at a remote airfield in Hertfordshire. I sat by the pilot and was very impressed by the smooth flight but, looking on the black side, I asked the pilot what would happen if one of the two engines either fell out or stopped working. 'Like this, you mean?' he said, and calmly switched one of the engines off. I nearly had a heart attack but the Dove carried on as if nothing had happened. That clinched the deal. The plane cost Rolls £24,414.

It was not many months after buying the Dove that I was involved in a genuine scare on a flight to Exeter with Anne and Goldbart. We had landed on a grass airstrip in Southampton to pick someone up, and Bell, our pilot, was preparing to land at Exeter airport when he noticed that the green light indicating that the landing wheels were lowered had failed to come on. He warned the airport about this and told us. I must say we were a bit apprehensive. We were expecting to be thrown all over the runway and we crouched down in our seats with our chins between our hands. Meanwhile, on the ground, there was a full-scale emergency alert with fire engines standing by. I could not believe it when we landed perfectly safely. It turned out that the wheels had lowered quite normally; it was just that our rough landing at Southampton had sabotaged the little green bulb by jolting it out of position.

I ended 1961 on a successful note with Rolls buying Electromatic, but 1962 started less successfully with my attempt to kill off resale price maintenance by setting up shops selling goods at less than the manufacturers' recommended prices.

84

Officially, under the Restrictive Trade Practices Act of 1956, manufacturers could fix the price at which their goods should be sold in the shops, which meant that if they got together they could give themselves enormous profits with no fear of being undercut. Yet in some fields, such as food, shopkeepers were offering a few pence off here and there and the makers were turning a blind eye to this trading. Resale price maintenance, RPM, was beginning to crumble. In the home appliances field, most manufacturers were still very severe on anyone trying to sell at a cut price—Sir Charles Colston had been a typical example before turning to direct selling—but I thought the time was ripe for someone to test the temperature of the water by going in with both feet.

Thanks to my conversion to air travel I was able to visit America over Christmas to see how tried and tested discount stores were run; there were few examples in Britain. Anne and I had an enjoyable four days with Lou Levin, the Rolls Distributor in the USA, who showed us round Chicago and Las Vegas. We packed in five shows including Harry Belafonte and Elvis Presley and I stayed up into the early hours fascinated by the 24-hour ten-channel TV. But I also managed to cram in visits to the big discount stores.

I decided that, rather than set up monolithic supermarket-like stores, I should do my discount selling from places much more like traditional British shops. The only difference was that I would have the minimum of assistants, no fancy display or packaging, just the goods themselves on the floor or on bare shelves—but always at an attractively reduced price.

One of the manufacturers' favourite sanctions against price cutters was to refuse to supply them, and when my plan leaked out in the trade I was told that some people were trying it on me. But because of the size of my orders I found no difficulty in getting wholesalers to let me have goods—and I usually got them at a substantial discount. The first of the projected Rolls Discount Store group opened on Saturday February 10th on High Street North, East Ham. Alongside Rolls products were such things as Hotpoint Supermatic washing machines, Berry coal-effect fires, Morphy-Richards irons, Bulpitt 'Swan Brand' kettles, Pifco hair dryers, Chalfont Warminster electric blankets —all with at least 15 per cent off their price.

The shop was an immediate success. When Reader Harris and I arrived half-way through the first morning to perform the official opening ceremony we could hardly get in, and the place took £1,200 in the first week. I soon opened other shops at Cricklewood and Southend and was busily acquiring places in Wood Green, Portsmouth, Nottingham, Bristol and about ten other areas with the help of Oppenheim, who, as head of City Wall Properties was perfectly placed to find suitable sites. However the manufacturers were quick to strike. Only 17 days after the East Ham shop opened Morphy-Richards told Mr Justice Cross in the High Court that two of their people had bought an M-R hair dryer at the shop at 11s 2d less than the listed price of £3 10s 6d. They were granted an interim injunction to stop us selling any of their goods at a cut price and this was later extended. It was obvious that the courts were going to have to stand by the letter of the law, which supported the makers, and we had various negotiations soon after this case which ended in our announcing that we had agreed not to cut the price of Electrolux and 'Swan Brand' goods. Really, although the shops struggled on for some time, the battle had been lost within three weeks. This was a great disappointment. I knew that the end of resale price maintenance had to come—as it did in 1964 —but I was simply too quick off the mark.

A much deeper disappointment came in April. Anne, who had learnt that she was pregnant in December had a miscarriage in the South of France and was rushed into hospital in Nice. I was very downcast and Anne was deeply depressed so I used to fly to see her every weekend.

Although Anne was much more important this happened at a particularly awkward time from the business point of view. The Stock Exchange had agreed that our shares could be quoted again, and the Rolls board was holding lots of crucial meetings about the prospectus that Kleinworts were going to issue giving details of the company's plans and financial position. Kleinworts, who were masterminding the 'reflotation', decided to fix the price of the requoted shares by offering 500,000 of them for sale by tender at a minimum price of 20s. This means that people offer any sum they like, over 20s, for a share and the 500,000 go to the people offering most. The price at which the shares become quoted when they then go on the market is the lowest figure at which one of the 500,000 was sold. The prospectus, giving details of the company's prospects and financial structure, is intended to guide potential buyers as to how much to offer.

At the many interminable meetings about the prospectus I only ever understood the operation in outline. I was utterly lost when it came to the detailed figures. I could not follow the various balance sheets and cannot read one to this day. I pretended to be following everything while I was actually working out new advert ideas. I thought that, as I was paying a good deal of money to have the whole thing handled, I should let Kleinworts get on with it.

Two days before the prospectus was due to come out and convince the world of our stability and respectability, John Read of Kleinworts rang with some staggering news. Oppenheim was thinking of resigning. Read explained that Oppenheim had told him he was discontented with the company. 'He would like you to see him more often and discuss affairs,' Read said.

'If he resigns,' I thought, 'the effect on the City will be disastrous and the whole thing will have to be postponed.' Which was true. I immediately rang up Oppenheim to try to appease him. I said: 'If you want weekly board meetings we can have them. Or we can have board meetings whenever you like. I am prepared to do whatever you want. If you want anything changed I will try to change it.' But he still did not seem very happy so Reader Harris and I decided to go down that afternoon to his place in 'Millionaires Row'—Winnington Road, Hampstead—to try and make our peace.

When we got there the picture became clearer. Oppenheim thought we had agreed earlier that in return for his introductions he should have 100,000 shares very cheaply. I had sold him 50,000, which meant he was still owed 50,000, he said. I was desperate to placate him and so agreed to sell him 50,000 shares. There was some argy-bargy about whether they should come from me or Reader Harris, or be shared between us. But to get the thing settled I agreed to sell him 50,000 of my own holding. After that Oppenheim never mentioned his criticisms and did not repeat to us his threat to resign.

There was, however, a bitter three-quarters-of-an-hour wrangle about the price he should pay. He knew that 20s was the minimum price at which people were going to be allowed to tender and that the unofficial dealings were currently quoting them at about 24s but when I offered them at 20s he refused.

Eventually I had to let him have the whole 50,000 at 10s. After the shares were actually offered for sale some days later, the official price of a Rolls share became 23s. In other words, Oppenheim paid me some £25,000 for shares which were worth £57,000 virtually overnight. Although he had been appointed financial director of Rolls he was unable to attend another board meeting from that day until his resignation the following January. And through his total dealings in Rolls shares he made over £125,000.

The arrangement with Oppenheim was a costly one, but it did save the situation. The offer for sale went through and the shares were requoted. My own holding became worth about £3.5 million. And that, at last, was official.

8

I FOUND MYSELF INVOLVED IN SEVERAL CHARITY ENTERPRISES in 1962 and it was through them that I had my first meetings with members of the Royal Family.

I met the Duke of Edinburgh at a greyhound meeting at Harringay Stadium, London, which was organised by the Grand Order of Water Rats, the show business charity group, run that year by Ben Warriss the comedian. I became involved through a fellow called Andy Neatrour who was introduced to me by Jack Hylton and who became my personal assistant. Andy was very good at everything to do with advertising and was a tireless charity worker. He had done a fair amount for the Water Rats and was a friend of James Orr and Commander Richard Colville who were private secretary to the Duke and Press secretary to the Queen.

The Harringay meeting, on May 7th, was in aid of the Duke of Edinburgh Award scheme and so the Duke was keen to attend. He designed a cup for one of the races, which was called the Prince Philip stakes, and the winner also received £1,000 from the *London Evening News* and a Rolls Rapide de luxe from me. It was one of three machines I gave away that night and I also met the meeting's miscellaneous expenses. Among the other people at Harringay were Jack Hylton and the holiday camp kings, Fred Pontin and Billy Butlin—all of whom had put up prize money and had races named after them.

When I was introduced to the Duke we only had time to swap conversational gambits, but when I met him over dinner later on we had a more serious discussion about business. He was interested to know how my direct-selling was working and advised me that there could well be a big opening for Rolls in South America which he had recently visited and where, he said, most household appliances, including washing machines, were in terribly short supply.

Apart from the social side of the evening, I found it particularly enjoyable because I had bought a greyhound of my own, called Snipe Island, not long before and apart from going to film and theatre premieres this was one of my main hobbies. For a time, I went pretty regularly either to the White City on Fridays or Wembley on Mondays and Snipe Island managed to win a handful of quite good races. I used to stay in the comfort of the restaurant most of the time since that is the only civilised way to watch the racing.

On another occasion, again in aid of the Award scheme, Andy and I organised a wrestling contest at the Royal Albert Hall which the Duke attended. He had never been to one before and for a joke Andy and I arranged that a wrestler in one of the bouts should be thrown out of the ring on to the Duke's lap as he sat in his front-row seat. The wrestler's aim was spot-on and there were several good pictures in the next morning's papers. It was all good publicity for the Award scheme—and the Duke never realised that the whole incident had been rigged.

It was July 14th when I next saw the Duke and when Anne and I first met the Queen. The scene was a race meeting at Lingfield Park in aid of the Olympic Games Equestrian Fund—in other words it was to raise cash to send a show-jumping team to Tokio. I had sponsored the main event of the day, the Rolls Rapide Handicap—which carried prize money of £4,073 10s—after being approached by the organiser, Geoffrey Cross, chairman of the Royal Windsor Horse Show.

When we arrived at Lingfield the morning's drizzle was starting to clear and a huge crowd was arriving. There were many celebrities of the horse world present, including Pat Smythe and Lt-Col Harry Llewellyn and the race-going Earl and Countess of Westmorland. As our Rolls was being parked I spotted the Duke of Edinburgh climbing out of a modest family saloon which he had driven himself. Anne and I recognised it as a car which had zipped past us a little earlier on the road. We met rather more formally when we were presented to the Queen in the Royal marquee. Anne was very worried about having to curtsey and the night before she had several practices. She would get it right, but if I left the room I would catch her curtseying again when I got back. She went through the whole rigmarole again before going to bed and then once more before setting out in the morning—although I must confess that I had a few nods myself. I cannot say how valuable all the practice was in the event. But at least neither of us fell over.

The main impression that I had of the Queen, meeting her in person, was that Her Majesty was much smaller than I had somehow imagined. At lunch there was just general conversation about racing and I found that Her Majesty was incredibly enthusiastic about racing and horses in general. Luckily there was some excellent racing to be enjoyed that afternoon. The most dramatic event was the Kirk and Kirk Stakes in which six of the nine horses were literally abreast as they passed the post. One of them, Aubusson, was the Queen's horse and all of us in the Royal party held our breath as we waited for the announcement of the winner. But Ron Hutchinson, who was wearing the Queen's colours for the first time, seemed in no doubt and rode Aubusson straight into the winner's enclosure. Aubusson was indeed the winner and the Queen was so delighted that she ordered champagne for all of us and we drank to her success.

The winner of the Rolls Rapide Handicap was just as big a thrill for Anne and I. Lady Sassoon's Young Lochinvar was most fancied but was perhaps a bit too heavily handicapped and it was Spartan General, owned by Freddy Laker, that made most of the running and kept his neck in front at the post. Without Freddy allowing me to pay off my Channel Air Bridge debt to him in instalments four years earlier I would probably never have been in a position to sponsor the race he won. It gave me great pleasure to repay him in this way—especially since, as a keen racing man, he had put a great deal more money into horses than he used to get out of it. So I followed the Queen's example and ordered champagne all round.

The villa incentive scheme was revived for the summer of 1962—but because it had improved salesmen's performance so much I had to raise the qualifying target to an average of $9\frac{1}{2}$ machines a week for four weeks. If I had kept it at seven a week most branches would be having a free holiday every month. This time we rented two different villas at Cap Ferrat—first, Mes Roches from the Singer family and then La Tour from Curt Jurgens. Anne and I were commuting again at weekends and on one occasion in July we went to a party on board a boat which was attended by Princess Margaret. We were with Jack Hylton and a very beautiful girl called Pat Marlowe with whom he seemed very close ... Jack was extremely upset when only weeks later—on August 26th—she committed suicide. This was the day after Marilyn Monroe killed herself.

Another person I kept seeing in the South of France was Sir Isaac Wolfson, the multi-millionaire financier, whom I met earlier in the year and who for the next two years became by far the most significant figure in my business life. Our first meeting, apart from a casual encounter a few years before, came at the beginning of the year after an article in the *Sunday Times* quoted Oppenheim as saying I was a second Isaac Wolfson. The meeting very nearly did not take place because when the switchboard operator at Cricklewood rang through to say Sir Isaac was on the phone I did not believe her. I was used to people playing practical jokes on me and, thinking it was probably Leslie Goldbart, I said jokingly: 'Stop messing about.' But the switchboard girl managed to convince me that it was Sir Isaac so I arranged to ring him back.

We had many meetings, sometimes at his fabulous flat in Portland Place, and the result as far as Rolls was concerned, was that one of Sir Isaac's companies, the General Guarantee Corporation, took over half of our hire purchase financing in March —that is, he paid me the advertised cash price of the machine and the customer paid him the same amount plus interest in instalments.

As far as I, personally, was concerned, the effect was that I came under Sir Isaac's influence. I regarded him as a father figure and, since he had amassed great fortunes, as the fount of all business wisdom. As time went by, the situation developed to the point at which I hardly made any move without consulting him. If he advised against doing something then I would not lightly do it—regardless of what many other people might say to the contrary. No matter how big the deal was—it might be something which I imagined would make millions—if Sir Isaac said 'No,' there was very rarely more to be said.

He, for his part, regarded me as his protégé and was fond of telling people that John Bloom was just like he had been 30 years before. I was given this build-up frequently—and in front of the most unlikely people from outside the business world such as Julius Nyerere and Jomo Kenyatta who were once having tea with Sir Isaac while attending a Commonwealth Prime Ministers' conference.

A typical example of the way I used to mix business and pleasure was the period from the 19th to the 28th of August. On the 19th we had a cocktail party at La Tour and entertained Jack Hylton and Rosalina Neri to dinner. The next day Sir Joseph Lockwood, chairman of EMI, came to stay with us and we talked business for a couple of days. On the 22nd Anne and I flew back to London so that I could keep tabs on people at Cricklewood and on various long-term projects I had in hand and we returned to Cap Ferrat on the 24th. Sir Charles Colston, who was over there, came to lunch with us that day. On the 25th we went to dinner at the Metropole Hotel, Beaulieu, with Felix Neubergh one of Sir Isaac's right-hand men. On the 26th we had lunch with Sir Charles again and the day after we had dinner with some friends of Jack Hylton aboard their boat in Monte Carlo harbour. On the 28th we went to a dinner party given by Sir Isaac and Lady Wolfson. Looking back, it seems for the most part a rather boring sort of routine—a more expensive version of the endless rounds of cocktail parties suburban neighbours arrange at each other's houses every Sunday.

Peter Ustinov, whom Anne and I tried to see as frequently as possible, was never boring, of course. I remember one incredible occasion when he came to dinner and acted out various roles which he had played in films—plus everyone else's supporting parts.

Later, in New York, Anne and I had a meal with Peter which lasted about nine hours. It started off as lunch for three in his Park Avenue flat. Then we were joined by Shirley MacLaine and moved on to the Russian Tea Room next to the Carnegie Hall. Lunch developed into tea, the eccentric surrealist painter Salvador Dali arrived, and tea became dinner. All the time, Peter was telling us tales of his trips across Australia and America. He was still talking when he had to rush off to record a spot on the Johnny Carson show. I can be as talkative as most people but on that occasion neither I nor anybody else in that strange group could get a word in. I still keep friendly with Peter and have been with him on many occasions since but I think that day in New York was his best performance ever.

In the autumn of 1962 Peter was very keen on breaking into industry. He was also very interested in cars and knew the history of Rolls-Royce and Bentley backwards. So we had put both interests together and were working on a project for taking over the AC car company. He was very serious about this—despite the fact that most of our business meetings continued into the early hours with everyone speechless with laughter. Our plan was to sell cars direct like my washing machines. Unfortunately we found that there were many problems, the main one being after-sales service, which is essential. I encountered this again later when I tried to obtain the selling rights of the little Daf cars.

The abortive exercise with Peter in the autumn of 1962 was very much on the fringe of my business activities. There was, however, a problem right at the heart of Rolls which I was trying to sort out at the same time. In some ways it was a very pleasant problem; sales were going so well—we were selling over 2,500 a week—that Cricklewood would soon be unable to cope. It was a case for urgent action.

One idea I had was to take over Jim Elvins' Duomatic which was still battling away at Romford. He was only selling about 700 machines a week, but that would have been a help. On the other hand he had no production capacity of his own; he was still importing from Holland. Although a take-over would mean I could sell his extra machines without the expense of duplicate sales and servicing organisations I was mainly concerned with the long-term production question. And there were people in a much better position than Elvins to help me there.

The best prospect at one time appeared to be Sir Joseph Lockwood to whom Jack Hylton introduced me after taking me to a dinner of the Saints and Sinners. He came as our guest to the Riviera, of course, and I asked him one night over dinner whether he could help to make Rolls washing machines. He said that he was sure something could be arranged because his company, EMI, had just taken over Morphy-Richards who had a factory in Dundee that would be just right. I had detailed discussions with him later in his office in Manchester Square and the City was quick to start the rumour that Sir Joseph was bidding for Rolls.

Patrick Sergeant, the city editor of the *Daily Mail*, whom I had got to know quite well, came on the phone to me about this. I denied the rumour and told him the real story. He then solved the whole problem for me. He said that the Pressed Steel Company had a huge factory in South Wales which was supposed to be making Prestcold refrigerators in unimaginable numbers but which was trundling along lamely producing at only about a quarter of its capacity. Pressed Steel as a whole, he said, were in terrible difficulties. They made bodies for the car industry and were supplying BMC, Rootes, Rover, Jaguar and Rolls-Royce, but during 1961, because of a big recession in the motor industry, Pressed Steel had lost £2,800,000. On top of this they had spent a lot of money developing the Beagle aircraft. The company should have been renamed Hard Pressed Steel.

I managed, through my brokers, to contact the chairman of Pressed Steel, Alex Abel Smith, and I discussed with him and his managing director, Joe Edwards, a possible agreement for them to turn out Rolls washing machines. Most of our meetings were, again, in the South of France—as far as possible from the inquisitive noses and fertile imaginations of newspaper men, whose activities in constantly concocting mergers and takeovers out of any meeting that I had with anybody were becoming a serious handicap.

When I eventually visited the Prestcold plant, which was in Swansea, I was completely staggered. It was the factory of my dreams—just as the Rolls factory had been three years earlier, only this time it was magnificent by any standards. It cost £4,750,000 to build, only two years earlier, and covered 50 acres. If they would agree to the deal, I thought, my capacity for producing washing machines would be virtually limitless.

Edwards and his technical team examined one of our machines and analysed the cost. Their report was astonishing. Yes, they could make an identical machine and they could let me have it for £23—which was £6 less than it was costing me at Cricklewood. This, obviously, was an extraordinarily advantageous deal. But what made it ten times better was that Pressed Steel also agreed that I could market their world-famous Prestcold refrigerator by direct selling. This part of the deal had even greater consequences for Rolls than the manufacturing agreement.

To seal the bargain, which was signed on September 9th, Pressed Steel and Rolls exchanged shares worth about £750,000. They took up 500,000, which gave them a 10 per cent interest in Rolls, and I took up over 900,000, which represented about 3½ per cent of their shares. We also set up a firm called Rolls Prestcold Appliances to handle the refrigerator business. The headquarters were the former Prestcold offices at Sceptre House, in Regent Street with the Royal warrant proudly displayed over the main entrance. As soon as the deal was announced I moved from Cricklewood and made the much more central Regent Street my headquarters.

Apart from Pressed Steel, the whole of South Wales was enthusiastic over the Rolls-Prestcold pact. It was an area of high unemployment and the Mayor of Swansea welcomed the prospect of 100 per cent productivity at the huge plant. The deal had the reverse effect at Cricklewood, however. It became obvious that production there would have to be wound down. Pressed Steel were making washing machines more cheaply and the Swansea plant was among the most advanced

Anne and John : an engagement picture

John and Anne cut the 'washing
machine' wedding cake, at the Savoy

John meets the Duke of Edinburgh at a
Harringay Charity greyhound meeting

John's brother-in-law Herbie Collins

Arthur Sowley, Rolls Razor secretary

Sir Charles Colston

John, George, John and Ringo

John and his one-time mentor, the
millionaire financier Sir Isaac Wolfson

Adam Faith and John in fancy dress

Party time : Bernard Bresslaw, John and
Richard Reader Harris

The fabulous La Fiorentina villa

La Fiorentina's private harbour

of its kind in Europe. In contrast, the 35-year-old Cricklewood factory had been adapted as best we could from making Rolls razors and would have cost an enormous amount to modernise. We decided to convert the factory space into a warehouse. We kept on 120 people who were making the razors plus about 200 office staff but about 400 assemblers and engineers lost their jobs. Predictably there was a lot of anger at the decision, announced by Irving Jacobs at the end of February, 1963, and this was not helped when, a week later, the board predicted that Rolls would make £720,000 profit on the year and would pay a 100 per cent dividend. I missed most of the commotion as I had been out of the country for about six weeks and did not return until April.

The Pressed Steel tie-up did not overjoy Sir Charles Colston either. For one thing, Pressed Steel were marketing a fully automatic dishwasher, using the established Whirlpool design from America, but his main worry was about the future of production at Tallent Engineering. He had very big ideas about their Aycliffe plant and was angling to take over the whole of Rolls' production himself. Now he had clearly been superseded by Pressed Steel. On top of this he did not get on with the Pressed Steel people on a personal level and in February he quit the Rolls board. But Tallent continued making washing machines and, in fact, turned out about 80,000 during 1963. Our joint dishwasher venture also continued as before.

The most antagonistic people of all, needless to say, were the rival refrigerator producers and the shopkeepers whom I was again depriving of what I considered unearned income. The first move from the opposing camp came the morning after the Rolls-Prestcold deal. Lord Nelson of Stafford's English Electric announced that they were ending 'by mutual agreement' the arrangement whereby they and Prestcold produced certain appliances for each other. They made a point of saying that they would continue to sell only through retailers.

Our first shot was fired a fortnight after the deal was signed. I slashed all the Prestcold prices drastically. The smallest model, 3.1 cu ft, went down from 39½ gns to 29½ gns while the price of the largest, 8.1 cu ft, model plummeted from 89 gns to 59 gns.

Only a few days before, the trade magazine, *Electrical and Retail Trading*, had been prophesying that our prices would stay as they were until a sales drive could be launched the following spring or even early summer. So the shopkeepers were stunned to find themselves lumbered with old stock, bought at the price at which we were now selling, and on which they could make no profit. The howl that went up was truly pitiful and we were deluged with retailers wanting us to take back their fridges and return their money. Such an operation for the benefit of people we did not think should be in business anyway would have been both costly and distasteful. We let them weep salt tears.

The upshot was that I was now hated by manufacturers and retailers on both the refrigerator and washing machine fronts. A bitter campaign ensued in which every sort of weapon was used against me, from anti-Rolls newspaper adverts, through price-slashing, to malicious whispers in the City. The immediate effect was nil; by the end of 1962 Rolls had sold 101,000 washing machines and had cornered 12 per cent of the market. But the war had another 12 months yet to run.

It was at this same time that I had the bitter experience of seeing a first-class piece of long-term planning become a fact and then blow up in my face. I foresaw that the automatic washing machine would completely take over from the twin-tub just as the twin-tub took over from the old boiler-type washing machine. The day has not yet come, although it is getting much closer, and in 1962 the automatics were only just being noticed. Nevertheless, my plans for entering the market were already laid.

The small development department at Cricklewood—which included Leslie Goldbart's brother, Barry, and which was headed by Irving Jacobs—had been trying to design an automatic for some time. Their task was particularly difficult as I had imposed on them three vital considerations. First, I told them that the machine would have to spin as dry as the spin dryer in a twin-tub. No automatic could do this at that time and I thought it would be our prime selling point. Secondly, the Rolls automatic would have to be almost as cheap as a twin-tub, and thirdly I warned them that the finished version would have to be light enough to be carried by one man. Automatics in those days, and even in these days, were usually pretty hefty since the weight was not a real consideration. But for direct-selling— where the automatics would be demonstrated in people's homes —it was essential that my salesmen could lift them in and out of their vans.

Late in 1962 Irving Jacobs announced that he had completed a prototype which would do all I asked of it. I was delighted. I saw the machine as a great secret ace which I could play against my rival manufacturers. Then came the bombshell: Irving Jacobs said that although he had been working on the machine at Rolls the big breakthrough, the idea for the suspension system which made the machine so small and so cheap, had come to him in his garage at home. Since this had happened outside working hours, therefore, he had patented the idea personally. Rolls, he said, would not be allowed to make the automatic except under licence.

I was so shattered I did not know what to think. I felt sure that Rolls were entitled to the idea and entitled to make machines. But perhaps Irving Jacobs had gone into this and had found that he was within his rights. I went straight to my solicitors, Norton, Rose, Botterell and Roche, who consulted counsel. I took the view that it might take a very long time to get a court decision and that during this period the development of the machine might have to stop. Obviously, by the time the matter was settled it would be too late from a business point of view whoever won the case.

I decided to come to terms, partly because if internal trouble had come to the surface in that way it would have damaged our share price and caused unrest in the City. The effect on the City was something I always had to consider. On December 19th I signed an agreement to pay royalties to a small private firm called The Washing Machine Research and Development Company which Irving Jacobs had set up without my knowledge on October 8th—just 20 days after being appointed to the Rolls board at the time of the Pressed Steel link-up. The licence to start production was to run from June 1963 and last for 15 years. I agreed to pay royalties of £1 for every automatic produced in the first year, reducing by stages to 5s a machine in the fourth and subsequent years—but I had to agree to pay a guaranteed minimum of £30,000 in the first year and £50,000 in each of the second and third years.

The prototype was sent to Pressed Steel who spent £110,000 on tooling up—for which Rolls eventually had to reimburse them. By the time Rolls went into liquidation 18 months later we had paid Washing Machine Research and Development around £16,000 under the agreement. Yet because of various technical difficulties, and our subsequent break with Pressed Steel, I never managed to get the automatic into production. All I had was three prototypes.

When we told Norton Rose of our decision to make peace with Irving Jacobs they replied, in a letter to Reader Harris: 'The company is treating Irving Jacobs very generously.' They could say that again.

One of the people who gave me full backing throughout the Prestcold manoeuvres was Sir Isaac Wolfson. A few weeks after the deal was signed I took him with me to Swansea to look over the computer-run plant. He was tremendously impressed and as we sat in our compartment on the way back to Paddington he suggested that Drages, his big finance company, should make a bid for Rolls. He said he was thinking in terms of around 33s a share—some 3s more than the current price on the Stock Exchange. I agreed in principle to this and told Hugh Robinson, my broker at Fenn and Crosthwaite. He was a bit alarmed because he thought the shares should fetch something like £5 in a take-over bid. But I told him that the deal had basically been agreed and the next day I gave a dossier on Rolls' affairs to Campbell Ritchie, one of Sir Isaac's associates, in the study at Sir Isaac's flat.

Inevitably there were Press rumours of some earth-shaking deal between Drages and Rolls and the share price rose in anticipation. But at the same time there were Press rumours of a different kind—surrounding the mention of my name in the

Blue Gardenia Club murder trial—and Sir Isaac was inclined to let these die down before proceeding with the take-over offer. It turned out to be several months before the rumours did die— and in the history of Rolls a few months is a long time. By then, even bigger schemes were appearing on the horizon and the take-over was passed by.

9

MENTION THE NAME JOHN BLOOM AND MOST PEOPLE, AFTER thinking of washing machines, will associate it with the Blue Gardenia Club murder trial. Which is not surprising considering how frequently I was mentioned in court. Yet the truth is that my name was just a red herring, dragged into the case to create publicity and to help the defence.

The facts of the case are simple. Harvey Holford, owner of the Blue Gardenia night club in Brighton, was arrested on September 18th, 1962, and charged with the capital murder of his wife Christine four days earlier. He pleaded not guilty. At Sussex Assizes on March 29th, 1963, Mr Justice Streatfield sentenced him to three years imprisonment for manslaughter on the grounds of provocation and diminished responsibility. He was released in December, 1964, and changed his name.

The basis of the defence case was that Holford had been driven to it because his wife, who had spent some time in the South of France that summer with a girl-friend called Valerie Hatcher, had been playing around with men and flaunting this fact in front of her husband. And the man she had been principally involved with was supposed to be me.

I was even dragged into the case before it began. A few days before the start of the magistrates court hearing, Holford, who was on remand in Brixton, took out a writ claiming that I had enticed his late wife away from him. *Man on murder charge sues millionaire Bloom for enticement*. It was bound to be the front page lead story. And it was. Yet nobody wanted to call me as a witness; the police said that I was only being brought in to confuse the issue and thought they would be better off keeping the case simple. I therefore had no chance of refuting the smears during the trial, and although several publications invited me afterwards to put the record straight, I was advised by counsel to try and forget about it and let the story die a natural death. I, personally, was in favour of making a statement but one has to do as one's advisers say. They were sure that, after a few weeks, everyone would lose interest. 'Today's news is tomorrow's fire lighter,' I was told.

Unfortunately, other people refused to forget about it. The Blue Gardenia smear was revived at various times before the collaps of Rolls and was always an uneasy memory in the mind of the City. Yet the story of my connection with Christine Holford, which I have never told until now, is absurdly simple and unexceptional. It is also markedly different from other people's memories of events as outlined by Holford's defence.

I first met her when she was sitting in Reader Harris' Bentley convertible one fine evening in Juan les Pins. Reader Harris had arranged a party of six to go to the Palm Beach casino in Cannes. Christine Holford, Valerie Hatcher and Reader Harris rolled up in the car and were joined by myself, Steve Solomons and Theo Coles. I had never met either of the women before but we started chatting and they said how much they were enjoying their Riviera holiday. We stayed at the casino for quite a few hours—and bumped into Sir Malby Crofton, a director of my stockbrokers, Fenn and Crosthwaite—before going on to Reader Harris' place at Cap Ferrat.

In all the stories at the trial this place was made to sound as if it were the epitome of high living—something akin to La Fiorentina. It is true that it was on the fringe of the Castelarras luxury estate, on which Reader Harris was having a villa built, but it was really like a small peasant's cottage. It was available to people who were waiting for villas on the estate to be completed and who wanted a base on the Riviera in the meantime.

The lounge was tiny and very sparsely furnished. What furniture there was would not be given house-room by the average

British wife. There was no television, not even a gramophone. An ordinary radio was the only source of entertainment. The so-called party we were supposed to have had that night consisted of us sitting around on the floor, talking. The only concession to a gay atmosphere was the occasional pop of a champagne cork—but I am not a drinker, anyway.

The only luxury that the cottage could boast was the use of the enormous swimming pool at the Castelarras club—to which all the villas were attached and which had been built by an American in the 20s to look like a château. At about 4 am Steven Solomons suddenly suggested that we should all go for a swim. Since I was a non-swimmer I opted out, and this gave Reader Harris a good excuse to stay indoors as well since he was not enthusiastic about an early-morning plunge. We stayed talking in the oppressive little lounge while the others went for a swim—with the women in the nude, since they had not thought to take swimming costumes for a night at the casino.

It was not long before they trooped back and we all started talking again. Christine Holford regaled Reader Harris and me with the story of her uneasy marriage. She said she was jealous of her husband because she believed he was having affairs, so she had been deliberately having affairs during her holiday to pay him back and make him jealous. She had been living for some weeks with a drummer in San Remo, apparently. But she said she was going back to England the next day to make it up with Holford. She seemed to be doing this mainly because she was missing her daughter Karen. She enjoyed the sun and the Riviera life but she desperately wanted to see her child. In fact, it seemed that she would put up with all sorts of indignities from her husband as long as she could be with her.

We talked until about 5 am, then the six of us dozed off in the lounge as best we could—which was uncomfortably. For various reasons we all had to be up early—I had to be at Nice airport to meet Anne—so at eight o'clock Christine Holford disappeared into the kitchen and fixed breakfast for six. Afterwards, I said a quick goodbye and picked up Anne. I mentioned that we had been to the casino and that we had spent the night at the scruffy little place that Reader Harris was using. I also told her of the trouble that Christine Holford was having in her marriage. She did not know her, of course, but felt very sympathetic towards her just the same.

Since I told Anne about the evening at the time, she knew all along of the existence of Christine Holford. She was therefore never in any doubt—despite what was said later—that the whole thing was perfectly innocuous.

I next met Christine Holford several weeks later in London. She had telephoned Reader Harris to say she wanted to see him urgently and they had talked together at the House of Commons. Reader Harris then took her to his house in Montague Mews for tea and invited me over. I was horrified when I saw her. Her hair had been cropped very short and she wore dark glasses in an attempt to conceal the fact that her eyes were bruised and cut. She told us that, a few days earlier, her husband had found a diary containing the names of everyone she had bumped into in the South of France and that he had then accused her of having several affairs. She said he had forced her into his car and driven out of Brighton on to the top of a cliff. He had then dragged her to the edge and threatened to hurl her over. Later, she said, he told he he was going to make her so unsightly that no man would want to look at her—whereupon he cut off her hair and beat her about the face.

She was petrified when she came to see Reader Harris. She wanted his legal advice on what she could do. He told her that there was nothing an outsider could do in a dispute between husband and wife. All she could do was to leave her husband. There was very little either of us could do to comfort her—her marriage was a disaster and that was that. I never saw her again and she was shot dead only weeks later.

On the evening of Friday, September 14th, Anne and I were dining at La Tour with some friends, Peter and Vicky Wise. As the subject turned to the colourful Riviera population I told them about the desperate and sad Christine Holford and how she had been intimidated by her husband. On that same evening 600 miles away in Hove the Holfords were having their last quarrel—as I learned next day. We were all lying by the villa pool in the autumn heat when a fellow arrived who turned out to be a journalist working on the Riviera for the *Sunday Pictorial*, since renamed the *Sunday Mirror*. We thought he had come to do an interview or to ask about the Stock Exchange rumours of a link-up between Rolls and Pressed Steel—which was announced only four days later. But he opened the conversation by asking: 'Do you know a Mrs Christine Holford?'

I said: 'Yes I do, slightly.'

Then he said: 'The late Mrs Christine Holford?'

'Not as far as I know.'

'Well, I'm afraid so,' said the *Pictorial* man, 'she was found shot dead this morning.'

I just gave a short laugh. My first reaction was that there had been some error. But the visitor seemed sure of his facts so I then said: 'How is this supposed to concern me?'

'I just wanted to get your comments on the matter,' he said.

'Well my only comment is that I have no comment to make,' I replied. 'I have only met Mrs Holford on two occasions.'

After the newspaperman left I rang through to tell Andy Neatrour to check the story absolutely. He confirmed it and then rang Freddy Debenham, an advertising chief in the Mirror group with whom I had always been on friendly terms. Through Freddy he found out that in the first edition of the *Sunday Pictorial*, which was printed as early as teatime on Saturday, there was a story mentioning the fact that I had been seen with Christine Holford at the Palm Beach casino in the company of Reader Harris and Sir Malby Crofton. Andy pointed out that it was hardly fair for our names to be gratuitously linked with her death in this way and Freddy agreed. He spoke to the editor and the reference was omitted in later editions. Though the Mirror group were helpful on that occasion, they later printed Holford's story. And when the first episode appeared in the *Daily Mirror* there appeared on the next page an advert for ... Rolls washing machines.

The writ for enticement that heralded the smear campaign came a month after the shooting—on October 17th, the day of my visit to Swansea with Sir Isaac during which he agreed to buy Rolls. As we stepped off the train at Paddington on our return I was collared by Theo Coles who told me that Holford was attempting to have the writ served that night. Apparently the man who was supposed to serve it was a friend of Theo and had tipped him off. Theo also said the Press had been told so that the writ would get maximum publicity, including pictures if possible. There was a posse of Pressmen waiting to corner me at the station but I ran straight past them to the Rolls-Royce where Anne was sitting.

I had a very tight schedule to keep since I was due to appear on Sportsview that night for the official announcement, live on TV, that I was joining the board of Queen's Park Rangers, who at that time were beginning to think big and had just moved from the dismal Loftus Road ground to the White City. They were planning to get into the first divsion, but since they were then in the third they needed some good players. My personal guarantee was going to get them the bank overdraft they needed.

On the way to the TV studios I decided that to avoid being hounded over the Holford writ, a Rolls-Prestcold sales trip that I had planned would have to be brought forward from several weeks in the future to the very next day. After the programme, I answered a few questions from sports journalists but I wanted to avoid their news-hound colleagues at all costs. I learned that they were staking out my flat at Aldford House so Anne and I drove to her parents' house in Ealing to pack a few things there as best we could. The refugee Blooms then stayed the night at the home of their solicitor Felix Nabarro.

An incredible piece of all-night organising by Jim Marsh, Pressed Steel's export manager, meant that our departure next morning on a sales tour of Greece and Turkey went like clockwork. To avoid any reporters who might be lurking at airports Jim had arranged with Alex Abel Smith and Joe Edwards that we should fly in the Pressed Steel executive plane—and that it would take off for Paris from the unlikely place of Bournemouth. It all seemed so simple. Anne and I met Jim, we all stepped into the plane, then we were off. And not a journalist in sight.

By the end of the ten-day trip we had got ourselves £360,000 worth of business. But I cannot say how we managed to do it. Even though we had escaped England the foreign Press had been tipped off about us and were chasing us in a way which made the British newspapermen seem like knights in armour. When we were staying at the Hilton hotel in Istanbul, for instance, Jim Marsh was trapped in the lobby by a gaggle of shouting reporters. Jim was completely taken aback, the only words he could hear sounded like 'murder' or 'murderer' and our Turkish representative had to rescue him. He then questioned the reporters and discovered that the Blue Gardenia story had become ludicrously distorted on its way from London —the Turks were convinced that Jim, Anne and I were a group fleeing from British justice after having committed a murder.

After all these alarms and excursions I had difficulty concentrating on the job—which was contacting long-standing Prestcold agents to see if they would also market washing machines and perhaps experiment with direct selling. In fact, I was in such a nervous state that it was the only time that I have had to take tranquillisers and sleeping pills. I felt I would not be able to carry on otherwise. A lot of credit for the business we did and for the day-to-day organisation must go to Jim Marsh. He was a wonderful companion throughout those nightmarish days. He was a very religious fellow, and his faith was a revelation to me. Several years later, after the collapse of Rolls, I turned on the Epilogue by chance and found that Jim was reading it.

Apart from our business meetings we spent so much time incommunicado in Greece and Turkey that when we got back to London we were astonished to learn that we were in the middle of the Cuban missile confrontation. I was also, of course, still in the middle of my personal crisis: the magistrates' hearing of the Holford case had ended and my name had been dragged through the mire—what should I do next?

Jack Hylton was the man who solved this problem and for that I shall always be grateful. He said that publicity was the best thing to wipe out the smears. I should appear in public as often as possible and try and get my photograph in the papers to show that I had nothing to hide or be ashamed of. He insisted that Anne and I should live in his flat over Hylton House in Savile Row—which is now the headquarters of the Apple organisation—and he took Anne and I out to a party or theatre every night. We went to a number of race meetings also, but the thing which really re-established us was our attendance at the Royal Variety Show, presented at the Palladium by Bernard Delfont. Jack managed to get us the box opposite the Queen and the Duke of Edinburgh. The audience was packed with the proverbial host of stars, and stars on the bill included Sophie Tucker, Bob Hope, Eartha Kitt and Harry Secombe—yet most papers found space to comment on our presence and the *Daily Express* printed a huge three-column photograph just of Anne and myself.

Alex Abel Smith was so impressed with my performance in Greece and Turkey that he immediately arranged for me to go on a much more ambitious two-month tour of the Far East, again with Jim Marsh. Anne came with me as usual, to act as my secretary. Abel Smith wrote to Prestcold's representatives over a wide area— Hong Kong, the Philippines, Japan, Australia, New Zealand—telling them to welcome me with open arms and proclaiming me as 'the salesman of the century'. It was just one of the superlatives that the City was later to remember with a wry smile.

The Philippines, our first stop, proved to be the most interesting. It seemed an incredibly lawless place. Anne and I once went for a river trip only to find that, at a certain point, the boat swung sharply round and took us back. I was told later that a group of pirates were in control of the river after that point and it would therefore have been foolhardy to carry on. The Prestcold representatives in Manila were part of the far-flung business empire of Walter Shriro, a large genial man whom I met over several meals. They looked after us well, and in the Philippines that meant providing us with two of their permanent staff of armed guards. Everyone seemed to have a gun and on the walls of the night clubs we visited large notices read: 'All guns should be left in the cloakroom with the attendant.' It was like the old Wild West days. Despite this unsettling environment I managed to set up a direct-selling organisation for marketing refrigerators and washing machines which is still going today.

We had considerable success in Australia too, and forged links with various manufacturers. We met most of the top Australian industrialists, including Rupert Murdoch who was then scarcely heard of in Britain but who burst on to the scene in 1969 with his typically forthright and swift acquisition of the *Sun* and *News of the World*. I had a letter of introduction to him from his fellow Australian, Alex McKay, whom I knew well as a *Mirror* advertising director. Alex, whose wife Muriel was in the headlines when she disappeared in December 1969, became deputy chairman of the *News of the World* after Murdoch's take-over. Murdoch contacted Anne and me at the Chevron Hilton hotel in Sydney and invited us to have dinner with him at his home down by Sydney harbour—which was reached by private cable-cars. We discussed the whole concept of direct-selling—and the amount of money I sank into Press and TV advertising sounded like music to his ears.

We returned to England just in time for the wedding on December 30th of Anne's brother, Malcolm Cass, who had become my accountant. But having put Rolls-Prestcold on the map in one half of the world, there was still the USA and South America to tackle. Only a fortnight later, therefore, Anne and I set off across the Atlantic, this time with Malcolm and his wife Barbara. Our aim was to set up a direct-selling organisation and to promote the sale of the new Prestcold 5 cu ft refrigerator with deep freeze which we thought would be an ideal second refrigerator for the US market.

The American tour kept me out of the country for ten weeks. This meant, fortunately for my blood-pressure, that I was away while the mud was flying during Harvey Holford's trial in March, but there were grave disadvantages too. With my earlier trip it meant I was out of the country almost continuously for five months. This was plenty long enough for my retail and manufacturing rivals' anti-Rolls campaign to get up a head of steam, for a plot to get rid of me, and for a firm called Bylock Electric Ltd., to be acquired against my judgment.

The price war became so keen that I was forced to take counter-measures which made a large hole in the company profits, and the financial problems of Bylock were an albatross around my neck right up to the collapse of Rolls. All the time that I was abroad, trying to expand into world markets, events were taking place back at home which marked the beginning of the end.

10

BYLOCK HAD BEEN MAKING MOTORS FOR ROLLS SINCE MAY 1962. Shortly after the reflotation of Rolls, when negotiations were going on with Bylock, there were rumours in practically every national newspaper that I was going to bid for them. This was totally untrue. It was, however, true that Bylock were ripe for a take-over.

For one thing almost half of the voting shares, 45½ per cent, were controlled by the four directors: Bertie Latham, Cecil Mathes, his father—who was one of the people to launch the firm in 1934 and who resigned as chairman in 1960—and L. W. Moscrop. The firm began as makers of various electrical appliances but when they went public in 1947 they decided to concentrate on vacuum cleaners. However, the credit squeeze of 1960 had forced them to diversify again and by the autumn of 1962 they were also making washing machines, floor polishers, hair dryers, automatic irons, food mixers and fan heaters. The only thing they were not making was money. They were losing about £70,000 a year and had not paid a dividend since 1959.

Cecil Mathes and Bertie Latham were introduced to me by Irving Jacobs who had known them a couple of years earlier when they were making the prototype of the washing machine he first showed to me. We had several meetings and they said they could make a very competitively-priced motor for our spin dryers and that they were developing a small motor which could be used on the wash side. At the time, spin-tub motors were costing us £2 10s and washtub motors £4; they quoted £1 10s for the spin-tub and £2 10s for the washtub. This represented a saving of £2 10s on every machine—and we were producing thousands every week. It was an attractive prospect. Irving Jacobs gave them the spin-tub motors which we were then using—from AEI and Delco-Remy—and asked them to produce a prototype that would match their performance. They did this, we tested it and they started supplying us in May, 1962.

In the autumn, after the backlash from doing the deal with Pressed Steel, I was worried that AEI and Hoover—who were producing our washtub motors—would freeze our supplies and that our production would be jeopardised. Even if they did not actually do this they would always have that lever and I would never feel secure. I decided that I could provide myself with a fool-proof supply by taking over Bylock and getting them to make washtub motors as well. I planned to sell off the assets of Bylock, keep its service division going to help cope with our ever-expanding number of machines, and to transfer the motor-making section to Pressed Steel's Swansea plant where it could help to reduce the amount of unused capacity. I discussed the whole idea with Sir Isaac Wolfson and I decided to go ahead. It was my first take-over bid.

I decided to make my move during my brief stay in Paris at the start of the tour of Greece and Turkey. I called Jack Jacobs over from London to discuss the matter and then told him to go back and tell the Bylock people that I was interested in taking them over. From the report on the affairs of Rolls produced later by the Board of Trade, it seems that when Jack Jacobs reached London he spoke to Leslie Goldbart and then rang Latham and asked him and Mathes to meet them in the bar of the Brent Bridge hotel at Hendon. Mathes, Latham and Goldbart told the Board of Trade inspectors that Irving Jacobs was also present but both Jacobs brothers denied that this was so.

Apart from discussing my proposal at that meeting, said the Board of Trade inspectors, Jack Jacobs also suggested that he was entitled to some sort of payment because he had brought Bylock the motor-making business and had introduced Mathes and Latham to me. It would be a kind of commission for good work on Bylock's behalf. Mathes told the inspectors that he agreed to let him have £6,000 and he made it clear that he would have to pay it out of his own pocket as Bylock 'were in no position to make a payment of this sort'. But he pointed out to Jack Jacobs that he was not in funds at that moment. He would have to await the outcome of a take-over bid. If it was successful he would then be able to afford £6,000. Some months later, when the take-over did go through, Mathes drew the £6,000 from his bank in £5 notes and took it in a case to Jack Jacobs' house where he found him alone.

In a memorandum submitted voluntarily to the Board of Trade inspectors, Jack Jacobs explained that the £6,000 dated from an arrangement that he had made with Mathes in 1960 under which he would get £10,000 as an introduction fee if a Rolls-Bylock merger could be fixed. In his evidence to the inspectors he said that after the take-over had been settled Mathes telephoned him out of the blue and arrived with a case of money. Jack Jacobs went on: 'I was delighted with this windfall even when, after Mathes had departed, I counted only £6,000 and not the £10,000 which had been the 1960 arrangement.' He denied that the £6,000 had ever been discussed at the meeting at the Brent Bridge hotel. In the end, however, he was sued by the Rolls liquidator, to whom he returned the £6,000.

Whatever else went on at that hotel meeting one concrete fact emerged—that Mathes and Latham would agree to a take-over. And on November 6th, after my return from Turkey, Arthur Sowley, the Rolls secretary, wrote offering one Rolls share for every 15 Bylock shares. There followed several meetings at Regent Street betwen Mathes and Latham, and Reader Harris, Jack Jacobs, Sowley and myself and soon afterwards I started my Far East tour, leaving Reader Harris in charge of all the arrangements. In between coming back from that tour and setting off for America we agreed with Bylock that our final offer should be two Rolls shares for every 25 Bylock ordinary shares and four Rolls shares for every 75 Bylock non-voting A shares.

The bid was announced on January 24th. Since the directors and their families had already agreed to accept we had 45½ per cent of the shares in the bag. Rolls also owned three per cent and as soon as the bid was announced I bought another two or three per cent to secure a majority. Bylock was mine, if I wanted it.

But I did not want it on those terms. My plan basically was to break up the firm and to do that, under company law, I had to have 100 per cent control. Fortunately there was a clause which said that if a bidder got 90 per cent of the shares he could make a 'compulsory purchase', as it were, of the other 10 per cent. But even 90 per cent was a tall order. Nevertheless, I did not for a moment consider making the offer unconditional—that is, finally agreeing to the take-over—unless I had 90 per cent.

Apart from the possibility of making motors at Swansea I planned to keep making certain of Bylock's other products such as vacuum cleaners, floor polishers and hair dryers. After securing the majority of shares in January I announced not only that I would continue selling these products through Bylock's old-established retailers but also that I would increase the retailers' margins. This was one in the eye for the retailers who had been so hostile towards me. It was also a shock to my manufacturing rivals. They were busy slashing the retailers' margins on their products in order to compete with my direct selling.

Perhaps the most interesting prospect that Bylock had to offer was a revolutionary vacuum cleaner called the Lewyt, designed by the American Lewyt Corporation. It had two motors, one at the end of a flexible hose and the other in its cylinder, which gave it the flexibility of cylinder models and the powerful suction of traditional cleaners. In happier days Bylock had secured the exclusive rights to sell and manufacture the Lewyt in the United Kingdom but they had not turned out a single machine since the agreement was signed in May, 1959. Meanwhile, fantastic though it may seem, they had been paying royalties to Lewyt, under the terms of the agreement, on every other vacuum cleaner they produced. No wonder they were losing money. I saw the Lewyt as an ideal product for direct-selling and decided to get my money's worth out of the agreement as soon as possible.

When I sailed for America at the end of January Mathes and Latham came down to Southampton on the boat train along with Jack Jacobs, Goldbart and myself. We were arranging the switch of production to Swansea and it was agreed that Mathes and several key technicians should move down to Wales to help provide the know-how. Mathes even started looking for a house soon afterwards. Pressed Steel knew of the proposed plan—although at that stage they wanted the whole thing kept very quiet—and later, during the voyage to America, I made a couple of ship-to-shore phone calls to Joe Edwards to discuss moving Mathes and his merry men down to Swansea.

When we got to Southampton, Jack Jacobs returned to London but the rest of us continued our discussions aboard the old *Queen Elizabeth* until we reached Cherbourg. By that time the outlines of Bylock's future had been agreed. I was happy that their products would be very useful to Rolls—always provided that overheads were reduced by manufacturing at Swansea and provided that we could raise a lump sum by selling off machinery and property. But first I had to have 90 per cent of the shares. Everybody knew this, from Reader Harris, who was going to see the deal through, downwards. Nobody was in any doubt that if I failed to get the 90 per cent then I would call the whole deal off. That was the crystal-clear position as I sailed from Cherbourg for New York.

In New York we stayed at the Plaza. I started trying to set up a completely new organisation to sell the small Prestcold refrigerator of which I had such high hopes. Meanwhile my brother-in-law Malcolm was holding various discussions with American finance companies about the possibility of their supporting a refrigerator venture. I had lots of meetings with Hambros, who were distributing Austin cars in the States, to see if they would handle the refrigerators, but they did not see the idea as a winner. I therefore tried to interest discount houses, some of which I visited with Sir Isaac Woolfson.

Several agreed to examine prototypes, but unfortunately they were not technically 100 per cent and they also fell foul of the regulations of the American Standards Association which were entirely different from British standards. In a short space of time I declared the New York operation null and void.

I turned instead to the West Coast where Prestcold had an agent called Norman Lee who ran the firm of Norcold in Los Angeles. I got on extremely well with him and I thought our 'second' refrigerator would sell very well in California as the place was saturated with money. Lee was enthusiastic and we ultimately agreed that Rolls would take over Norcold which would then become our American subsidiary and our base for expansion.

During my stay at the Plaza I met a fellow with whom I later had several dealings. This was Lew Levy, a big music publisher who went on to sell his company Leeds Music, to the Music Corporation of America for £2 million. However, at that time I remember him principally for his introduction to Edward St. George who was the right-hand man to Charles Hayward, chairman of the Firth Cleveland group of companies. Although I met St George in New York his real base was in the Bahamas and he told me that there were incredible opportunities there for making huge profits. Anne and I accepted the invitation to stay as his guests at his luxury home in Nassau.

He wanted me to put money into Freeport—a part of Grand Bahama Island which had been mainly forest but which was being developed into an ultra-expensive tourist resort by a consortium called the Grand Bahama Port Authority. Hayward had a quarter share in the Port Authority, his son Jack was at one time administrative vice-president and St George was legal adviser. When Hayward was persuaded to sink money into the scheme it was intended that Freeport should be an industrial township, but there were few takers and in 1960 the Port Authority was allowed to start building houses on land earmarked for industry. After this, the project really began to take off and a hotel and casinos were built which made millions.

St George offered to fly me over to Freeport where I could meet two of the brains behind the operation, Lew Chesler and

Wallace Groves—the 'King of Grand Bahama'. I refused for what now seems the ludicrous reason that the plane had only one engine—and to me, one engine seemed an inadequate safety margin. It is true that I would not have been impressed by the small amount of work that had been done by then, but if I had invested only a modest few thousand in land I would have made a fortune. Every £100 invested in 1963 must be worth almost £10,000 today. This was one of my first really gargantuan errors of judgment.

St George was a well-known figure in the Bahamas and introduced me to several millionaires including Bernard Sunley the financier. He also introduced Anne and me to Mrs Dorothy Killen who was a legendary and elderly multi-multi-million-airess. She invited us to stay at her house, which was as fantastic as La Fiorentina, and when we explained that we were already guests of Edward St George she invited us to dinner instead. She had only ten guests but during the meal, served in the spacious dining room overlooking the sea, I counted about 40 servants.

Although Mrs Killen was old she was still very shrewd and questioned me about my business. Anne and I were sitting next to Walter Annenberg, who is now the American Ambassador in London, and his wife. Mr Annenberg also was intrigued by my coupon-return system and he told me about his Philadelphia newspaper and TV empire. The ladies spent a lot of the time talking about the problems of hostessing but although Anne had done a great deal of entertaining none of it had been at the Killen level of sophisticated extravagance and she therefore felt rather out of the conversation. She also felt as though she were trailing rather badly in the jewellery stakes. Sitting around the table was like spending an evening in the jewel house at the Tower of London and Anne later said that she felt as though she had nipped into Woolworths on the way to buy a few sparklers.

Mrs Killen was interested to hear of our villa life as she was thinking of buying herself a Riviera villa for her even older age. She was on the brink of making an offer for La Leopolda, a villa in the Fiorentina class, which was owned by the

Agnellis, the Fiat millionaires. Soon afterwards she bought the villa for a reputed £1 million. But she died before ever staying there.

The Bylock bombshell dropped on March 31st. In the two weeks since leaving the Bahamas Anne and I had visited New York, Chicago, Los Angeles, Acapulco and had wound up in Mexico City. It was from there on March 31st that I made one of my periodic calls to Andy Neatrour in London, and asked him what the news was on the Bylock front. He then told me that on March 29th, the closing date for the offer, Rolls had got 71.3 per cent of the ordinary shares and 35 per cent of the 'A' shares. The offer had however been made unconditional on March 30th—the day before I spoke to him. I became almost demented. This was absolutely contrary to my specific instructions.

While I was away there had, apparently, been some trouble from a rebel group of Bylock shareholders, led by one Sebag Cohen. He was a director of Nicolle, an investment trust which held 8,500 'A' shares, and one of his main objections was that ordinary shareholders were receiving one and a half times as much as 'A' shareholders. Cohen had circularised Bylock shareholders urging them to oppose the bid and had formed a shareholders committee which held its first meeting in London on March 26th. Only about 40 people turned up, but Cohen had letters of support from over 500 shareholders—some 10 per cent.

He told the meeting that his argument was not with Rolls, who had driven a legitimately hard business bargain, but with the Bylock directors for accepting. His opinion of the board was not improved by the fact that on November 19th—only thirteen days after our first official offer—Mathes and Latham had acquired new service agreements with Bylock. Latham's was to run for 10 years at £4,000 a year and Mathes' for 19 years at £3,000 a year. 'I feel this is a suitable matter for a Board of Trade inquiry,' Cohen told his meeting. 'In all my years as a company lawyer I have never heard of such a long service agreement as 19 years.'

Apart from these rebel non-sellers there was a group of people who obviously had decided to hang on to their shares on the grounds that, although my offer was reasonable bearing in mind the state of Bylock, if Rolls injected life into the firm the value of their holding would improve startlingly.

Since there was this solid group of non-sellers, Andy reported to me across the crackling long-distance line, the impasse had been accepted and it had been decided that the offer should be made unconditional. The offer for 'A' holdings had been stepped up to one Rolls share for 15 in Bylock and the offer for both 'A' and ordinary was going to be kept open until April 22nd. But I considered this a waste of time; it would hardly produce the 20 per cent more acceptances we needed. I was right. Rolls finished with 77 per cent of the ordinaries and 53 per cent of the 'A' shares.

In all the years since, I have never been able to find out how the offer came to be unconditional, except that everyone assured me that it had been on the advice of Kleinworts. But really it is a mystery to this day. During our phone conversation, Andy also hinted to me that there was a plot to take over my power within the company. To get an outside opinion that I respected I then telephoned Patrick Hutber of the *Financial Times*, who is now city editor of the *Sunday Telegraph*. He confirmed Andy's story and added that there was a rumour being put round that I had left England altogether because of the Holford case, and had no intention of returning. Telephone calls to Hugh Robinson, of Fenn and Crosthwaite, and to Reader Harris produced substantially the same story. I decided to fly home as quickly as possible.

Anne and I caught the first plane out of Mexico City to New York and from New York I flew to Paris. I telephoned Andy from New York to tell him where I was, that I intended making inquiries about who was responsible and to impress upon him the secrecy of the whole scheme. I need not have bothered. Anne and I were spotted by representatives of the *Daily Express* in New York and photographed. The picture appeared in late editions of the newspaper the next morning, April 1st, complete with details of our American tour and the fact that we were heading for Europe at once.

In fact, wherever we went, throughout the whole history of Rolls, the local representative of the *Daily Express* always managed to trace us. The paper seems to have more agents than the secret service. Within 24 hours of our arriving anywhere somebody would roll up to say: 'Good afternoon, Mr Bloom. I am from the *Daily Express*. How long will you be here? What are you doing?' When the *Express* want to know where you are, nothing will stop them. And nothing will stop their photographers getting their picture.

Although the *Express* had blown the gaffe on our flight, I carried on with my plan of campaign. The minute I got to Paris, Anne and I checked in at the Georges V hotel and I asked Jack Jacobs to come over from London to see if he could throw any light on the plot. He had heard about it but was not able to say who was behind it. After this I decided there was no point in bringing everything out into the open in any case. With all the competition we were facing from outside it would have been absurd. However I did reorganise the board, reaffirming my control by putting both my brothers-in-law, Herbie and Malcolm, on the main board of Rolls. With Sowley, Reader Harris, myself and Al Palmer (our hire purchase director) I then outnumbered the Three Musketeers as they had become known at Rolls—the Jacobs brothers and Goldbart, who had been made director in charge of buying in January.

I also asked Jack Jacobs to step down as deputy managing director in order to put a stop to his apparent megalomania which had been reported to me. Apparently he had told Geoffrey Lewis, one of my assistants, that he should bar two of the directors from having lunch in the boardroom at Cricklewood because they left crumbs on the table by the side of their plates. He also complained to Lewis that Goldbart was arriving five minutes late in the mornings and said that he would have to reprimand him for such unpunctuality. As well as this behaviour he wanted to take over my role at Queen's Park Rangers and became involved in negotiations to buy players. He once had his picture in the *Daily Mirror* talking to Phil Woosnam the West Ham inside forward.

To drive the message home, I issued a memo on April 18th, which went to everybody in any position of authority at Rolls. It said quite simply that I was chief executive of the company, that all departmental heads were responsible to the board through me, that I was in charge of the company's policies and that Reader Harris and I would carry out all contracts with our merchant bank, brokers and any other City institutions. The rest of the memo set out the responsibilities of all the other directors and executives. In this way I put on record the fact that Jack Jacobs was barred from dealing with anybody—including the Press.

I had been dissatisfied with him for some time and had tried to get a fellow called Sidney Roberts to be my deputy instead. Roberts was getting £20,000 a year as managing director of Hoover when he was deposed as the company's chief in late 1961 by a Canadian, Arthur Earle, sent over by the parent company. In February, 1963, Roberts quit Hoover so I sent a confidential message inviting him to join Rolls—officially as export director but unofficially as my deputy. He decided that it was not his cup of tea and turned down my offer. As I was abroad I never had the opportunity of asking his reasons, but he did confide in the *Sunday Express*. 'I am not interested in joining that outfit in any capacity,' he said. And, loyal to the end, he added : 'I would not dream of doing anything that would harm the Hoover business.'

After my hasty return from Mexico I was even more determined to get Jack Jacobs off my back and I had talks with David Rettie, a director of my other rival, AEI-Hotpoint. Patrick Hutber acted as a go-between in the initial stages and I then had some hush-hush meetings with Rettie at the Dorchester Hotel. He agreed to join me later in the year.

We then went through the motions of taking over the Bylock boardroom. On May 6th Reader Harris, Malcolm Cass, Al Palmer, Herbie Collins and I became directors while L. W. Moscrop—a partner in the firm's accountants—resigned. As old man Mathes had finally retired the previous November this only left Mathes and Latham of the former board—and at the Bylock annual general meeting on May 31st Mathes failed to secure re-election, although he continued to manage the day-to-day affairs.

But the total Bylock situation was grim. At the same annual meeting Reader Harris, as the new chairman, announced that the firm had lost £175,000 on the year up to July, 1962, and that the bank was pressing for its £155,000 overdraft. He said that the board was thinking of raising money through a 'rights issue'—whereby new shares are issued and offered for sale to shareholders. This was another Kleinwort, Benson idea. The theory was that nobody would buy the new shares after the announcement of the enormous loss and that Rolls would therefore be able to snap up the whole issue. This would then give me the elusive 90 per cent of the shares. In practice, however, shareholders were so sure that I could work wonders with Bylock that they bought their new shares and again ruined the whole break-up operation.

The plan to move the motor division to Swansea never got off the ground for technical reasons that were thrashed out while I was in America. Much later, at the Board of Trade inquiry, several people, including Sir Charles Colston, Irving Jacobs and Joe Edwards stated that they had predicted much earlier that it would not be practical. Yet I do not recollect their raising such objections.

My practical problem was this: I had been saddled with Bylock, what was I going to do with it? I decided that they should press on with developing the Lewyt and making the traditional vacuum cleaner for their usual outlets while starting to make a smaller vacuum cleaner which they could sell to Rolls for a mere £4 and which I could give away with my washing machines to help boost sales. These little cleaners were the first of my free gifts—or premium offers, as I called them. The trouble was that they were phenomenally successful. In the first week they were advertised, Bylock made 1,000 of them—but we had 9,000 inquiries and sold 4,000 washing machines. This left a backlog of 3,000 vacuum cleaners to deliver. In three weeks we were 9,000 behind and the administration people were becoming frantic. As premium offers became more numerous later that year so their stranglehold on administration tightened. In the end they choked the company.

11

BY SLASHING THE PRICES OF PRESTCOLD REFRIGERATORS IN 1962 I proved once and for all that I was a major threat to the rest of the industry and to retailers. It had been bad enough when I was selling washing machines direct but now that I was going to repeat the dose with refrigerators it was too much. For all they knew I might start on cookers. I threatened to win an increasing number of customers from the other manufacturers and to wipe domestic equipment shops off the map. I would have to be stopped.

I had the element of surprise in my favour, however. After stunning my rivals with my tremendous price cuts I followed up swiftly with a full-page advertisement in the *Daily Mail* which told the housewife that 'despite the blandishments of Britain's High Street middlemen she is entitled to buy at the very lowest price consistent with large-scale quality production.' I also pointed out that 'up to 40 per cent of the cost of most electrical goods on sale in British shops and stores is taken by the middlemen. On a quality washing machine their profits can amount to more than £30.'

This was the first salvo of a propaganda war. On the other side the 7,000-member Radio and Television Retailers Association, under their director Michael Keegan, announced that they were setting up a fighting fund aimed at getting £100,000 to launch a campaign against Rolls. They planned adverts on TV and in national, local and trade papers; posters, windowstickers, leaflets and a public relations campaign aimed at putting their point of view to MPs, consumer associations and other bodies.

The trade magazine, *Electrical and Retail Trading*, in their issue of October 11th, urged retailers to smarten themselves up, and printed an open letter setting out the alleged virtues of buying through a shop. It claimed that shops, unlike direct salesmen, had a wide range of models to show—in fact many shops could only afford to carry a handful of models spread over a wide price range—and that shops did not employ high-pressure salesmen but 'salaried experts'—surely a grotesquely distorted description of the average shop assistant. The magazine suggested that retailers should duplicate this farrago and distribute it to houses in their area.

At the same time an independent group of London retailers led by three fellows called Pomper, Robinson and Hough, and calling themselves the Appliance Trade Association, launched another fighting fund by asking for £1 a week from every independent dealer and £100 a week from every appliance manufacturer for a minimum of three months. They, too, had visions of an all-out anti-Rolls attack in the national Press. But their grand design ended with an advert or two in the worthy but nationally insignificant *Croydon Advertiser* and *Croydon Times*.

At first the retailers were worried that some manufacturers —especially Hoover, which started in Britain as a door-to-door vacuum cleaner operation—would throw over the shops and turn to direct selling themselves. But all the makers entered the propaganda battle on the retailers' side. Even Pomper and Co., had the backing of Hoover, Hotpoint, Parnall, Servis, English Electric and Electrolux in their little Croydon foray. However, this touching concern for the small shopkeeper was very much a piece of self-interest: if the little man went to the wall only the big distributors would remain—and they were already extracting crippling discounts on large orders.

Arthur Earle of Hoover was first to put the retailers' minds at rest in a provocative letter to his 17,000 dealers, in which he said: 'We are convinced that the best method of protecting the interest of the consumer is through complete co-operation with the trade.' He added: 'Our sales and merchandising policy will continue to be governed by the maxim, "Every sale a dealer sale".' And he promised the shopkeepers 'full co-operation in all aspects of aggressive sales activity to counteract direct selling methods.'

Soon afterwards Robert Craig Wood, chairman of Hotpoint, announced that his firm would be contributing 'a four-figure sum' to the £100,000 fighting fund and, casting a slur on my sales methods, he said: 'We do not support any technique which could persuade people into a hasty decision which they may come to regret.' To justify his backing of the retailers' campaign he added: 'It is in the public interest that they should know more about the advantages of buying from a shop and the dangers of buying on the doorstep.'

Despite all the fighting talk little actually materialised from the notoriously fragmented and apathetic retailers. It took a month before Keegan of the RTRA managed to convene a meeting of the various sections of the industry—from the National Federation of Ironmongers to the London Electricity Board. This was a month in which, from their point of view, a big counter-blow was urgently needed. Yet they spent the time fiddling around, investigating the possibility of setting up a central body while several organisations, such as the Electrical Contractors' Association, refused to join in as they thought the scheme 'unwise and doubtful of success'. The whole operation was typical of the retailers' lack of aggression and was a very good example of why I was by-passing them. Even my rival manufacturers, who publicly stood by the shop men and applauded the customer's right to make a calm and sober decision, secretly wished there was more aggressive selling in the shops.

The whole counter-propaganda campaign was such a failure that the editor of *Electrical and Radio Trading*, Owen Pawsey, was prompted to remind his readers that direct selling was a success because it provided better service than that on which the shops prided themselves. Rolls salesmen, he pointed out, sold to people without forcing them to leave the comfort of their home. They gave a demonstration in the housewife's own kitchen. They visited people in the evening and on Sundays—

at any time that suited the potential customer.

Although the anti-Rolls campaign flopped eventually it had a serious effect in its early stages—when retailers and manufacturers were still talking big—in that share prices tumbled across the whole industry. Rolls shares, which stood at 35s when I announced the Prestcold price cuts, were down to 22s by the end of October. But in our case the fall was accelerated by a series of rumours that mysteriously started to sweep the City. These reached such a pitch that we arranged with Fenn and Crosthwaite that they should issue in their monthly letter to clients, 'an authoritative denial of all the adverse rumours affecting Rolls Razor'.

This statement, which was widely publicised, said: 'A number of rumours regarding Rolls Razor, its methods of trading, the quality of its products, its ability to meet its accounts and its general solvency (have begun) to circulate. These rumours have reached considerable proportions and there has been some nervous selling which the Cuban crisis brought to a climax. Although it has nothing to do with Rolls Razor as an operating company, the fact that Mr John Bloom, the managing director, has been mentioned in a recent court case and widely headlined may also have had its effect.

'We are glad to be able to tell our clients that the chairman of Rolls Razor, the chairman of Pressed Steel and the chairman of Drages authorise us to say that Rolls Razor has operated and is operating successfully, that it is entirely solvent, that all its creditors are being and have been paid in the normal way and that all its salesmen are, and always have been, expressly forbidden to attempt "switch selling".'

The shares were never again as low as 22s until immediately before the collapse of the company.

Even the manufacturers had to admit that their propaganda was ineffective. They were backing the retailers' campaign, and were also spending large sums advertising their own products—Hoover, for instance, launched a series of television adverts—but they were making no inroads into my buoyant washing machine sales and my rapidly-increasing sales of refrigerators, which averaged 566 a week during November.

The only solution for my rivals was to take direct action. Which they did, by slashing their own prices.

There were some reductions in the price of existing washing machines, and English Electric brought out a revamped version of their Liberator automatic with the price down from £110 5s to £96 12s, but the main attack came in the shape of new models at new economy prices. Hotpoint brought out a twin tub costing 64 gns, Hoover launched a new machine without a heater at 65 gns and a few months later English Electric brought out a twin tub at 42 gns. These compared with the 59 gns for our best-selling Rolls Rapide de luxe.

There were also newcomers cashing in on the anything-goes atmosphere. Phillips, the Dutch electrical giant, announced that they were launching a 78 gns twin tub to be made for them by Ada of Halifax. But by far the biggest sensation was the announcement on November 2nd that GUS had reached an agreement with Acme, the Glasgow manufacturers, under which a 57 gns machine—appropriately called the Acme Challenge—would be sold through GUS mail order catalogues, the 2,700 retail outlets in the group, and the 5,000 GUS salesmen-collectors. There was immediate speculation about the fact that Sir Isaac Wolfson was, as chairman of GUS, launching an attack on Rolls while, as chairman of Drages, he was supplying me with £10 million of hire purchase finance. The answer to this apparent riddle was that the GUS deal was arranged as a result of an independent marketing policy.

Most of these rival machines were successful only to a minor degree, while others like the Acme turned out to be a flop. Our sales still forged ahead. On November 7th came our forecast of a 100 per cent dividend for the year instead of the 80 per cent predicted previously, which must have had a demoralising effect on my rivals. But it was more than borne out by our profits for, instead of being cut back, our sales topped 3,000 a week for the first time ever in the last week of January, 1963.

It was at this point that I left on the *Queen Elizabeth* for New York. While I was on board I talked to Jack Jacobs on the ship-to-shore radio and he told me that Rolls shares were again taking something of a dive. So on February 14th I wrote to Hugh Robinson, at Fenn and Crosthwaite, suggesting a way to remedy the whole situation. I thought we could display our confidence by predicting, in the chairman's annual report in July, that our dividend for 1963 would be 200 per cent—double our prediction for 1962, which was confirmed in March. Although only six weeks of 1963 had passed Rolls was doing so well that I planned to double the number of washing machines sold in 1962—which I did, selling 201,400 by the end of December. And since Pressed Steel were making them £6 cheaper than Rolls had been I anticipated a profit increase of some £1,200,000. Furthermore, as I wrote to Hugh Robinson, when the Swansea plant became fully operational, turning out vast numbers of refrigerators and the various Bylock products which I envisaged, this also would make a colossal difference to our competitiveness. The Board of Trade, in their report, some-how decided that this letter was part of a ploy to push up the price of the shares.

With a further view to building up confidence Sir Malby Crofton suggested that it would be useful for Rolls to have some support in America. If we became entrenched on Hoover's home territory it would also be another warning salvo in the price war. Sir Malby joined me in America and we addressed meetings in Wall Street which roused the interest of several leading American institutions and unit trusts.

Eventually I sold 250,000 shares to Investors Diversified Ser-vices, the biggest of the American mutual funds, who intended holding the shares as a long-term investment. The shares were placed for me by International Bond and Share Inc, stock-brokers with the Pacific Coast Exchange, and I also made arrangements for Rolls shares to be quoted on the New York exchange through Morgan Guaranty American Depositary Receipts.

I did not want to sell a quarter of a million of my own shares for the US deal. I did use about 100,000 belonging to myself and my family and relatives, but for the remaining 150,000 I looked elsewhere. Eventually it was arranged that I should buy them from Sir Arthur Frederick Pullman Wheeler, a Leicestershire farmer known to his friends as Sir Derek—perhaps because his father, the original baronet, was also called Sir Arthur. The first Sir Arthur, who was a stockbroker, became one of the first shareholders in Rolls Razor. Sir Derek who had watched their value disintegrate refused to part with them when Gilbert Southall made his offer of 1s a share in 1959. When I bought them I had to offer 26s a share. By hanging on to them for three years Sir Derek therefore pocketed the best part of £200,000 instead of £7,500. The local papers described him as a quiet man who seldom visited the City. He seemed to do very well without bothering.

At this period, while I was still in America, several instances were discovered of Rolls employees being taken out for drinks and being pumped for any information they could give about future sales tactics. And people in our development section were approached to see if they would reveal anything about new products. It seemed to be a case of industrial espionage on a small scale, and we never found out who was behind it. However no worthwhile information leaked out so that when I sprung my big surprise in April it set my rivals reeling.

I decided to offer a washing machine and a Prestcold Packaway refrigerator together at a knock-down figure. The price varied depending on the size of the Packaway—three, five or eight cu ft. The cheapest package deal with the Packaway 3 with the basic Rolls Rapide. Together they cost only 59 gns. But the other packages were equally incredible value right up to the enormous 8 cu ft refrigerators and the Rapide de luxe which still cost only 103 gns. This offer was a measure of the kitchen revolution I had brought about. When I took over Rolls only three and a half years earlier a washing machine alone had cost £100. This double offer was the high point of my operation as far as the housewife was concerned.

The war itself had forced my rivals to cut the price of their expensive models and to bring out the economy models in an attempt to cash in on the market which I had proved existed. Once they had tasted the turnover from this mass market and once the housewives had become used to reasonably-priced washing machines and refrigerators there could be no going back, even after the demise of Rolls. Since then the whole range of kitchen equipment has come down to the same price range. The only things still in the semi-luxury class are dishwashers. I am convinced that they would sell if they could be made more cheaply. But that means selling them in great numbers. It is a vicious circle which no-one has yet broken, and in early 1963 the prospects for Rolls Colston were starting to look bleak.

The dual offer brought in an unprecedented number of coupon replies. In April, for the first time, washing machine sales averaged over 4,000 a week—and at that rate I was going to finish the year by supplanting Hotpoint as Britain's second-largest seller of washing machines. In the same month the weekly average refrigerator sale shot up to 1,289.

But although my turnover was racing ahead I was actually having to buy the washing machine sales since I was losing about £5 on each Prestcold Packaway. The Bylock vacuum cleaner which I started giving away soon afterwards was also costing money and eating into the washing machine profit margin. As an alternative to these premium offers I was offering a part-exchange allowance, which again cost money but which shocked retailers since they assumed that people in direct selling did not want to burden themselves with old machines. On top of all this, it was shown when the figures were worked out much later that the basic washing machine, costing the housewife 39 gns, was being sold at a loss. This was something else that had to be absorbed by the profit on the de luxe. And as we fought for more and more sales at the bottom end of the income scale we started selling more and more basic models. In 1962 five out of every hundred machines were basics. In 1963 fourteen out of every hundred were basics. And, again because we were dealing with the lower income bracket, we got more bad hire purchase debts than we had been used to.

One cost which stayed constant was the salesman's commission. They were paid no wages—just £3 10s for selling a de luxe, £1 10s for a basic and 10s for the 3 gn table top which we sold as a profitable extra. Refrigerator commission varied from £2 for a Packaway 3 to £3 for a Packaway 8. I insisted that salesmen must make a minimum of 50 sales out of every

100 leads and Jack Jacobs struck fear into the heart of any backslider. Often he did this publicly in the Rolls weekly newsletter. He once wrote: 'Bournemouth's disgusting contribution can offer no valid excuse.' And on another occasion he lambasted two managers, whom he named, by saying that their 'benign personalities ... must have more than a little to do with the mediocre results of these two branches ... the advice I have given these gentlemen has varied from a suggestion that they wear tight shoes and thus be forced to dispense with some of their inherent good nature to establishing the whereabouts of the nearest labour exchange.'

Over-riding all other expenses were the staggering amounts that I spent on advertising—some of it on television for the first time, but most of it in the Press. I started 1963 sensationally by announcing that for the following year I would be spending about £2 million by putting an advert once a week in every national daily newspaper and in every Sunday paper every Sunday. I also announced that I planned to become Britain's biggest national advertiser in 1964. To show I meant all I said I signed a contract with the *News of the World* for £238,000 which was the biggest single advertising order ever placed in a national newspaper.

At the start of the year I was producing adverts which looked like news pages. They carried headlines, such as 'Housewife pockets £35', had names over the various 'stories' and had adverts within the whole-page advert. These were highly successful and the cost of leads went down from £5 to about £1. But the Advertising Standards Authority started a fierce attack on adverts which 'masquerade as editorial or news matter'. To pacify them we had to put 'Advertiser's Announcement' over the top of our pages and remove the adverts within the advert. These and various other modifications took away the edge of editorial-style advertising and I stopped using it.

This was not the only way in which my advertising methods were controversial. For one thing I booked all my own spaces in newspapers—a job normally done by the agencies. The placing of an advert was vital—if it was on the left-hand side of page two it might bring 50 coupon returns whereas the same advert on the right-hand of the eye-catching page three might bring in 500. I knew from experience which adverts were suited to which papers and I built up good personal relations with several key men in newspaper advertising departments. Whenever somebody else took this job over, the coupon returns fell noticeably.

This was at least partly because I had an instinct for a good advert. And to give me a wide choice I used four agencies in competition with one another—Roger Pryer, Stowe and Bowden, Hausman Langford and Reid Walker. This, of course, was another unheard-of practice, but the commission on even a quarter of my £2 million expenditure was still nice work if they could get it. It was also gruelling work. I liked to make the presentation entirely different every week—so that even if the information and offers were the same two weeks running people would still want to read them.

On Fridays I would tell the agencies what was going to be in the next week's adverts and the copywriters would chew their pens dreaming up a good hard-sell headline such as 'Get your £5 now', 'Four great offers' or 'You win all ways'. I then dictated all the information in detail and the visualisers would fit it all into the various advertising shapes booked for that week. They often worked through the night on Mondays, producing several versions for every shape and each agency had 30 or 40 dummies to present to me on the Tuesday. If I was abroad an executive from one of the agencies, taking it in turn, might fly out to me with everybody's dummies but normally I rang them up to tell them to come over to Sceptre House. They then pinned up their offerings for me to see round the walls of my office. As they would not all go on the walls some had to be spread out on the carpet but each agency tried to make sure that the ones on the floor were not theirs as they thought that I might walk all over them without looking at them properly. I then used to go through the list of spaces I had booked choosing an advert to fill each one.

Sometimes it happened that one of the agencies would have a bad patch, but unless their offerings were really terrible I would try to award them one or two small slots to help to pay the telephone bill. But after all the sweat they put in to it I always felt a bit apologetic. 'Sorry,' I used to say. 'Better luck next week.'

12

I THINK THAT ANNE AND I ENJOYED MEETING SHOW BUSINESS people because, subconsciously, we recognised how much more glamorous their lives were—even though we might have more money. The business people I dealt with were often twice my age and I was becoming old before my time. And dining with people such as Sir Isaac and Lady Wolfson, Anne and I became used to wearing clothes which were, although we did not realise it at the time, at least ten years too old for us. Now that we are freed from the demands of business convention and the burden of keeping up contacts we find that we are much more relaxed and wear the sort of clothes we must have been wanting to wear all along. Our friendship with show business people obviously stems from the fact that they were the people we ourselves really wanted to be like.

My connection with this other world started in 1961 when Bud Flanagan asked me to join a charity committee he was forming to raise money and to visit the East End's elderly and poor. At the inaugural meeting in the Café Royal the other members of the committee included Alfred Marks, Tommy Steele, Bernard Bresslaw, James Booth and Lionel Bart. Through them I got to know many other entertainment people including Jimmy Henney, the music publisher and disc jockey. Jimmy was helping to run the Showbiz XI—the football team that plays for charity—and he invited Anne and me to watch them one Sunday at Chelmsford. Tommy Steele was playing outside right for them that day and Billy Wright, the former England captain, was making one of his regular appearances. I knew Billy already; he and his wife Joy Beverley were plugging my washing machines at the time—doing an endorsement, as it is politely called. After the match I invited the team and several spectators back to my flat for drinks.

Among them was Sean Connery who at that time had not made any James Bond films. A few days later I invited him round to dinner and he told us he had bought one of my machines for his Hampstead mews flat only a few weeks before. He was quite put out that he had not met me in time to get a discount out of me, but he seemed very happy with the machine all the same. The next time I saw him was during my tour of America in 1963 by which time he was living in rather more opulent circumstances in the Beverley Hills Hotel. He was busy promoting James Bond, but I had been so busy promoting Rolls that I regret to say I knew very little about 007. But despite this, Anne and I have seen him quite a few times since.

Parties, like our wedding, were always a good opportunity for entertaining business contacts, but I thought it would brighten things up if I invited a few celebrities and made fancy dress compulsory. As time went by the number of celebrities mushroomed startlingly, but at the first revamped party, my thirtieth birthday, they were vastly outnumbered by the strictly business faction. The theme of that party was China and guests were told that they must arrive in Chinese costumes to match the catering from the Lotus House. To complete the setting we also managed to borrow a rickshaw and Anne, wearing a cheongsam, was taken in it along Park Lane and got her photograph in several papers. Afterwards, we managed to get the rickshaw up the stairs to the top floor of Aldford House and parked it outside the flat. Throughout the party whenever people vanished I always found them carrying each other up and down the small landing.

Although there was not much damage to the flat, considering the number of people there, Anne decided that in future we should remove the lounge furniture entirely and lock it in our bedroom. We could then turn the lounge into a mini-ballroom.

To make a proper job of this I got some friends of mine in the timber business to make a collapsible wooden dance floor which could be put up in about twenty minutes, covering the whole of the carpet. This scheme was a great success when we tried it out a few weeks later at our New Year's Eve party. We had a pop group to provide live music and Beryl Bryden, the fantastic but heavily-built jazz singer, joined in with them. As she stamped her foot to the music the floor seemed to shake and I feared for its safety. However it survived this first ordeal and has never looked back.

We decreed a fancy dress free-for-all at this party and there was the usual number of beachcombers, Helens of Troy, Buddhist monks, and Red Indians, plus one Cleopatra, one Invisible Man and Shirley Bassey who just came as Shirley Bassey. Anne was a harem girl and I was a man from outer space with a huge inverted paraffin funnel as my helmet—an unconscious tribute to earlier days. Several guests caused a distraction by arriving on an ordinary London Transport bus in full regalia. Among them were Adam Faith and Colin Berlin, the pop manager.

On the business side, the guests included the Jacobs brothers, Reader Harris and Hugh Robinson but I found I could not invite everyone at Rolls who thought they ought to be invited. As time went by an increasing number of these people felt they were being snubbed and there was a lot of jealousy at Rolls. But there was nothing political about my motives for excluding top people, it was just that there was not enough room.

There was always a tremendous amount of noise at my parties—especially at my New Year's Eve party in 1961, when I paid handsomely in cash and in whisky for four pipers to play in the New Year. Two of them nipped round the corner from the Dorchester Hotel after piping in the New Year there. They paced up and down the corridor avoiding people sitting on the floor and weaving in and out of guests carrying drinks from the bar to the lounge, and created a devastating din. But I never had any trouble from neighbours. Underneath our flat was a young couple whom I always used to invite, while on our floor there was Bertie Green of the Astor Club and a record company chief who always used to come along with interesting visitors such as Hank Mancini.

Apart from my own parties the ones I most enjoyed were undoubtedly those given by Jack Hylton. At least part of their success was due to the catering by Jack Isow of the Jack o'Clubs in Soho and I was so impressed that I later arranged for him to handle a couple of mine. One of Jack Hylton's parties was at the Jack o'Clubs itself and was attended by the Crazy Gang, who were his close associates, Charlie Drake and Dr Stephen Ward who was on the same table as Anne and I. We found him a very sophisticated and pleasant man. He was a friend of Jack's because he was such a good osteopath. He was called in whenever Jack got backache—which was frequently because he was a 68-year-old who ran about like a boy of eighteen. Once, when I suddenly found that I had a pain in my back, Anne said: 'Why not go and see Stephen Ward?' He cured me completely in no time. He seemed to have a remarkable natural gift. He was also well-known for his portraits and had done several drawings of members of the Royal family. At Jack's dinner party he said he knew all about me and would like to paint my portrait also. I heard nothing more about this and dismissed it as dinner table talk until one day, to my astonishment, Anne came home with a painting of me tucked under her arm. Stephen Ward had done a very good likeness and I had it hung in my office. Anne had given him some photos to work from—a difficult method of portrait-painting—and had made several trips to his flat in Bryanston Mews West to see how it was getting on. On several occasions she met Christine Keeler, who did not make much impression on her. She spent most of the time sitting in a corner while Anne and Stephen Ward discussed the portrait. I did not visit his flat myself and although he invited us down to his cottage on Lord Astor's estate at Cliveden we never managed to get there.

At the same Jack o'Clubs party I met Maurice Woodruff, the clairvoyant. This was very early in the evening, before we had been introduced, so he did not know who I was. He had one of his intuitive feelings and said: 'You are worth a great deal of money. And you will make even more money out of something in connection with water and valves'—which I took to be a reference to a new semi-automatic machine we were developing at that time. We got to know each other better over dinner and I later kept in touch with him. After the collapse of Rolls he assured me that everything would work out for the best. He was the only person who felt that was so—but although it has taken a long time he has now been proved right. I believe that he truly has some rare power.

Jack Hylton's parties were usually held at Hylton House and were particularly impressive because they were staged in the vast ballroom—a legacy from the days when the building was the Albany Club. The most incredible party he ever held was in May, 1962, after the last-ever Crazy Gang show at the Victoria Palace. The Crazy Gang had been a legend for years and everyone in show business—and a host of people outside show business—wanted to pay tribute to them at Jack's party. But even Hylton House could only accommodate so many and the invitations were like gold.

Even so, I could not think of anyone who was not there and champagne flowed at an impossible rate through until six in the morning.

It was one of those parties where Anne and I seemed to chat briefly with hundreds of people without having a substantial talk with anyone in particular. However I do remember meeting Dr Max Odens, the doctor who specialised in rejuvenating injections. Jack Hylton was one of his patients—and they certainly seemed to work on him. I said to the doctor: 'I hope you keep yourself alive until you're over 100 because when I reach 65 I'm probably going to need you.' I had a long talk with Donald Campbell and his wife Tonia Bern. I told him I had seen the Monte Carlo grand prix and thought it must be terrifying to drive at such a speed. Yet he was going even faster on water. He said that a few hundred miles an hour more or less did not really bother him. 'Once you go over a certain speed it makes no difference.'

On New Year's Eve 1963 I turned my flat into a little Bulgaria to celebrate a holiday enterprise I was starting with that country. So among the usual mix of guests I invited people from the Bulgarian Embassy who had supplied Anne and me with traditional Bulgarian costumes. We laid on liberal supplies of Slivovitch—the potent national drink which is served in little coffee cups—and everyone became convivial in a very short space of time. As an instant party-warmer it is to be recommended. The Embassy men said that it was their first experience of a capitalist party and they made the most of the opportunity. Since the Bulgarian holidays were something I was keen to promote I invited several Fleet Street people including Alex and Muriel McKay, Freddie Debenham and his wife, Rex North the columnist, and Hugh Cudlipp and his wife. The place was packed to the doors.

When it came to our third wedding anniversary in February, 1964, we found we had invited so many people that we had to abandon the flat altogether and hold our party in the Jack o'Clubs. There was an incredible combination of people with totally different backgrounds, including Lord Thomson of Fleet, Sir Isaac Wolfson, Bobby Butlin, David Jacobs the show business solicitor, Lance Percival, Suzy Kendall, Adam Faith and Vera Lynn. As the evening wore on Dorothy Squires got up and sang—several times. This started off an impromptu cabaret which became compered by Al Mancini and which lasted two hours. Most of the stars chipped in with a party piece including Vera Lynn and Adam Faith who rarely performed except in perfect conditions. But even in the midst of all this, business intruded. Marian Massey who, with her husband, had a few discotheques told me she had discovered an amazing little girl singer who went by the name of Lulu. They were managing her but were thinking of changing agents so I suggested that they should get together with Adam Faith's managers Eve Taylor and Maurice Press. I believe they did have some discussions but nothing came of them.

These parties, which all the guests enjoyed so much, never went down very well in the conservative City. Businessmen were supposed to stay out of the public eye and those who had money were supposed to enjoy it in private and in moderation.

I suppose Sir John Ellerman would be their ideal. Similarly my yacht was regarded as unwarranted ostentation. I bought it in June, 1963, as a substitute for the villas the company had been renting. I decided that a yacht would be just as good for entertaining my friends and business contacts and I thought that since I was keen on the sea I personally would enjoy it more.

Finding a suitable vessel turned out to be more difficult than I had expected. I took a trip to Cannes harbour to see what was for sale and found a 75-foot boat called Apollo which looked about right for £50,000. I was taken out to Eden Rock to see how it went but the answer was: not very well. When a speedboat zipped past, its wake was enough to send the Apollo rolling viciously. I decided to play safe and start looking for something bigger.

I then discovered a boat which was huge enough, but which cost £300,000. I felt I did not want to pay so much but I looked her over to see what I would get for that sort of money. I had an unpleasant surprise—the boat was rather like a whaler and was very austerely fitted out. The elegant yacht moored next to it, the Ariane III was much more my line, and although I thought it would probably cost an astronomical amount I was forming the opinion that I would have to pay heavily for what I wanted. Out of curiosity I asked Harvey Langer, who had become one of my personal assistants, to make enquiries about it and he reported that it was owned by a Greek shipbuilder called Pandelis B. Pandelis. It had been built in 1961 at Newport, Monmouthshire, to Pandelis' own design and, at 375 tons, it had been the biggest yacht built in Britain since the war. It had cost £250,000 but Pandelis now wanted £400,000. The figure seemed a bad joke but Langer was so enthusiastic about the boat, having been on board to see Pandelis, that I went down to the harbour to look at the outside again. I was still tempted and when Langer produced the brochure that Pandelis gave to people who wanted to charter the Ariane I decided I would take it if I could get the price down. I arranged for Anne and me to see Pandelis aboard the Ariane one afternoon.

Anne was no boat lover but she fell for the Ariane as soon as she saw her. A tour of the yacht did nothing to change her opinion. It was just like a five-star hotel with all the furniture and fittings built-in. The elegant dining room was panelled in wood and silk. There was a large master bedroom, two double and one single guest rooms, each with its own bathroom—plus individual cabins for the 10-man crew. There was even a lift from the main bedroom to the bridge, which always impressed visitors. It was not really a luxury, however. Pandelis suffered with his heart and the lift was to save him the strain of climbing stairs. Anne and I never used it; it was quicker to walk.

After looking round the Ariane we were taken for a short trip in it and then had tea with Pandelis, his wife and children. His daughter obviously did not want to sell and kept drawing our attention to alleged faults. 'You should hear the noise the air conditioning makes when you're under way,' was one of her gambits. But Anne and I were determined to have the yacht and after some bargaining I agreed to pay Pandelis £330,000 for her plus £46,000 to compensate him for the charters he had fixed and would have to cancel. I wanted the Ariane at once; I had no intention of waiting until the end of the season before being able to use her.

I immediately changed her from the Panama registry to the British. Under the Panama flag you avoid things like PAYE for your crew, but I preferred to sail under the British flag. I never became eligible to fly the blue ensign. All the exclusive yacht clubs, whose members fly it, clearly thought that they were too exclusive to include me. Eventually I applied to join the Royal Air Force yacht club, but they too decided, for reasons they did not have to disclose, that I was ineligible.

Although I took over the predominantly Greek crew they were replaced fairly rapidly by Britons under Captain Christie and soon afterwards we had a few test trips to neighbouring Riviera resorts before setting off on our first major cruise to Venice. We worked along the Italian coast for several days until we were caught in a terrible storm and had to hole up in a tiny fishing port. It was unbelievably windy and at the same time unbelievably hot. There was absolutely nothing to do in the village and nothing to do on board except watch films. We were stuck there for 48 hours and were driven wild with boredom. We were compensated however when we finally reached Venice and parked the yacht in St Mark's Square. It is a beautiful city and we spent days seeing the sights in the speed-boat we always had with us.

Anne and I flew back to London for a few days while the Ariane was taken down to Athens. We then flew out to Greece to meet up with the boat and continue our voyage—to the Lebanon. Leaving Athens, we had great difficulty getting our supply of films past customs officials who, even in those days, seemed to match the Russians for suspicion, and we were delayed for 12 frustrating hours. But we then set sail through the Greek islands, putting in at Rhodes, and on to Beirut in the Lebanon where I had talks with the Rolls agent for the Middle East, Fuad Salim Saad, who entertained Anne and I royally.

Because of Arab-Israeli hostility no-one was allowed to sail from the Lebanon to Israel, so when we arrived in Beirut we registered our next port of call as Malta. But several days later when Langer went ashore on his way to the airport to take some advertising material back to London, he was cornered by a group of policemen who again asked him where the Ariane was bound, Langer assured them it was Malta but they were still not happy, probably because I am Jewish, and they quizzed him for about five hours at a police station. How much fuel did we have on board? they wanted to know. Where had we come from? What exactly was my business? Eventually they let him go. Since Lebanon appeared to be the friendliest of the Arab countries towards Israel they did not treat the possibility of a voyage to Israel too seriously. If they had done, Langer may have been wasting away in some arid prison cell to this day.

Anne and I arrived off the Israel coast late on a Friday evening. I had business to conduct with various branches of the GUS empire and I was expected by their representatives. As we hoisted the blue and white Israeli flag and went in to Haifa,

Anne and I were saying how thrilling it was to be visiting Israel and I predicted that the royal reception we had in Beirut would be nothing compared to our welcome in Israel. I was wrong. We were not even allowed to enter the harbour as it was too late in the evening. There was a ban on admissions after a certain hour for security reasons. We were told that we would therefore have to spend the night anchored at sea. Hardly the reception I had anticipated.

We were mollified next morning, however, when we were welcomed ashore and the Ariane became the talking point of Haifa. It seemed that she was the first luxury yacht ever to visit Israel and she was featured in all the Israeli newspapers. As a result the Arabs immediately announced that the Ariane had been slapped on the Arab League black list and would never again be allowed to call at the ports of member nations. Later, after the collapse of Rolls, when I was negotiating the sale of the Ariane to King Hussan of Morocco he invited me to take the boat over for him to inspect. I decided against this because, since she had been blacklisted, I thought she might be seized as soon as we arrived in Moroccan waters.

In Israel we were shown round by one of the most interesting people in the country, Chaim Hertzog, a former head of Israeli military intelligence. In 1963 he was in charge of GUS interests in the country. He was an urbane and charming man and fascinating on the subject of Jerusalem which was then still a divided city. He took me to all the secret Israeli posts where the Israelis kept a watch on Jordanian movements. And he also pointed out the supposedly-secret Jordanian installations which were doing a similar job. He introduced me to the then Prime Minister Levi Eshkol and to Mrs Golda Meir, the present Prime Minister. On another day he took me to see a passing-out parade for members of the Congolese army who had been trained in Israel and I talked to Colonel Joseph Mobutu who took over power in the Congo in 1965.

Later that summer I took the luxury yacht idea to extremes by adding expensive refinements. One of these was an electronic instrument called the Melotron which looks like a single-keyboard electric organ. The right hand plays the melody in a

145

choice of many different instrument sounds while the left hand plays accompanying chords and percussions in a choice of twenty rhythms. It can sound like a complete band yet needs little musical ability. It also provides a variety of sound effects.

On several occasions the sound of the Melotron astounded people as we came into harbour—especially in small places where the population thronged the quayside like African tribes greeting the first radio. I had the Melotron in the bar of the top saloon so it was clearly audible outside, especially across water. On our first cruise with the Melotron we went to Elba with Adam Faith, Bernard Delfont and several other people, including the works engineer from the Melotron factory. As we sailed in to the island we were displaying the Melotron's virtuosity—and the mixture of music, blood-curdling shrieks and animal noises made it sound as if Ted Heath and his band were being savaged by a pack of hounds in something by Hammer Films. The islanders looked astonished as a small group of surprisingly ordinary people disembarked. The magical Melotrons are quite common today, especially in pop groups, yet mine, which I now keep in the living room of my flat, still fascinates new visitors.

An even more dramatic toy which I had was an amphibious car—the Amphi-car—which, I was told, was the first ever fitted on a boat. It was designed for inland water, not sea water, but I had a few modifications made and it became an impressive substitute for a speedboat. Wherever I used it I could see crowds on the beaches looking aghast as it was lowered into the water; they used to think we were dumping an old car in the sea. They were even more amazed as I swished over the water, drove up on to the beach and disappeared down the road.

Unfortunately the car was not always reliable. On one particularly hot day we were in Monte Carlo harbour not far from the boat of Prince Rainier and Princess Grace when I noticed that the Prince was looking at the Amphi-car through his binoculars. So I said to Adam Faith : 'Come on. Let's drive ashore and show Prince Rainier what a fantastic gadget it is.' We lowered it into the water with our royal audience watching intently and were half-way to shore when it stalled. Adam and I toiled away in the baking sun for what seemed like hours before we managed to get it started again and complete our journey. It took us so long that there was plenty of time for some cameraman to take a picture of us which appeared in numerous motoring journals.

Along with 99 per cent of the Riviera population I spent a lot of spare time playing roulette in the casinos. As a rule I did not spend a lot and so did not win a lot. However I learned of a system whereby you watched the table for about an hour and if a number did not come up in any combination during that time—say, neither the 1, 11, 21 or 31—then you started betting on all of them in ever-increasing amounts until the number did turn up, the theory being that it would turn up pretty soon. I decided I would give this system a try at the Beaulieu casino and, starting with nothing and betting on the 4, 14, 24 and 34 I won £4,000. They gave me £1,500 in cash and a £2,500 cheque and I walked out absolutely elated. It was much the biggest win I had ever had—and nothing used to give me such a lift as a casino coup.

A few days later I bumped into Charlie Drake in the Cannes casino. On the spur of the moment I said to him: 'Do you fancy going for a quick cruise to Corsica?' And he said: 'All right. When are we leaving?' I replied: 'Let's go now.' And we did. I drove him down to his hotel where he threw some clothes into a bag and from there we went to the Ariane in Monte Carlo. I had made a point of having crew on stand-by 24 hours a day so there was one officer and one crew waiting. Charlie and I lent a hand and the four of us got the yacht under way. It was about four in the morning as we pulled out of the harbour and we were in Corsica eight hours later. But it turned out to be a totally unexciting place and after a few more hours we decided to put to sea again and head for San Remo.

When we arrived there we had the usual pantomime with the Amphi-car. But I have to admit that this time the gaping spectators had something extra to gape at—the sight of Charlie Drake, curls blowing in the breeze and with a sailor's hat perched on his head. He looked like something Walt Disney had dreamed up for the occasion. We headed purposefully for the casino and, by operating my new-found system, we both won quite handsome amounts.

After that I thought my system was infallible and I decided to hare back to Beaulieu at once to repeat my success of a few days earlier. We sailed along to Cannes, took the speed-boat ashore and, just before midnight, Charlie and I were in Beaulieu casino. After watching the table I decided that the sixes were the numbers to back. But they were slow to come up and the longer they took the more money I was putting on—that was how the system worked. In the end the sixes did not come up all night. I lost the evening's winnings from San Remo, plus the cheque from Beaulieu, plus the £1,500 in cash, plus a little bit more. So at the end of my biggest-ever winning streak I was out of pocket. As Charlie and I left, feeling a bit low, the casino manager and director met us. They were always very cordial and on this occasion they commiserated with us and insisted on escorting us to our speed-boat. Presumably they then laughed all the way to the casino.

It was at the roulette table at Beaulieu that I first met Robert Maxwell. I cannot say that we were ever introduced. We were just standing near each other. Later he and I were on the same plane back to London and he came over to talk. We discussed his businesses and he said he might have an idea in which I would be interested. However I never got round to ringing him and he never contacted me. Apart from a few chance meetings at Beaulieu I did not see him again until 1970 when we discussed the ins and outs of Board of Trade inquiries.

Chemin de fer was another game I played for a time. But I more than met my match when I found myself at a table with Fiat millionaire Gino Agnelli, Dino di Laurentis, the film director, and the actress Anna Magnani. It is usual for players who draw a winning hand of eight or nine to show it to the banker to stop him drawing cards unnecessarily at great expense, since he cannot win. But on several deals Agnelli and di Laurentis failed to show their winning hands when I was banker because money was of no importance to them. They were merely playing as a hobby and if someone had done the same thing to them they would not have turned a hair. It taught me the foolishness of playing against those sort of people and it completely cured me of casino gambling.

13

IT WAS DURING THE SUMMER OF 1963 THAT I PLANNED THE MOVE
that was intended to put me in the Isaac Wolfson class as a
financier. I had the very best professional assistance available.
But because of a legal wrangle that caught up with me from
three years previously, the grand design was only partly completed.

The project centred on English and Overseas Investments, a
company which started life in 1910 as the Higgoda Rubber
Estate Ltd, running a rubber estate in Ceylon but which in 1963
was running hire purchase businesses. I first became involved
with them in 1961 when one of their subsidiaries, Finance and
Service Insurance, backed a Rolls sales venture into Northern
Ireland. Malcolm Cass became a director of E and O in June of
that year and became secretary a few months later. Al Palmer,
who had been Rolls hire purchase director for only a few
months, became an E and O director at the same time. I took
an option to buy 100,000 E and O 2s shares for 4s—an option
which I took up in August, 1962.

Soon afterwards the chairman of E and O, Arthur Mitton,
asked if I would be interested in some further financial link
with his company and I suggested that E and O could buy a
couple of companies which were connected with Rolls and in
which I had an interest. One of these was the Slough Die-Casting Company, an old firm which made castings for Rolls and
in which I had a 55 per cent interest; the other was Mercon
Metals which was incorporated in October, 1961, to trade in

metals with Rolls and Rolls suppliers. I had an option to buy 55 per cent of their shares on May 30th, 1963. I took up this option and the next day sold the two companies to Arthur Mitton for 217,000 shares in E and O. We agreed that I would receive more shares, up to a maximum of one million, over the following three years depending on the financial success of the two companies. This would give me a 40 per cent stake in E and O, but for the time being it raised my holding to around 16 per cent.

Al Palmer then suggested to me that it would be a good thing for Rolls if I became a director, or perhaps chairman, of E and O as they were still a hire purchase firm. I could also, he said, make E and O my personal investment company—like Sir Isaac Wolfson used Drages—to finance any other enterprises I might dream up which would not fit into the Rolls set-up. This system worked quite simply: in my case I would, as it were, 'buy' E and O shares with Rolls shares, leaving me with E and O shares and leaving the Rolls shares as E and O's main asset. This meant that the dividend on the Rolls holding would flow into E and O where I would leave it—escaping surtax and financing new projects.

This was an exciting prospect. I already had an idea, picked up in America, which I thought E and O could run. This was a home movie kit—an 8mm camera, a projector, a special light for indoor filming, a roll of colour film ready to be used and a short cartoon film so that people immediately had something to put on the screen. I felt that many people wanted to do their own amateur cine-photography yet were daunted by the thought of photographic shops and by the expense of the equipment. If they could have demonstrations in their own home and if the cost could be kept down I felt home movies would be a huge direct-selling success. In fact, earlier in the year, I put a coupon advert in the Southern editions of the *Daily Mirror* which produced so many replies that I had to stop advertising because we only had a small sample stock. It was an ideal scheme for E and O if I made it my personal investment company.

Several of the other Rolls directors were enthusiastic about the idea because they already owned E and O shares and felt sure their value would rocket if I took over. I consulted Toby Hoffman, and worked out a detailed scheme for the share-swap. Then I took over as chairman of E and O. Arthur Mitton resigned because the inclusion of Slough Die-Casting and Mercon Metals had altered the whole structure of the E and O operation and the only other old-guard director, Lt Col Harry Ross-Skinner, resigned at the same time. This left a board comprising Malcolm Cass, Al Palmer and Bernard Conway—an old school friend who ran Mercon Metals and who joined the E and O board at the same time as I did.

The news of my take-over passed virtually unnoticed. The *Daily Telegraph*, for instance, carried a mere eight lines under a miniscule heading: *New Job for Mr Bloom*. That was on the morning of July 20th—exactly a year before the board meeting at Cricklewood confirming the collapse of Rolls. A great deal was to happen in those 365 days.

A few weeks later, Toby Hoffman and Malcolm Cass went to see Sir Isaac who was staying at the Hotel de Paris in Monte Carlo to talk over my E and O plan. He was very enthusiastic and came up with an even more sensational scheme: not only would E and O assume control of Rolls by virtue of taking over all my Rolls shares, but Sir Isaac and I would form a joint company to control E and O.

As they worked it out, there were three steps to this holding company scheme. First I would receive something like a million E and O shares and £1,135,000 convertible loan notes in return for all my Rolls shares; second, Drages would buy £1 million worth of E and O loan notes from me; third, I would transfer 925,000 shares to a holding company in return for 50 shares of £1 in that company while Drages would transfer an equivalent value (£740,000) in loan notes in return for the other 50 holding company shares. All this was contained in an agreement signed in the utmost secrecy by Sir Isaac and myself on October 17th. We even formed a joint company called City and Commercial Developments to act as the holding company.

Unfortunately however, a major obstacle had arisen. In September an action had been brought against me by the executors of the estate of Lewis Jackson. Jackson, the man with whom I had signed an agreement in 1960 after his work in finding Rolls for me, had died a few months later. Now his executors— a solicitor called Asher Oldschool and, ironically, Toby Hoffman—were claiming that 318,500 Rolls shares rightly belonged to Jackson's estate and threatened to take out a High Court injunction preventing me disposing of any Rolls shares until their action had been heard. Not only was I unable to carry out my share exchange with E and O therefore—I did not even know how many Rolls shares I would end up with. For this reason, although we decided to announce my proposed Rolls and E and O share-swap on November 1st, no figures could be mentioned. It was however announced that if the Jackson litigation had not been sorted out by July 31st the whole share-swap agreement would lapse.

In view of all this uncertainty the Drages agreement had to gather cobwebs. Clearly Sir Isaac could not pay me £1 million for E and O loan notes which I did not have.

This was not the only business setback of the year. The Rolls-Colston sales gradually deteriorated until it became clear that the artificially low price was costing money without benefiting us. We therefore hoisted the price back to around £80 in an attempt to reduce our losses. Even so, by June, the joint venture had cost Rolls £85,000 and Sir Charles and I agreed to unscramble. We sold Sir Charles our £125,000 half-share in Rolls-Colston Appliances for £40,000—a loss of £85,000—and Sir Charles renamed the company Colston Appliances. All the Rolls people, and Oppenheim, withdrew from the board, and within a week Colston Appliances were arranging to sell again through retailers. However I did not sever all links with Sir Charles. Indeed, I stepped up my washing machine order with Tallent Engineering and they had to build themselves an extra 20,000 sq ft of space to cope with production.

Away from the business scene I had given up the directorship of Queens Park Rangers that had been announced on Sportsview. Because of my world tours I had been unable to attend a single board meeting, and so, having promised to help in any way I could, I considered it unfair to stay on. Although, at the end of April, I issued a statement jointly with QPR's chairman, George Wodehouse, explaining the position there was quite a bit of bad feeling among certain sections of the board. This was typified by a comment made by Wodehouse to the *Sunday Express*: 'When someone makes an effort to take up a directorship one expects him to show keenness.' This I felt to be totally unjust and led to an explosive situation later in the year when I was involved in an attempt to take over the club. For the moment I was happy to accept an invitation from Freddy Debenham, who was also chairman of the Athenian League club Hendon, to become involved with his club in a non-executive capacity. I was made vice-president for life and to show my appreciation I gave them £1,000 towards a set of floodlights.

In another sporting sphere I donated £10,000. This went to the Royal Windsor Horse Show to cover the prize money for the next three years—an arrangement largely made with Geoffrey Cross, the show club chairman, by Andy Neatrour. It was the first time a commercial enterprise had given all the prize money at a British horse show. They were especially grateful as the cost of staging the annual show was running at about £20,000 and they had made a loss the year before. The Queen, the Duke of Edinburgh and Princess Anne all attended, and among the competitors were teams from all over Europe and the cream of British riders—Pat Moss, Pat Smythe, David Broome and Alan Oliver. With such company, it was money well spent in terms of Rolls-Prestcold prestige. I am only sorry that for both the 1963 and 1964 shows Anne and I were out of the country.

One sport seemed to be very popular with certain Rolls employees. It was the one that you play with someone of the opposite sex. And 1963 was a particularly active season. On one occasion a salesman was found by a night watchman literally with his trousers down and with one of the office girls in close attendance. As a result he was given a warning and the girl was sacked. This incident did little to deter others however. Shortly afterwards a night watchman found Jack Jacobs in his office with a female companion at eight o'clock in the morning. He tipped the watchman £1 and told him to phone his wife

154

Myrtle to say that Jack had been found asleep at his desk after working assiduously into the night. Myrtle appeared to believe the story, which I found incredible.

I expect that, as usual, she inwardly blamed me. It was one of the causes of friction between Jack Jacobs and myself that he was continually telling his wife in the evening that he had to go out on all-night work sessions with me. Often when I met her she would accuse me of being a slave driver and say: 'How is it that you keep Jack working 24 hours a day?' I always used to smile weakly and mumble into my beard to cover up for Jack. This used to make Anne very indignant but Jack was so convinced that he was a Don Juan and spoke about it so often that he had convinced me too that he was good-looking.

One day when Anne was annoyed at the way I had again covered up for him I explained to her: 'You mustn't blame Jack. He can't help it. He's just such a good-looking fellow that women are all over him.' Anne was incredulous. She said: 'You must be joking. Try looking at him properly one day.' A little later I took her advice and studied some photographs of him taken during a party. Rosalina Neri, who was with us at the time, said he looked like another Gandhi. She was not far wrong. It had been another of my errors of judgement.

The price war, which had been simmering during the summer months, boiled over again in October when I gave Hoover a broadside for which they never forgave me. They should not have been so surprised for I was provoked by no less a person than Arthur Earle during the company's annual meeting in April. He announced that Hoover were being clever and were diversifying by introducing a floor-level fan heater, called the Hoover 3000, which was going to be a world-beater. He went on to assert: 'One of the weaknesses in the direct sales technique is its limitation in the type and variety of products which can be promoted.' This was a claim I could not allow and I decided that the most dramatic way of showing it to be false was by handling exactly the same product at Rolls.

I examined the Hoover 3000 and discovered that it was

powered by a 3 kw turbo-fan unit for which Charles Hayward's Firth Cleveland group held the world licence. There were several firms in Britain making these units under licence and I asked Edward St George if he could tell me who was supplying Hoover. He told me that it was a company called Solartron which was actually part of the Firth Cleveland set-up. I asked if they could supply me with the units and they said: 'Of course. We supply all the manufacturers in the industry.'

Edward St George then put me on to the Welsh company, Airfix Industries, one of whose subsidiaries was assembling the motors and shells to produce the Hoover 3000. I spoke to a fellow called David Senaglia who was in charge and he agreed to produce a replica of the Hoover 3000 only in a different shell which I had designed. In a few weeks Senaglia had produced some prototypes which I provocatively called the Rolls 3333.

Having produced it, I decided that the biggest impact would come not from launching it in competition—although that would have caused a stir—but from giving it away. At a Press conference on October 3rd I announced that I would offer 50,000 or 60,000 heaters free, while stocks lasted with Rolls washing machines, both de luxe and standard models. Since Hoover were selling the heaters in the shops for 14 gns, this created a sensation. And it was all the more sensational since the announcement was deliberately made in the middle of Hoover's annual sales conference week. My Press conference was not a flamboyant affair—it did not need to be. I handed out the extract from Earle's speech attacking the alleged limitation of direct-selling. Apart from that I simply had on display stripped-down versions of the Hoover 3000 and the Rolls 3333. They spoke for themselves.

My announcement made such a good story that it was even on the BBC radio's 1 o'clock news. The announcer said: 'Rolls-Prestcold, the washing machine manufacturers are planning to give away a fan heater, described as costing at least 14 gns in the shops, with every one of their machines bought.' He went on to explain about the limited stocks and said that the price of the washing machines would stay constant.

There was an immediate flood of letters to the papers protesting about 'advertising' on the BBC news—which is prohibited. Some people said the BBC obviously realised they were wrong because the Rolls item was not broadcast on subsequent bulletins—but the real reason was that later and more important news had squeezed it out. The shop men were predictably apoplectic about the item and such organs as the *Hardware Trade Journal* and *The Ironmonger* frothed with indignation and printed swingeing attacks on the BBC. The Radio and Television Retailers Association and the Electrical Appliance Association protested both to the BBC and to the Postmaster-General, Reginald Bevins, and were reported in the national Press as having done so. The BBC replied with commendable coolness that such items were 'not advertisements but items of news interest ... You will perhaps have noticed the considerable coverage of the subject given in the Press. It would be quite wrong if, in such circumstances, our bulletins failed to report the facts.'

The Sunday after the fan heater announcement we had our own national sales conference in the London Hilton. Since it was also to celebrate my first five years in washing machines I invited lots of show business friends in addition to the 380 salesmen and we had a champagne party and dinner for some 700 people. I hired two large rooms and the main ballroom and the whole thing cost £3,000. As another part of the Rolls Razor cut-throat competition all the branches had been making a superhuman effort during the week to outsell each other and reach a record weekly total. Many salesmen even went out on Sunday morning to add a few sales to the branch total. To enable them to do this I had laid on charter planes from all over the country to bring them all down to London and the salesmen got into their dinner jackets during their flight.

Before the dinner came the sales conference itself when I had my usual question-and-answer session. And, after that, Tommy Trinder presented me with a large illuminated scroll from the advertising managers of the national Press in appreciation of the business I had put their way. At the top were three quotations from Shakespeare, the first of which, from Henry IV part one, I thought was particularly appropriate: 'Yet doth he give us bold advertisement.' I was also presented with a scroll

157

which read: 'The chairman, directors, executives, branch supervisors, branch managers and staff of Rolls Razor Ltd, together with the directors of the company's advertising agencies presents with wholehearted congratulations this address to commemorate the occasion on which you, John Bloom, were declared the Salesman-industrialist Extraordinary of 1962-3 in Great Britain.' Beneath this were the massed signatures of countless Rolls people with, in the middle of the top line, the unmistakeably large signature of Jack Jacobs.

That evening during the dinner, each branch manager stood up to announce his week's sales. The total came to a staggering 7,442. This meant that many salesmen were earning £100 or more in commission and that we were bidding fair to overtake Hoover who at that time were claiming about 9,000 sales a week. The figure was so impressive that the *New York Times* devoted a whole column to my techniques.

The figure was in fact too good. I was blinded by it. I thought that if we could do it for one week we should be able to do it every week. I therefore decided that in 1964 we should aim at 8,000 sales a week which would make 400,000 during the year. I was sure that this could be done since it would double the expected 1963 total and up till then I had been doubling my sales every year. To be precise, I sold 201,400 machines by the end of the year—19.7 per cent of the year's washing machine sales in Britain—and therefore knocked Hotpoint off their perch as number two to Hoover.

To bring in the coupons for 1964 I stepped up my advertising from £1,720,000 in 1963 to a planned £3 million. I also ordered manufacturing materials based on a turnover of 8,000 machines a week. All the time I was spurred on by the 25,003 machines I sold in October—but the monthly total never again reached even 20,000. On advertising alone therefore I began paying out twice as much as was warranted by sales. And Rolls just had not got that sort of money to spare.

14

BUT ALL THIS WAS IN THE FUTURE. FOR THE MOMENT I WAS surging forward on a tide of euphoria and planning major essays into various new fields, including trading stamps, mail order and TV rentals. I was also working on an important breakthrough for Rolls—to market washing machines and refrigerators direct in the Common Market countries. Although David Rettie did not join Rolls until October 1st I consulted him during the summer since he was managing director of AEI Appliances (Overseas) Ltd and had a first-class knowledge of the export game. I started by thinking that I could sell direct in Italy since there were several domestic appliance plants in that country which I could take-over. But Rettie thought that we should invade the whole of the Common Market.

He then introduced me to Biff Gale who was the chairman of Studebaker International. His parent company the Studebaker Corporation, of South Bend, Indiana, had a year earlier bought up a Minneapolis firm called the Franklin Manufacturing Company which controlled a new domestic appliance plant in Turin. It was round this plant that our talks were based. I had preliminary discussions and then, when David Rettie joined Rolls, we got to quite a serious stage—even to the point of agreeing to form a Rolls subsidiary company in Europe in which Studebaker would have a stake. The virtually limitless opportunities for a major direct-selling operation right across Europe were just about to become a reality when the board of the main Studebaker Corporation, under its president Sherwood H Egbert, suddenly announced that they were withdrawing from all their international commitments. The news was as much a shock to Biff Gale as it was to me, and the whole deal collapsed literally overnight.

It was after this reversal that I started to concentrate on diversification—a policy I believed to be the key to continued success. I planned to move into two of the fastest-growing areas at that time—TV rentals and mail order—and announced my intention at a lunch given to celebrate my 32nd birthday on November 8th in the Hilton penthouse. The mail order idea I intended to introduce around the middle of 1964, but the TV rentals were a much more immediate proposition. I had formed a firm called Rolls Rentals with a starting capital of £10,000 and to start the venture I was already negotiating to take over several local rental firms such as the nine-shop Leytonia chain in London which I bought for £125,000. I felt sure that the advent of colour television and 625-lines would give the booming rentals business a further boost and I intended being there ready to cash in. My theory was a little ahead of its time in that colour TVs are only now getting off the ground and it may be another five years before they are for mass consumption. But even so I had an instant market to tap by circularising the 1,250,000 people who had bought washing machines or refrigerators from me and inviting them to call in at their local Rolls Rental shop.

To take advantage of this it was clear that I would need a nationwide chain and that would take time to build up. (John James, the Bristol millionaire, had taken two years to build up his TV-dominated chain of 150 shops—which was generally regarded as a cracking pace.) Apart from the small chains I was planning to take over I therefore needed a large group. I set my sights on the 474-shop retail division of Charles Hayward's Firth Cleveland empire. This division contained the Wolfe and Hollander stores but mainly comprised the Max Stone and the Broadmead radio and TV shops. The Broadmead chain had been built up by John James, who sold it to Firth Cleveland in 1959 for close on £6 million in cash and shares, which made him the second-largest shareholder to Charles Hayward. But there had been a policy disagreement in December, 1961, and he resigned.

In November, 1963, I discussed with Edward St George the possibility of making an offer and he made the approach to Hayward. I made a bid of £10 million through English and Overseas with Sir Isaac putting up the money. This would cost me £900,000 a year in interest but I calculated that the shops could make me an annual profit of £1,750,000—a clear margin of £850,000 and the sort of shot in the arm that E and O needed for my expansion plans.

But on November 18th, only a day after my bid was announced, Hayward and his board threw it out of the window. That night, ironically, Anne and I went to the premiere of 'The Victors' at the Leicester Square Odeon. The board valued the division at £20 million. They added that they had plans for expansion and did not intend to sell. There was much comment in the financial Press about the right of a public company to refuse to sell in such categorical terms, and it was considered that the retail division would have to improve its profits to justify the no-sale decision.

The next day John James himself put in a bid of £11 million and had it rejected within 24 hours. Hayward explained that it was not in the shareholders interests to give up the division's potential earning capacity. It was, he said, the board's expressed intention 'to expand this division whenever possible'. But as John James commented: 'Why hasn't Mr Hayward done this in the past year or so, when, starting from scratch, I have built up another chain of 150 shops?'

During the whole of November I was working a 25-hour day. Not content with major take-over bids I also announced, only three days after my birthday lunch, that I was entering trading stamps since I saw them as a good way round retail price maintenance. At that time there was a national trading stamp controversy with stamp companies falling over each other to sign up retailers and at least half the trade bodies banding together in a stop-the-stamp movement called the Distributive Trades Alliance. Its members represented such varied facets of trade as the National Hairdressers Federation and the Wine Merchants Union.

Green Shield, the entrenched British firm, were grabbing petrol stations and were on sale at Tesco supermarkets while King Korn, having formed a British subsidiary, had brought over their vice-president, Richard Ettelson, to run it, and were using Morris Cohen's Victor Value stores as outlets. Sperry and Hutchinson pink stamps were just going on sale at Garfield Weston's Fine Fare supermarket chain and were putting girls in pink capes outside the stores to distribute explanatory literature to housewives.

On the other side of the fence, Lord Sainsbury, as joint chairman of the Distributive Trades Alliance, was steadfastly refusing to have anything to do with stamps in his shops and took full-page newspaper adverts to explain why. Many large store chains lined up on his side and Wilf Proudfoot, Labour MP for Cleveland, planned a Private Member's Bill banning stamps. Garfield Weston was facing a boycott of his bread and other foods by members of the Distributive Trades Alliance and the bakery business was in turmoil. Weston's men were having their hours cut and other bakeries were being asked to work around the clock seven days a week.

It was into this seething situation that I plunged. I announced that I was going into the business by giving stamps with all my direct-sale goods and offering them to those small retailers who at that time were being overlooked in the rush to sign up the big groups. I also said that my stamps would give colossally more value for money than any other firm's. I intended that housewives would have to spend between 40 and 60 per cent less than with other stamps to get the same article. It seemed to me monstrous to expect people to spend £378 before being eligible for an electric toaster.

Towards the end of November I acquired a controlling interest from Frank Lewis in his family firm—the Supa Yellow Stamp Trading Company—which had quietly been in business for 36 years and used about 20,000 small grocers as outlets. Soon afterwards I spoke to Sir Isaac who offered to sell me his four-month-old Golden Eagle stamp company. I planned to run both companies until I could produce my own stamps and saving books, at which point I would merge them and call them Supa Golden stamps. Part of my arrangement with Sir Isaac, and one that he hoped would cement some sort of relationship between Rolls Razor and GUS, was that I should buy from GUS the articles offered in our stamp catalogue. This turned out to be a disastrous move. There were delivery problems and our distribution got into a bad tangle as a result.

At the beginning of December I stunned the other stamp firms, who were having a tough enough battle with the retailers, by launching a broadside against them from within the stamp enclave. What I was starting amounted to another price war: I announced that I was going to offer cash for trading stamps as an alternative to goods. I was the first British stamp promoter to make this move.

It was all part of my previously-announced plan to offer the best value for stamps. In return for one of my books, which cost £32 to fill, I intended giving 10s in cash, or goods worth between £1 and £1 10s. This compared with goods worth between 15s 9d and 16s being offered by my rivals. In practical terms, I intended offering a vacuum cleaner for nine books as opposed to 25 identical-value books from another company; an iron for five and a half books instead of seven; a 44-piece cutlery set for ten books instead of 19. I felt sure that my offer of better goods and cash convertibility was so much better than anyone else's that even retailers dealing in other stamps would start using mine. The Consumer Council was already lobbying for a bill to make cash convertibility compulsory but my rivals saw it as a threat to their whole operation. They were making a hefty profit by bulk-buying their offers at a discount and offering them at the full retail price. But they could not buy bank notes at a discount.

Immediately after my preliminary announcement that I was entering the stamp business I received a telephone call from the BBC asking me to appear with Bernard Levin in an interview about trading stamps on 'That Was The Week That Was'. I had heard about the famous satirical show, which was facing the axe for its irreverence, but I had never seen Bernard Levin's spot and did not know he used it to launch vitriolic attacks on the subject of his so-called interview. I therefore agreed to appear on the show. When I told my friends to make sure that they were watching they were astonished. They said that I was mad, that Levin would crucify me. And Rex North and Jack Hylton both told me horror stories about his other interviews with Randolph Churchill and the hairdresser Teasy Weasy Raymond.

Everyone seemed so unanimous that I decided I would have to arm myself with as much knowledge as possible—first about Levin's programmes and second, about trading stamps. If Levin indulged in one of his personal diatribes—I was told he might refer to my personal appearance, pending lawsuits or anything to make me lose my temper and make an exhibition of myself—I would have to fend for myself as best I could. But if he launched a full-scale attack on trading stamps I would have to be ready.

My assistants prepared a list of questions which Levin might put, making use of every possible anti-stamp argument. And I examined a shoal of verbatim reports, prepared by Tellex Monitors, of TV and radio programmes in which stamp trading had been discussed so that I could pick up points that had been made for and against. In this way I had the answer to any point which Levin could possibly dredge up, plus a lot of statistical material. I committed all this information to memory and kept asking my assistants and Anne to put questions to me so I could rehearse the answers. On top of all this the BBC agreed to let me have the transcripts of Levin's previous interviews and on November 15th, the day before the show, I went to the BBC theatre where they screened the Churchill and Teasy Weasy interviews so that I could watch Levin at work.

All this may seem much ado about nothing. But Levin was a professional TV interviewer and it seemed foolhardy to hope that I could get away with answering off the cuff. My efforts paid off. When we had the interview I seemed better prepared than he was and so, deciding that attack was the best means of defence, I led the discussion. I completely floored him with facts which demolished the generalised basis of three or four of his questions. The verdict of almost everybody was that this was the first time that anyone had got the better of Levin.

Ned Sherrin, the producer, wrote to thank me for 'putting up what I thought was the best show we've had in these encounters'. And Granville Tompkins, the founder of Green Shield, sent a telegram of congratulations 'on a terrific personal success'. There were many letters from ordinary viewers, a letter from Colin Kingham, the former Rolls chairman, thanking me for dealing with that 'aggressively objectionable interrogator', and some roses from Harry Wheatcroft.

Perhaps the most significant point from this TV confrontation was my answer when Levin suggested that housewives would be paying more at shops using stamps. I said : 'The British housewife can make up her own mind. The public are not idiots.' This phrase was quoted back at me so often that soon afterwards I started incorporating it in all the Rolls adverts underneath a photograph of myself in a TV screen. People later pointed to this as a piece of megalomania but I had been pictured in newspapers so often and had been seen by so many people on TW-3 that market research found that my photograph was immediately identified by over 75 per cent of the population. It was therefore felt that people would identify themselves more with adverts carrying my photograph—and any idea for drawing more coupon replies was worth pursuing.

After the TW-3 show I was introduced to the resident members of the team such as David Frost, Al Mancini, Willy Rushton and Lance Percival. We had a few drinks and the next day I was invited to a party at a flat in Grosvenor Square along with most of the cast. After that I went to a number of parties given by the same group and became friendly with most of them, especially Al Mancini who performed so marvellously off the cuff at our wedding anniversary in the Jack o' Clubs. David Frost, who was the TW-3 linkman, was very amusing. I have not met him for some time but he seems to be much less lighthearted than he was six years ago. Perhaps his seven-day working week is proving a strain. I know the feeling.

Not content with launching several business ventures, I became involved in an attempt to take-over Queens Park Rangers —the club of which I had been a director about a year earlier. This was not business—people do not make money out of football clubs, and I had no desire to increase the 2,000 shares which I still held. I simply wanted to make the club into a big name— as big a name as Arsenal had been when I used to pay 9d to see them every Saturday as a boy.

In November, 1963, QPR had a long way to go. They were grovelling around on one of the lowlier rungs of the Third Division. The White City gamble had failed, the team was playing badly and they had moved back to the squalor of Loftus Road. They had lost £25,000 in the previous season, had a bank overdraft of £64,000 and had not paid a dividend for ten years. To raise cash they were about to sell two of their best players— Peter Springett and Mark Lazarus—and start from scratch by training their own young players.

On November 14th—twelve days before the annual general meeting of QPR shareholders—I received a letter from Bill Clow, the honorary secretary-treasurer of the Rangers Supporters Club which had been officially disowned by the board of directors. He said that since no organised body of shareholders existed many supporters and shareholders, who were dissatisfied with the board, had come to him asking if he could set in motion machinery 'to register and implement a vote of no confidence in the present board of directors'. He suggested that if this happened I might like to become chairman and said: 'I am sure that the many hundreds who have a financial interest in the club would welcome someone with wide business interests, such as your good self, who would lead them and help them reverse the downward trend of the company.' He added: 'There are thousands of supporters, I am sure, who do not think that any real progress can be made with the present administration.'

I decided that if the shareholders disposed of the board leaving the way open for me to become chairman and implement my policies I would put £150,000 cash into the club. To measure the exact support I could expect I decided to put adverts in the *London Evening Standard* and the *London Evening News*, appealing for shareholders to contact me. But the papers refused to insert the advert so I had the names and addresses of every one of the 2,000-odd shareholders copied out of the shares register. By ringing up many of them personally and by sending telegrams or express delivery letters, I contacted every shareholder with more than 100 shares.

The stories about this in the papers brought in several letters of support, one of which expressed concisely what seemed to me the opinion of many of the fans and shareholders. It said: 'The history of QPR over the last ten years leaves much to be desired; at no time in this period have QPR progressed beyond the third round of the FA cup. It seems to me that QPR is run by a board who think Third Division and act Third Division. We have probably the most "slum type" ground in the league—the stand is literally covered in rust—the poorest floodlighting in the league, the worst and most grass-free playing surface in London, no adequate cover for spectators. Shepherd's Bush fans deserve better and I wish you luck.' It was letters like this which convinced me that my decision to attempt to take-over the club was right—despite the allegations in certain quarters that I was doing it for personal glory. There was no prospect of glory at QPR—only years of hard toil.

The annual general meeting, which was usually attended by about 30 people and held in the boardroom, was, on the evening of November 26th, attended by more than 200 shareholders and was therefore held in the battered stand with the floodlights on. The national Press and photographers seemed almost to outnumber the shareholders.

I had worked out that at the rate of one vote per share I had 22,000 votes on my side while the board held 13,900 personally. They had therefore quite a leeway to make up. The two-hour fixture was very heated with boos and jeers both for me and the 61-year-old Chairman George Wodehouse, a former QPR player, who was my chief protagonist. There was much fist-shaking and shouting among the assembly. 'You can't buy a football club,' shouted my opponents. 'Resign, get out,' my supporters yelled at board members. On a show of hands my supporters twice defeated the board. First they refused to adopt the directors' report and accounts and secondly they refused to re-elect the retiring director, Bert Farmer—an issue which Wodehouse had said he would regard as a vote of confidence. However he then demanded a paper ballot and the votes were taken away to a solicitor's office to be counted. After this Wodehouse told everyone: 'If you want to stay in the stand arguing you can, but the meeting is closed.' As he spoke, at least two shareholders were attempting to make a speech and the evening broke up in angry confusion.

I was still confident because as I was quoted as saying in many papers earlier: 'It is impossible for the voting to go against me.' But I was wrong. Forty-eight hours later I was staggered to learn that the board had swept to a crushing two-nil victory. There had been 28,408 votes for the adoption of the directors' report and 8,400 against. For the re-election of Bert Farmer there had been 26,918 votes and against only 5,969. These results only began to make sense when it was revealed that Jim Bonser, the 58-year-old chairman of Watford football club, had just bought 6,000 spare QPR shares. As Rangers director Reg Starnes explained to a baffled public: 'When we announced that we might have to sell players because of our financial problems Mr Bonser offered to help. He was going to give us the money as a loan but we offered him shares.' Thereby boosting the pro-director votes by 6,000. This, with a certain amount of predicted support from old-guard shareholders, accounted for the board's showing but the disappearance of my backing was harder to explain. Although numerically I had more supporters than Wodehouse—as shown by the hand votes—they clearly did not possess many votes each and many people who had pledged their support must have stayed away. Also, on each motion, there were 1,284 and 1,216 votes against on spoilt papers. On the other side there were only 18 and 139. It was possible for me to call an extraordinary meeting and try again to dispose of the board but it was a fact that the board had more than half the 52,000 shares behind them. Before the annual general meeting I had said that if the board received 50 per cent support I would back down. And so I did.

This however did not stop me supporting the club and I

was back in the stand that Saturday to watch the team play Coventry. But there were no trading stamps being given at the turnstiles—one of my ideas. And none of the players would have received a holiday in America—another of my ideas—for their performance; they were given a 6-3 drubbing. Afterwards there were angry scenes on the forecourt outside and hundreds of spectators shouting 'We want Bloom' were hustled away by the police.

This failure to win control of QPR was, of course, totally unimportant in itself and totally irrelevant to Rolls. However I had made the mistake of being over-confident and of rushing the whole operation. It had also taken place from first to last in an enormous and disproportionate blaze of publicity so that when I was beaten the headline writers had a field day. '*QPR 28, Bloom 8*,' was the graphic *Daily Mail* banner. '*Bloom Washed Up*,' said the *Herald* dramatically. While the failure of the Firth Cleveland bid was mainly confined to the City pages the failure to take over QPR was blazed all over much more widely-read pages. It was the first time that the word 'failure' had appeared over stories concerning John Bloom. And it was printed in the largest type available.

15

I MET THE BEATLES FOR THE FIRST TIME DURING THAT SAME
frenetic month of November. Leslie Conn, an artists' manager
friend of mine, knew them well and asked me whether I would
like him to invite them to my birthday party on Saturday the
9th. I was always interested to meet people at the top of their
own particular tree and since the Beatles were the undisputed
kings of the pop scene—and in a much more flamboyant way
than later—I told Leslie to go ahead. He immediately rang the
theatre they were playing and got through to them. Paul could
not come but the others said yes at once. And it was all settled.

At least, it was settled until John, George and Ringo actually
set foot in the hall of Aldford House. Although they were all
wearing suits and ties—which can hardly be imagined today—
they were not looking devastatingly smart. Ringo for instance
wore a dark shirt with a button-down collar. As a result, one
of the porters downstairs, a 68-year-old fellow called Arthur
Dyer, refused to let them in. He recognised who they were by
their Beatle haircuts but, perhaps because he did not approve
of their standard of dress, he did not believe they had been invited to my party as they claimed. The porters had dealt with
would-be gate-crashers often enough in the past and he was
therefore only looking after what he thought were my interests.
It was several minutes before some rather more familiar guests
of mine arrived and assured the porter that the Beatles had been
invited.

They created a sensation when they finally reached the party.

170

Shoals of people surrounded them, trying to talk to them and the photographer that we always had at our parties seemed unable to stop taking pictures of them. He must have got through dozens of rolls of films. The most amazing point about it was that although many people in public life did not approve of the way Beatlemania was sweeping the country, at my party representatives of those people formed an enormous queue to get the Beatles' autographs. For a time the party seemed to stop while MPs, men from the City and their wives cornered John, George and Ringo. Afterwards all the women wanted to dance the twist with them but the wife of music publisher Lou Levy seemed to be their most frequent partner. It was through Mrs Levy meeting the Beatles at this party that Lou acquired from their manager, Brian Epstein, the American publishing rights for '*I wanna hold your hand*'. It netted him a fortune.

The Beatles were used to fans, but at a distance. After a time I thought all this close-range adulation was exhausting them so I asked them and Max Bygraves to join Anne and me in the dining room. There we had a small party of our own and they told me about the pace at which they lived. The next night, they said, they were giving a concert in Birmingham where they expected yet another battle with the fans.

In the early hours of Sunday morning after all the other guests had gone, the Beatles were still in the dining room. We were idly chatting when John remembered that the *News of the World* were due to print an article about them so I said: 'Why don't we drive down to Fleet Street and get a copy?' I got out the Rolls-Royce Phantom V and we set off. The Beatles sat in the back playing with the gadgets such as the tape recorder that I had in there and all the time I was driving I could see out of the corner of my eye that the electrically-operated partition between me and the back seat was going up and down. It was John who had adopted this as his plaything, and later on one of his first cars was a Phantom V. Perhaps he bought it for the push-button partition.

After leaving Fleet Street the Beatles decided that they would call it a night so I drove them back to their flat which was in Green Street not far from mine. Anne helped Ringo make us all coffee while John showed me some pictures which were going to be used on the front of a new album. It was totally informal —they were still very ordinary Liverpool lads who in many ways were still unsure of themselves. They wanted me to tell them all I could about America as they had never been there and were about to go on their first visit. They told me what their manager, Brian Epstein, had obviously told them—that there was going to be an incredible reception waiting for them. Just sitting there in their flat drinking coffee with them I just did not see that it was going to be anything like the dramatic success they were imagining. And yet, from the moment their plane touched down, their tour was one long triumph. I was in America myself some of the time and saw it at first hand. After that I had tremendous respect for Brian Epstein's handling of publicity and advertising.

While we were at Green Street the Beatles invited us to go with them to Birmingham later in the day. Unfortunately I did not have the time because I am sure I would have enjoyed the experience—it turned out to be the famous occasion on which, to avoid the frantic fans, they were disguised in police raincoats and helmets and were driven into the yard behind the Hippodrome in a Black Maria. To make up for not being able to accept their offer I invited them to have dinner with Anne and me at Aldford House. Only two of them could make it: George brought a girl-friend and John brought his then wife Cynthia who had hardly been heard of at that time because Epstein was still trying to pretend that they were bachelor boys.

Over the meal we talked about stocks and shares. But when I tried to explain the intricacies of finance and how people came to make colossal sums of money they did not seem to follow properly and lost interest. I also tried to get some information about the financial structure of the Beatle empire as I had vague plans for some sort of deal with E and O. John seemed to be the business brains of the four at that time but he could not help me much. They could have helped me by revealing how much they personally earned—but they were far too canny to divulge much information on that.

We then moved into the lounge and talked further—mainly

about my records. When I suggested putting some music on, George and John suddenly became animated and wanted to know what I had in my collection. Unfortunately the only record out of a large collection which they liked was an early LP by Stevie Wonder. The others were, like our clothes, a reflection of the tastes of our usual, rather older, guests. We began discussing the whole music scene and George and John talked enthusiastically of many singers who were unknown to me. Not that it was very difficult—I had not even heard of Bob Dylan at the time. This conversation marked the beginning of a reassessment of my records which ended in my replacing the whole of my collection. I have kept it bang up to date ever since.

A few weeks after that dinner I was introduced to Brian Epstein. We had several further meetings and I eventually asked him if he would let the Beatles do a television commercial for Rolls. He said that he was not very happy about the idea and that the Beatles themselves were not very keen on doing adverts—no matter how much money they were offered. I thought about this and had an idea that I might tempt them with a novel sort of payment such as the Rolls boat called the Blue Rose which had cost £30,000 and with the extras that had been added must by then have been worth £50,000. I told Epstein this and he said it might make a difference and that he would consider it. He probably spoke to the Beatles about it, but the next morning he phoned to say the advert was a non-starter, even for a £50,000 boat.

My next contact with the Beatles' world was at a dinner in aid of hospitals at the Adelphi Hotel, Liverpool. I was originally invited to be guest of honour but had to refuse as I expected to be out of the country in connection with the Studebaker deal. But when this collapsed I got in touch with Jack Rubens, who was running the dinner, to tell him that I would be happy to go. By that time, he had fixed himself up with another guest of honour—Brian Epstein, who was born in Liverpool. But he invited me to attend as an ordinary guest and I accepted.

Anne and I flew up to Speke airport in the De Havilland Dove and when we arrived at the hotel we found that there were several other guests from London including Bernard Delfont, Alma Cogan and Lionel Bart. Friends of Brian and members of his own family were also heavily represented. Before the meal I was talking to several of them and I was amazed to hear that Brian had been regarded as the black sheep of the family until his success with the Beatles and other artists. Later on, one friend of the Epstein family became rather drunk and insisted on telling me all sorts of anecdotes about Brian's homosexual activities. His parents, he said, had worried themselves for years in vain attempts to 'cure' him. But to no avail —that was the way he was made.

Several of Brian's friends said that everyone was worried that undesirable characters might latch on to him and, if he became interested in them, get money out of him by persuading him to launch them on careers that were doomed because of lack of talent. This unfortunate attraction for men was probably one of the causes of Brian's undoing.

It was not long after this dinner that Leslie Conn came to me with the suggestion that Dick James would consider selling his shares in Northern Songs, the company which owned the rights to the Lennon and McCartney songs. Leslie said that an offer of about £300,000 would do the trick and that Dick James would be happy to have the money in E and O shares which were doing so well on the market. At that time the E and O 2s shares were changing hands at about £2 each, so to pay £300,000 in shares would have meant spending only £15,000 as far as the capital of E and O was concerned. I thought I would enjoy working with the Beatles and I considered this a first-class deal. I was right. The enduring success of Lennon and McCartney songs has made Northern Songs a great money-spinner. However when I discussed the possible take-over with Sir Isaac—who was to be a partner in the E and O holding company when the Jackson estate was settled—he considered that the pop world was not one in which E and O should get involved. So, since I still regarded him as my absolute adviser on the suitability of investments I rejected the idea against my own judgement. I have been regretting it ever since.

16

THE BULGARIAN HOLIDAY ADVENTURE STARTED WITH SOME colour photographs of the Black Sea. It sank beneath the weight of international air regulations seemingly designed to stamp out tough competition. It was another of the promising ideas which turned sour on me in the first half of 1964.

I became a convert to Eastern European holidays when a fellow called Bertie Littman and the Bulgarian commercial attache in London approached me with some photographs of Bulgaria's beautifully unspoilt beaches and asked me if I would be interested in promoting holidays there. I found it hard to believe that these superb beaches were in Bulgaria; in common with most people I automatically assumed that Iron Curtain countries were as cheerless as Moscow on a winter's day. Yet the photographic evidence showed that the country was every bit as attractive as Majorca. And I felt instinctively sure that it could in fact be made as popular as Majorca or Spain and that there was a great deal of money to be made by the person who first realised this.

Soon afterwards I investigated the possible prices and, co-operating with the official Balkantourist holiday organisation, I worked out that a fortnight's holiday would cost from 45 gns by plane and only 29 gns by coach. This was competitive by any standard—and there was the added attraction for the holiday-maker of going behind the Iron Curtain. Having therefore decided that the idea was a winner on paper, the next step was to visit the country myself. When I discussed the trip with my advertising agents they said: 'Can we come as well?' So I agreed to take them along. In fact everyone I spoke to was interested, which augured well, and by the time I had finished I had to charter a Viscount and Anne and I visited Bulgaria with the chiefs of the advertising agencies, representatives of Sir Isaac Wolfson and Fenn and Crosthwaite, photographers and members of the Press such as Patrick Sergeant. We left London on December 6th taking a special train to Gatwick and champagne was served during the flight to Sophia. When we landed Anne and I were treated as if we were royalty. We had been promised a warm reception but had not anticipated the bouquets of flowers. It was, after all, a business trip.

We were greeted by the Minister of Tourism and shoals of other government officials who steered us through the VIP section of the customs and then entertained us to a champagne buffet at the airport. Later we all drove in a fleet of shiny black limousines to the former royal palace where we were all to stay. This was a particular honour as the immense palace was usually kept closed and had only previously been used for the visits of Nikita Kruschev and Alfried Krupp, the German arms manufacturer.

That same evening the friendly Bulgarians plunged us into the first of four state banquets given in our honour during our week-long stay. After the banquet I made a brief speech ending, in Bulgarian, by wishing everyone peace and friendship. This brought the house down and the Bulgarians really thought that I was going to learn their language. Afterwards, the British Ambassador came up to Anne and me telling us to be careful of what we said during our stay as all parts of the palace were bugged with microphones and all conversations were recorded. I took this rather jokingly—although I did speak with some caution, just in case. However several other people later on told me the same thing and I was led to believe that bugging was pretty well standard practice all over the Iron Curtain countries. On the last night of our stay the Ambassador invited Anne and me to an embassy party being given at a hotel. He told us that it could sometimes be depressing living in a communist country. It was probably the necessity for caution in the diplomatic field which made it so—Anne and I had enjoyed ourselves immensely.

Our visits to various parts of the country to examine the resorts and the hotel facilities convinced me that the holiday scheme would work. All the Bulgarians seemed eager that the tourist industry should get a lift and their natural hospitality augured well for future visitors. Anne and I particularly enjoyed their restaurants where we used to be greeted with a type of hot bread which we then had to break off and dip into a delicious salt. As we ate, girls would dance round the room to traditional Bulgarian music.

While away from Sophia we were still staying in royal accommodation. The overthrown dynasty had thoughtfully provided themselves with a great number of summer palaces— enormous stately homes in the countryside—and hunting lodges which had something of a British flavour with the deer heads displayed around the walls. There was no permanent staff in any of these buildings, of course. But by an impressive piece of organisation one complete entourage was moved from place to place so that they and the accommodation were ready for us wherever we went. At first Anne and I did not realise that one set of people were being whisked round the countryside for our benefit but there was one waiter who started trying out his few English phrases on us and wherever we moved he kept popping up at our shoulder. Eventually he gave the game away.

It was the same situation with cars. There appeared to be only a handful of the impressive Zims in the whole country. On our arrival in Sophia Anne and I thought that all the cars had been kept off the streets during our triumphal procession. The Bulgarians were capable of going to so much trouble that nothing was beyond the bounds of possibility. But, again, it was not until later that we realised the truth. What gave the game away this time was the consternation of the Balkan-tourist officials if I decided to change my itinerary. This concern was followed by frantic telephone calls. It turned out that there was only one fleet of cars and it had to be redirected to our new destination.

Having studied the country I had several talks with Bulgarian government Ministers and eventually met the Prime Minister, Todor Zhivkov, whose private plane we had been using to hop around the resorts. I had some reservations about the possible political problems of tourism. I felt that any country abounding with bugging devices must have some internal unrest—and this was confirmed on one occasion in 1964 when several young Bulgarians swam out to the Ariane, which was anchored quite a way from the shore, seeking political asylum. But since the holiday arrangement was then just getting going, and since I happened to have several Bulgarian officials on board at the time, I felt it was hardly the moment to get involved in a political situation I did not understand. I am afraid that Captain Christie was told not to allow any would-be refugees on the yacht.

But my main worry was that some British tourists might get themselves arrested for contravening some law of which they were ignorant. During one major discussion which I had with Zhivkov—and which was filmed for television—I said quite clearly that if arrangements were made to bring in thousands of visitors I wanted an assurance that there would be no arrests of that sort. He told me I need not worry. There were already thousands of tourists visiting Bulgaria from West Germany every year without anybody being slapped in jail. It was well known, he added, that Bulgaria was a place where East and West Germans could meet—and often families were reunited there. It was also a place where spies could meet contacts, pass on information or leave messages. He said that several West Germans had been found taking pictures of military installations but that these cases had not been closely examined. The police had merely taken the film out of the cameras and told the would-be photographers to leave the area. Anything rather than risk upsetting the tourist business.

Bulgaria had 400,000 visitors in 1963—but they were mainly people driving through on their way to Turkey. Only 50,000 were on the Balkantourist fortnight's holiday. And of these only 1,500 were from Britain. The Bulgarians' plan was to get the number up to 1,500,000 visitors by 1970. The final deal that Zhivkov and I agreed on was that if I sent 8,000 tourists before October, 1964, I would be given the travel concession for Britain—in other words, from 1965, people would still be able to book individual trips but I would have the only package-deal holidays available. Apart from the profit I would make on the holidays Zhivkov agreed that 60 per cent of the money that would be made out of the increased tourism would be spent in the British market with English and Overseas Investments acting, in effect, as his agents. This meant that I would be getting a percentage on everything from aeroplanes to tins of rice pudding. I would therefore make two lots of profit if the deal came off.

As usual, those already in business in my next chosen sphere of operations were up in arms. The major travel agents, except Cooks, were disgusted at the way Zhivkov and I had sewn up the country under their noses and announced within two or three days of my return that they were withdrawing package-deal tours to Bulgaria even though Black Sea resorts were in the pamphlets which they had been circulating for months.

I did not have any experience in the holiday business but I did not see that as an insuperable problem. I could always buy the know-how. And soon after my return I realised that I would need it. I announced that I would offer two-week holidays from 49 gns, flying from London to Varna, and a coach tour across Europe, including a week in Bulgaria, for as little as 29 gns. But I got a nasty shock almost at once. I was told that I was not allowed to advertise holidays so cheaply when they included a flight direct from London since under the International Air Transport Agreement the minimum permitted fare from London to Varna was £70.

As usual my plan depended on a mass sale—this time of visitors to Bulgaria—and so I had to keep the price down. Somehow I had to get round the IATA regulation. On December 21st I signed up the two Lord brothers, both well-known travel agents in their own right, to manage the administration of the company I had formed to promote the travel—English and Overseas Tours. They were to have nothing to do with the finances or with getting the bookings and they still carried on

179

their own business. They agreed to fill this role in the first instance for nine months and I agreed to pay them each £5,000 a month. When Rolls collapsed I had to pay the balance on their contract out of my own pocket.

Their first piece of advice was to transfer my flights to Ostend since Belgium was not bound by the IATA regulations. In this way we managed to get down the costs to 45 gns for the cheapest holiday. The drawback, of course, was that travellers had to fly first to Ostend and then transfer to a Bulgarian airliner. Although it was cheap, many people who liked their holidays simple and carefree were against the arrangements. This much was predicted by the Lord brothers who said that if I was to meet my 8,000 target I would have to offer a direct flight from London even if it was quite pricey.

The basic point about chartering is that a certain number of bookings pay for the costs after which each traveller represents a profit. With the 128-seat Britannias that we were using on flights direct from London we found, as time went by, that we could not get enough passengers to cover the cost. These expensive London flights were disastrous and were one of the main reasons for the lack of profitability on the whole tour project. A further reason was that, since the travel agents had washed their hands of Bulgarian holidays, we had to sell them all direct. In a progress report dated February 2nd it was revealed that in the first few weeks of the operation only nine bookings had been received from travel agents. Although direct selling meant a saving on commission—travel agents received 10 per cent, almost twice as much as the £2 10s our representatives received—it also meant that there was a heavy advertising cost to be borne. In that February report it was said that some £13,000 had been spent on advertising—which worked out at an average cost of £11 1s a booking. Something had to be done to boost sales but since I had launched the operation so rapidly I had not had time to saturate the market with brochures as the other package holiday merchants had been doing since the previous summer, and so Bulgaria had received too little promotion. In addition, February, the month when we really began to get the firm off the ground, is usually regarded as the last month for summer bookings. From all aspects, circumstances were against us.

This was not my only headache at that time. For it was in March that the production arrangement with Pressed Steel ended in an unfortunate public shambles. The break had been on the cards for some months. In fact for most of the time Pressed Steel had been supplying us there had been rows between their boards and the three musketeers on the quality of machines and the flow of supplies. In addition the musketeers had become increasingly involved in the Tallent side of our supplies—Leslie Goldbart in particular becoming very friendly with Aaron Wright. Goldbart was constantly arguing that we should stop dealing with Pressed Steel and switch over entirely to Tallent. I did not feel inclined to do this—for one thing it would kill the Prestcold link—and in any case the agreement could only be terminated by one side giving a whole year's notice. However towards the end of 1963 Pressed Steel started telling us that they could no longer afford to make a twin tub for as little as £23. It was this cheap production which gave Rolls its attractive selling price and its profits. I had linked up with Pressed Steel, at least partly, because their £23 quotation was cheaper than the machines I was making at Cricklewood. I therefore told Abel Smith that I could not agree to raising the price I was paying—especially since Tallent seemed to be managing perfectly well at the same price. Furthermore I told him that I was not at all happy with the way that the still-controversial Beagle enterprise was being run and that in view of my large shareholding I would like a seat on the board of Pressed Steel to see what I could do. However I was coolly told that there was no seat on the board for me and that the price they were charging for twin tubs would have to be increased.

This was the background to the announcement on December 12th that Sir Charles Colston was rejoining the Rolls Razor board, this time with Aaron Wright. If Tallent were going to take over the whole of our production—and that was how things were shaping up—they would have to be on the board. Meanwhile the situation was becoming more difficult with the

Swansea people and we agreed to unscramble our financial links. On Christmas Eve we announced that the interlocking directorships were being abandoned while I was selling my shares in Pressed Steel and they were selling their Rolls holding. As a sign of the times it is interesting to note that I lost about £40,000 on the deal while Pressed Steel made a profit of around £250,000 on their Rolls shares. Our announcement said that the interlocking directorships 'had served their purpose' and that both sides considered that our joint business could be best continued on a manufacturer-customer basis. All the financial pundits nodded sagely at this and there was no hint of any behind-the-scenes wrangling.

On February 12th Pressed Steel gave us a year's notice that they intended ending the manufacturing agreement but we released them from their obligations on March 2nd. Soon afterwards—appropriately enough on Friday the 13th of March —Joe Edwards told the workpeople at Swansea that the super-factory was to close at the end of May when the link with Rolls was being severed. For the 1,450 workers the announce-ment meant that they had to look for new jobs in an area that already had a high unemployment problem. For me the closure meant that I would be relying on one supplier, Tallent, who immediately started taking on extra staff, and that if I was to continue selling refrigerators I would have to find an alternative supply. But the announcement also had rather more far-reaching effects for Rolls.

The linking of our name with the shock closure—which was partly blamed on our failure to reach a high enough level of productivity to make ends meet—reflected badly on us. The whole closure operation was, in fact, a very bad piece of public relations from our point of view and caused a crisis of confidence which only served to push us a little further down the slippery slope.

17

THE LOSS OF CONFIDENCE IN ROLLS CAME AT A MOMENT WHICH was already serious. Although in the first three months of 1964 we sold 54,794 washing machines, so keeping a 21.5 per cent share of the British market, this was only half of what I set myself and only half of what our production and raw material supply was geared to turn out. Also, the sales in March fell to 16,104 which heralded the slump. In January they were 19,452 and in February 19,238. And again, the percentage of basic models—on which we lost money—to de luxe models reached an all-time peak of 15.4 in December followed by 14.5 in January and never again fell below 11 per cent. A year earlier, in January 1963, the figure had been a mere 6.7 per cent.

But my biggest problem was my huge advertising budget—again geared to a sale of about 32,000 washing machines a month. At the level of actual sales that was being achieved each machine I sold cost £9 12s 5d in advertising in January and £8 18s 5d in February. Although this was a lot of money it was not totally absurd. But in March, when sales dropped, the average cost shot up to £14 9s 6d a machine.

On top of this there was the cost of my premium offers—all of which cost me about £5 a sale—and the ever-increasing administrative cost. The premium department under Leslie Goldbart was taking on additional staff all the time and as the offers multiplied and the customer had more choice so the problems mounted. Supplies failed to arrive or there were not enough of a certain offer to go round. The headaches were endless. I was giving away a complete set of kitchen tools, the fan heaters, cutlery, crockery, hi-fi radiograms and vacuum cleaners. At Christmas I had several seasonal gifts including a 4ft high Santa Claus—supplied by a trader in New York, called Lenny Stoegel—which proved a great success. I sent a lorry-load to Great Ormond Street children's hospital where they were welcomed by the matron and all the children. I also sent three round to Buckingham Palace where they were eagerly accepted. Another royal link we forged at about the same time was to supply Princess Alexandra and Mr Angus Ogilvy with one of our washing machines for their home in Richmond, Surrey. They filled in a coupon in the usual way but we gave them an undertaking that we would not seek any publicity at all from the sale.

After taking my first steps in the air charter holiday business I went over to Belgium to arrange the even-cheaper coach trips to Bulgaria. It suddenly occurred to me that I could use the same coaches to take people on trips all over Europe and that I could offer such trips as premium offers with Rolls washing machines. These holidays turned out to be sensationally good value. There was a choice of eight days touring France, Holland and Belgium for 3 gns, ten days in the Austrian Tyrol for 7 gns and ten days in Venice for 9 gns. These prices could be offered because most people buying a machine and getting the cut-rate holiday wanted to take a husband or wife who had to pay the economic fare and so subsidised their partner.

I was still looking for new fields into which I could expand and I was considering several offers—one of which had nothing to do with business at all. It started in June 1963 when a letter came from Jeremy Thorpe, the present leader of the Liberal Party, who had been trying to get in touch with me by phone for some time. His letter said: 'I would very much like to take 20 minutes of your time to suggest a project (political) which I think may interest you.' I was intrigued, naturally, and surmised that he must have read a comment of mine in the papers that I was very keen on the Liberal Party.

Because of all my business commitments, however, it was

not until December that I eventually met him at his small office near the Houses of Parliament. Since I took the meeting to be top secret I went alone and there were just two of us present across the top of a desk. The project, he revealed, concerned a committee of three which he was organising for the party and which was intended to spearhead the Liberal effort at the imminent general election. I was invited to be one of the trio, which would, of course include himself and another person and he explained that his basic plan was to win a further thirty seats additional to those already held. In this way Jeremy Thorpe anticipated that the Liberals might well hold the balance of power in the next Parliament. He had analysed the 30 seats in great detail and he gave me various documents which showed who the prospective candidates were and gave a break-down of the expenses the Liberals would have to incur in order to be fighting the seats at full strength. If I joined the committee, and the idea paid off, I would have had a hand in what could have proved a major turning point in 20th century British politics—the revival of the Liberal Party as a potent force. I gathered that in such a case my efforts would not go unrewarded and that any aspirations which I might have towards getting a seat in the House would receive a sympathetic hearing.

I told Jeremy Thorpe that I would examine the documents, think the whole thing over and give him my answer soon. However I became swamped by the Bulgarian and the Pressed Steel matters and did not have time to give the committee decision the attention it deserved. As a result I received several telephone messages asking if I could make up my mind and these culminated in a handwritten letter on House of Commons notepaper dated February 12th. In it Jeremy Thorpe said:

'Dear JB,
    'I shan't bother you again—since a spate of letters and telephone calls is boring for both of us! But I am anxious for reasons of time finally to resolve the matter we discussed last December.

185

'You are, I know, inhumanly busy! But the question resolves itself into 2 short points:

'(1) I should be delighted if you were to become the third member of our Committee—and have so invited you. If successful the Committee could have a lasting impact on the political scene. But if you are unable to join then with the prospect of a Spring Election I am anxious to fill the 3rd place immediately.

'(2) Without reading through the long document I sent you, I have totalled the financial help needed by the 30 winnables, in addition to their existing income on the basis of total war between now and polling day. I hoped that you might feel disposed to help us here financially.

'Naturally I hope your answer may be "yes" but even if it is "no" to one or both propositions could you let me know?

'Time is now our most precious commodity and the problem of raising the wind is driving me "bonkers".

'If you say "yes" however it will be an even better restorative than a Bulgarian holiday.

Yours,

Jeremy T.'

Unfortunately I could not see myself having enough time between February and a spring election to help much. And this turned out to be correct. So I turned down the place on the committee and sent back all the documents. I regretted having to do this as I considered that I would have found the operation stimulating and could have helped behind the scenes even after the election. As the *Guardian* suggested in an editorial that January, people like myself, who know how to make capitalism work, should be invited to sit on government advisory committees if anything to do with money is at issue.

While this was going on I was approached by Bob Goldstein, a former managing director of 20th Century Fox Productions, who suggested that I should get together a consortium to bid for British Lion films which was being offered for sale by the Government-run National Film Finance Corporation. He said the company could very well reap large profits for the consortium and I decided that I was prepared to put up a good part of the necessary £1,600,000—on a personal basis, with no connection with any of my companies. I enlisted the help of Jack Hylton and between us we produced an imposing group comprising Jack, Bob Goldstein and myself, plus the Hollywood writer-director Nunnally Johnson, and two other directors—Anthony Mann who made 'El Cid' and 'Fall of the Roman Empire', and Terence Young who directed 'Dr No' and 'From Russia with Love'. Our consortium was recognised as a bona fide bidder on January 30th—only 24 hours before the closing date for bids—when Goldstein and I had an hour-long meeting with the board of the National Film Finance Corporation at their office in Soho Square. Unfortunately, there were six other consortia which also contained some pretty powerful guns. The rival groups were headed by film men Sydney Box, Sir Michael Balcon, and Sam Spiegel (with John Woolf and Leslie Grade), agent Stanley Dubens, the Federation of Film Unions under their president Sir Tom O'Brien and the Freedom Group of Edward Martell.

However our enthusiasm was cooled by the ban on the sale of any of British Lion's assets by the successful consortium and by the fact that the Government retained the right to veto anything it liked. So we decided not to continue with our bid. When March 11th—the closing date for the actual bid documents—came round only the Balcon, Box and Martell groups were still interested. Edward Heath, who as President of the Board of Trade had to make the final decision, chose Sir Michael as expected. He had as supporters the five directors of British Lion including the Boulting brothers, John Osborne, Peter Sellers, Jack Clayton, Tony Richardson, Lady Wooton of Abinger and the former Attorney-general Sir Lionel Heald.

Just after my consortium was accepted as a bidder my own trading stamps came out and the name Supa Golden was officially born. Frank Lewis, from whom I bought Supa Yellow, the cornerstone of my stamp enterprise, was in charge of operations and he decided that my face should appear on the stamps. He considered that it would be advantageous since it would make the stamps recognisable and would mean that the shoppers would identify with me. The thinking was much the same as the thinking behind the inclusion of my face on adverts, but I was not happy about it as I was aware that a large part of City opinion still regarded Rolls shares as a wild speculation and mistrusted the amount of publicity I was still getting. In fact, if anything, I was getting more mentions in the Press than ever before. *Punch* summed up the situation neatly in their issue of January 30th. This carried a cartoon showing two commuters reading newspapers, with one commuter saying to the other: 'I buy mine for the regular contributors—William Hickey, Beachcomber, John Bloom.'

So, partly because I wanted to cut down a bit on the personalised publicity and partly because putting my face on a stamp looked like a particularly bad piece of egocentricity, I refused to have anything to do with the idea. Frank Lewis and his advisers were convinced, however, they ought to do this to give the stamps a distinctive impact. I therefore told them that as they were supposed to be the experts they could go ahead on their own—but that I was going to do nothing towards publicising the launch. Consequently, when the Press party was held on February 2nd to unveil the Supa Golden stamps I was not even present—but this was a fact which seemed to go unnoticed. The part of Lewis' official statement which claimed that I was the first person in Britain, other than the monarch, to have his face on a stamp, was seized on for much withering comment. But, unfortunately, the impression ever after was that this had been my personal proud boast. And the almost saintly aura of light which surrounded my head likewise caused much mirth—quite rightly. The whole personal stamp idea therefore boomeranged disastrously and only served to confirm the worst fears of certain elements in the City.

It also proved fatal to the expansion plans of Supa Golden. The main outlets that we hoped to capture were the small retailers who were feeling disgruntled at the extra competitive edge which the stamp-carrying supermarkets had gained. But since these shopkeepers, whether they were in the electrical goods business or not, considered me to be the archenemy of the little man, a neat piece of salesmanship was going to be needed to persuade them to carry Supa Golden stamps. The task would have been difficult enough without putting me on the stamps, but having my face as a visual reminder of who was running the stamp company was too much for most retailers to stomach. As a result the number of Supa Golden shops stayed almost static and prevented the venture from becoming the almighty success I had anticipated.

For some time I had been discussing with Lou Levy the possibility of setting up a direct-sales record company in Britain on the lines of the big American success, the Columbia Record Club. I had talks with Louis Benjamin of Pye and with Norman Lonsdale of Concert Hall records, and in January, 1964, I formed the Rolls Record Club and the Rolls Record Company. Working to the old formula that I already had on file millions of potential customers I was sure this would be a big success and indeed there are several prospering record clubs going today. The operation was a complex one and took months of planning. I attempted to get a record label of my own by buying Ember Records from its owner Geoff Kruger. But first I wanted to have its success assured by having some top talent signed up. Adam Faith was being considered, but most important was John Barry the composer who had as assets his ability plus the royalties of his companions. Geoff Kruger attempted to get John Barry to join Ember but failed and as a result I decided not to go ahead with my Ember deal. The whole record club project was just one of several that were still in their embryo stages at the time of the Rolls collapse.

There were of course many more 'million-making' enterprises that were put to me and that I did not pursue. One of them came from Vic Lownes who was living at that time in another part of Aldford House and who, in the *Playboy* warren, was one of the right-hand men to Hugh Hefner, the guiding light. I went to one or two of Vic Lownes' parties which were always well-stocked with Bunny-class girls and he showed me the profits made by *Playboy* clubs all over the world. He was planning to open a *Playboy* club in London and was at that time looking at a building in St James Street. He asked if I would be interested in financing the project and I looked at the figures. I was quite interested but Sir Isaac did not think it was a suitable investment for E and O and a detailed examination of the proposal rendered it less attractive than I thought, so I turned down Vic Lownes' offer.

Cyril Stein of Ladbrokes, the well known firm of bookmakers, came to me soon afterwards with a suggestion that I should take over his firm. I was extremely interested in that idea also but again when I put the idea to Sr Isaac he thought it was not appropriate to our plans for E and O and I therefore decided to turn it down.

18

ONCE THE ROT SET IN ON OUR SALES EVERYTHING SEEMED TO go wrong for Rolls. But the big question is: why did the rot set in? Even today nobody is certain. The usual reason given for a sales slump in the domestic appliance industry is mild weather—it is a fact that housewives do not bother with such things as cookers and vacuum cleaners during the summer months. This is possibly because the pleasant weather makes them feel happier with their lot; it is only when it becomes cold again that they start thinking how to make their life more bearable. In 1964, spring came early which would account for some falling off in coupon returns for March.

Secondly, automatic and semi-automatic machines were beginning to make their mark. Pressed Steel had not been able to get ours into production and when we broke with them Tallent had to take over the operation, which meant another delay while other firms were stealing the market.

But probably the most important reason for the sales slump was the breakdown of confidence in Rolls. In a firm whose movements were made as public as ours this lack of confidence was not confined to the worlds of industry and finance, it spread to potential customers. And once people started asking themselves: 'Will we ever get our machine or will we have to wait for months, and will we ever get that cheap holiday bonus?' Rolls was done for. They would not buy until they were sure that the company was safe and the more they did not buy the less safe we became. The Pressed Steel break was not the only thing to shake people's faith in us. On March 22nd the *Sunday Times* devoted a large part of their colour magazine to my life story, under the not altogether flattering title 'The Electric Man'. In it I was pictured at the wheel of the Ariane and reading the papers in bed with Anne. The article itself, which I regret to say I co-operated in, contained various nicely-phrased criticisms of the way I worked, the way I lived and the people I had working for me. The short financial section of the piece claimed that my Rolls and E and O empire was in the form of two inverted pyramids, one on top of the other. It added that although this structure had been highly successful in the case of Sir Isaac Wolfson it had also been calamitous in the famous cases of the Insul crash in America and the Clarence Hatry empires in Britain between the wars. As Kenneth Fleet, the *Sunday Telegraph*'s City editor, remarked the week after, the article marked 'the end of the attempt in the City to understand and come to terms' with me.

At the beginning of March in an attempt to prune costs, we stopped our premium offers and concentrated instead on offering holidays and Supa Golden stamps—with extra stamps for people who disposed of their second-hand machines since we were being inundated with them. We also brought out a new machine called the Rolls Concorde—an improved version of the Rapide. The Concorde was tested by *Which?* and was included in a survey of washing machines on April 8th—just a fortnight after the *Sunday Times* feature on me. As far as losing public—as distinct from business—confidence was concerned this report was crucial. The Concorde did not figure as the best buy. *Which?* said: 'We think it is expensive to buy the direct sales twin tub by hire purchase. If you do pay by instalments over three years as the advertisements suggested, the final hire purchase price of the Rolls Concorde de luxe comes to £83 1s. This is equivalent to a true rate of interest of about 23 per cent.' The most damaging part followed: 'If you buy a twin tub from a shop or electricity board showroom you will find that, although hire purchase charges vary, it is not difficult to find a shop that will charge you a true rate of interest of about 9½ per cent. And you can get a policy cover-

John and Anne celebrate after his Old
Bailey acquittal

Footballer John at the time of his
bid to take over Queen's Park Rangers

Left: John and Anne : reflections in
tranquillity

John negotiating a deal with the
Bulgarian premier (top of table, left)

Brian Epstein, Christina Foyle, John and
Helen Shapiro at a Foyles Literary Lunch

John with 'Steptoes' Harry H. Corbett
and Wilfred Brambell

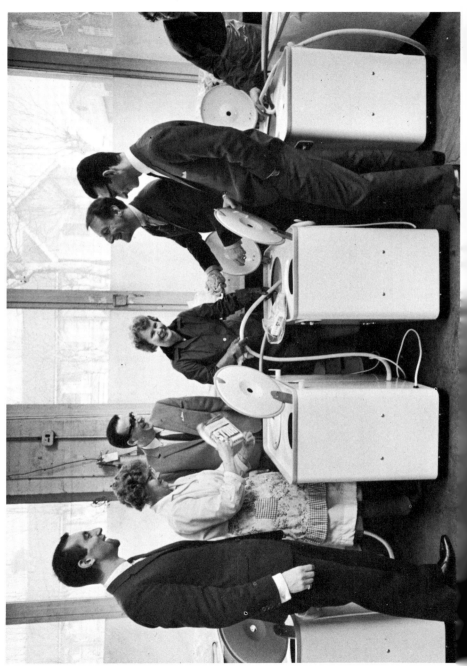

Leslie Goldbart, Jack Jacobs, John and
Irving Jacobs supervising a demonstration wash

The £330,000 *Ariane*

The *Ariane*'s master bedroom

John in the Rolls-Prestcold offices, Regent Street

Keeping in touch : John on the factory floor

ing accident and sickness' (but not unemployment which was also covered in the Rolls HP agreement) 'for 6d in the pound on the total sum outstanding. This might come to £1 12s on a £61 19s washing machine, making a total hire purchase price of £72 2s; £10 19s less than Rolls.' This report was followed two days later by the BBC television programme 'Choice' which was based on the *Which?* report but which pointed up even more strongly the hire purchase disparity. As we did not handle our own HP we could do nothing about this.

A bizarre but equally unfortunate side effect of the *Which?* report was that they criticised an English Electric twin tub as being potentially unsafe electrically. English Electric who had thousands of these machines in stock disposed of them in a bulk deal with the result that a machine went on to the market complete with heater and pumps, looking very similar to ours, but only costing 39½ gns as opposed to our 59½ gns. This clearly ate into some of our potential sales.

For all these various reasons the sales slump continued. Whereas it had been 16,104 in March it became 14,334 in April although the saving on premium offers improved the profit situation slightly. But the price of shares continued to fall—mainly because of rumours of a rift between Sir Isaac and myself. This was true to a slight extent. I had settled the dispute with the Jackson executors by buying from the estate 159,000 shares at £2 0s 3d each and the details of my share-swap between Rolls and E and O had therefore been finalised. There was now nothing to prevent the Drages agreement going through. I spoke to Sir Isaac about it three times but he had been advised not to proceed. (I later learned that his solicitors and accountants had been advising him to wait until our accountants had produced the Rolls accounts for 1963.) I had been told by Norton, Rose, the Rolls solicitors, that the agreement was legally enforcible but it would take an enormous amount of time to settle if I did take it to court. In any case the publicity attached to any legal dispute between Sir Isaac and myself would have been the death blow to Rolls. Since there was no way of bringing the issue to a happy conclusion I agreed finally to let the agreement lapse—and waved goodbye to the biggest deal I had ever planned.

At the same time I was having discussions with Sir Isaac's General Guarantee Corporation who were financing the Rolls hire purchase operation. They had agreed in 1962 to finance us to the tune of £10 million and as all but £1.5 million had now been taken up I was keen to negotiate a new agreement. Since all the hire purchase profit—about which *Which?* had complained so bitterly—was going to General Guarantee with Rolls just getting a small commission, I wanted a much better slice of the cake. For one thing, it was Rolls who were creating the business in the first place; and for another, the hire purchase was proving much more profitable than the manufacturing—especially since Rolls were responsible for paying any bad HP debts.

Not surprisingly, Sir Isaac did not want to concede any bigger share of his profits to me. Rumours inevitably started that the General Guarantee agreement was about to cease and the shares were hit once again. Eventually, on March 26th, General Guarantee had to issue a statement saying that there was no change in the £10 million hire purchase finance agreement of 1962. This assured people that I was not going to be left suddenly without any backing—but equally it did not say that there would be any more finance coming from them. So the overall effect on the share slide was not very great.

It was at this time that Capital Finance came strongly on to the scene. A finance house based in Edinburgh, Capital was backed by the London merchant bankers Guiness Mahon and quoted in Liverpool and Edinburgh. They had been doing small pieces of financing for Rolls for some time and they came to my attention again through a fellow called Douggie Bayle, a Canadian whom I first knew in 1961 when he was running a few garages. I gave him the contract for hiring to Rolls as many vehicles as we needed and from this he emerged as a would-be tycoon. He eventually sold the contract business to Capital and became very friendly with Bertie Veitch, Capital's joint managing director.

In February, 1964, I was having a talk with Douggie Bayle

about the hire business, which he was again running having bought back a share, when he mentioned that Capital would be interested in taking on some of our hire purchase business. I had talks with Bertie Veitch and he said he would like to take over entirely from General Guarantee. But when I examined the legal aspect it appeared that General Guarantee had everything sewn up and that Capital could only be allowed to finance new businesses. Towards the end of March, however, I had further discussions with Veitch and Bayle and on March 29th the three of us finally met on board the Ariane in Monte Carlo to complete arrangements. We agreed that money should be borrowed from Capital by a company called Finance Services and Insurances which was a wholly-owned subsidiary of E and O. Under the new scheme of things, this company would double its share capital to £100,000 and would become 50 per cent owned by Rolls, 22½ per cent by E and O and 27½ per cent by Capital. Finance Services and Insurance would then re-lend the borrowed money to Rolls at a higher rate of interest. In this way, I got the share of the hire purchase proceeds that I felt I ought to have. As for Capital, they had boosted their business with us, and, more important, were on the scene to offer much greater financing facilities in the future. They also took 285 £1,000 loan notes in E and O.

The emergence of Capital, when our deal was announced on April 10th, took people by surprise—but favourably. It was generally felt that I had pulled off something of a coup. As a result there was a scramble for my shares and Rolls went up over 2s to 28s 3d with E and O rising by around 1s to 18s 6d. It was the last time, at a tolerable price level, that either share showed an appreciable rise.

The spheres which Capital were to finance were TV rentals, the revival of the home movies scheme and a new cheap washing machine to be marketed under Tallent's own name.

The rentals never really got off the ground. I had bought the Leytonia chain and also the nine-shop Downs chain in Bristol which I intended expanding to 50 shops within 18 months. But the Rolls empire collapsed before the enterprise had an opportunity of proving itself. The photographic idea, which I still

195

considered a winner and which I used as a dual offer with washing machines, did have time to prove itself—but unfortunately failed the test because of technical difficulties. The projectors were being made by Spectro, a firm to whom I lent about £40,000 to help capitalise. They were tested at Cricklewood before going on offer and seemed fine, but a little later, when I went to the northern and western area sales conferences, representatives complained that the projectors were burning out or slowing down. I told Leslie Goldbart, who was in charge of the home movies offer, and he got on to Irving Jacobs who had organised the earlier testing.

The projectors were re-examined and we found that although they were all right when one or two reels of film were running through them, some motors became strained when a whole set of, say, ten holiday reels were run. And if a motor was particularly defective it might break down after a very short time, perhaps actually during a demonstration. In that case the salesman would almost inevitably lose the sale so it became vital to check as many as we could before they left Cricklewood. We had men from Spectro and our own people working all the time testing them and they found that about one in three had to be rejected. The whole operation was therefore very costly and wasteful of man-hours, ruining its chances of being a success.

The Tallent washing machine idea was another semi-failure. When our sales began to fall quite markedly in April I had the idea that we should spawn a 'rival' to Rolls which we could market with lower advertising costs, lower hire purchase deposits and no special offers. They would therefore sell more cheaply and if the name Rolls was beginning to work against us perhaps we could pick up our missing sales with another name. The machine, called the Tallentwin, came out at the end of April at 36 gns and 56 gns as opposed to the 39 gns and 59 gns of the Concorde. But precisely because it lacked promotion it did not have the desired impact. We did not get enough coupon returns and we found that many of those who did fill in coupons were curious about the cheapness and low deposit rather than serious about the possibility of buying one. The percentage of coupons converted into sales was therefore poor; and of the people who did buy the machines many were not good risks.

I was at the stage where I was trying anything to keep sales buoyant. But the amount of cash that was available to promote sales was fast running out. We had no financial representation on the Rolls board, and we were beginning to regret it. Our accounts were also continuously behind the times at a period when we could have done with up-to-date information on which to base decisions. I decided to ask Patrick Hutber if he would work for Rolls as financial co-ordinator to assess the situation and advise us. He agreed and I paid him £10,000 a year on a contract out of my own pocket.

His appointment was passed by the board on May 14th—the day that Reader Harris announced the year's results which the City had been anxiously waiting for. In the circumstances the delay in producing the results had in itself been the source of damaging rumour which the results did little to alleviate. Although we declared a final dividend of 120 per cent thus making a total of 200 per cent, as forecast, the profits were disappointing. The actual trading profit had gone up from £797,461 to £1,160,366 yet the net profit after various provisions for tax and so on showed an increase of only £11,873 over 1962 at £475,799. In hectic after-hours dealings following these results Rolls shares sank 4s 6d to 23s 9d.

In a further attempt to improve sales I asked Tallent what hopes they had of producing an automatic machine, but they said they had not yet even received the tooling from Pressed Steel. In desperation I turned to Jim Elvins' Duomatic who were marketing a sort-of automatic machine. Talks dragged on for a few weeks to absolutely no avail and became a standing joke in City circles. My accountants were unable to produce any meaningful report about Duomatic, and it looked as though their liquidity situation was much like ours. I decided to break off the talks. Instead I tried to arrange an instant supply of automatics from the Continent but could not find a suitable machine. In the end I turned to Leon Seltzer's Imperial Domestic Appliances who had been having a quiet little success story of their own; they had sold, direct to the customer, 10,000 fully automatic washing machines in ten months. They were imported from the Italian manufacturers Zanussi and were sold at 79 gns—deliberately to appeal to the top end of the market. Imperial's financial director was Bernard Rader, a Rolls shareholder and chief of Bernard Rader and Co, the auditor of various E and O subsidiaries.

Our tie-up was good for them since it increased their turnover but it was not very advantageous for us. We were only doing it to get into the automatic market and since we were buying the machines from Imperial instead of straight from Italy it did not leave us much of a profit margin—unless we charged more than Imperial themselves, which was out of the question. But even with this disadvantage I decided that I could still offer an automatic at less than the Imperial price by cutting down on the finish and the speed of action, and by substituting a 1½ kw heater for the 3 kw. I called this model the Rolls Robot and advertised it at 65 gns; the Rolls Robot de luxe, which was identical to the successful Imperial, was marketed for 79 gns. The automatic operation was announced on June 12th but by that time there were only weeks left to Rolls and it therefore turned out to be more of an academic exercise.

The self-perpetuating spiral of falling share prices, weakening public confidence, and dwindling sales, was creating an increasingly desperate situation. And just how desperate was shown by the May figures. In the whole of the *month* we sold 6,504 washing machines (in that single record-breaking *week* in October we sold 7,442) and each machine cost £21 17s 2d to sell in advertising alone.

I then came up with two more sale-pushing ideas. The first was a scheme whereby anyone who bought a washing machine from us would be able to buy many other goods from us at far below the shop price. Apart from providing an incentive to buy machines this was also another knock at resale price maintenance and as an ironic joke I named the operation the Rolls Privileged Member scheme—so giving it the same initials, RPM, as for resale price maintenance. This scheme, launched on May

24th, was a good idea because it would have provided the germ of a huge mail order business, again using all our previous customers as the basis of the business. I had talks with David Clore, Charles Clore's brother, about expanding into a mail order company and he put me on to one Leonard Sainer with whom I had more discussions in June, but by then things were moving so quickly that I just could not keep up with everything and this was something which fell by the wayside. Although the mail order business would have benefited all Rolls customers, the RPM scheme itself was confined to new buyers as its whole purpose was to boost sales. However many people did not grasp this point, which led to the breakdown of the scheme. So many coupons came flooding in that we ran out of catalogues and had to have more printed. It was the middle of June therefore before we discovered just how large a percentage of the replies came from housewives who already had a Rolls washing machine. They merely wanted to have one of our catalogue offers—anything from a set of saucepans, through bedroom furniture, jewellery, sewing machines, golf clubs and garden sheds to mink stoles. Alternatively the salesmen would discover that although the inquirer was not a Rolls owner she did not want to become one either—she was only interested in the cut-price goods. This meant that the salesmen were wasting a great deal of their time and at the beginning of July we decided to suspend the whole operation as it was totally uneconomic.

The second idea that I had at the same time was the Recommenda Rolls scheme which simply rewarded people for filling in a little coupon introducing us to a friend—provided that friend then bought a washing machine. The rewards were very attractive starting with a watch, children's clothes or a hair dryer for one successful introduction, and progessing to various sizes of refrigerator and several increasingly glamorous free holidays. There was a motor scooter or a Colston dishwasher for a dozen introductions and for hitting the jackpot of 50 introductions a white Mini saloon. This scheme would again put costs up through having to provide the various rewards but we could contain the expense if sales rose. The drawback

199

was that although the recommended people were supposed to be willing to have the Rolls Concorde demonstrated, this did not always turn out to be the case. Sometimes they had not even been asked by the person recommending them or they had only agreed to please somebody and did not intend actually going through with it. The basic flaw in the idea was that it ignored the basic concept of successful direct selling—that my salesmen should follow up only genuine inquiries. But the scheme operated for such a limited period that it scarcely affected the general situation, one way or the other.

While my hopes were still pinned basically on remedying the sales situation it was also obvious that there would have to be a trimming of costs. With the small rise in actual profit for 1963 the shareholders would expect to hear that economies had been made by the time the annual meeting was held in July. The obvious thing to be done was to amalgamate some of our branches. In the West Country we decided to make Bristol our headquarters and to shut down Bournemouth and Swansea altogether. Our Birmingham office and one of our depots in Manchester were closed while our Glasgow office was streamlined. Since coupon returns were down the sales force was top heavy and so I had to sack about 80 men. In addition I and all the other paid directors took a salary cut.

The effect of this when it all became fully effective was to save Rolls around £10,000 a week on our £32,000 overheads. It should also have indicated to the world at large that we meant business and should have helped restore confidence. In fact it had the opposite effect. 'Bloom Sacks 80' was front page news —and in some cases was the main splash story—when we announced our streamlining on May 25th. The extent to which any Bloom story became over-emphasised cannot be better illustrated than by this incident. For, the very next day, Hoover announced that they were bringing in economies which would mean that 1,000 of their sales and service force would lose their jobs by the end of the year. Yet the story went comparatively unremarked in the Press.

But all these sales schemes and cost improvements could only be part of the answer. As Patrick Hutber had been pointing out since his arrival the company desperately needed more cash. We had therefore sold stocks of gifts for £160,000 and borrowed £200,000 from General Guarantee, £440,000 from Capital and £200,000 from E and O. But it was not enough. We were owing money on all sides—to Tallent, to Pressed Steel, for Income Tax, for Purchase Tax and the bank overdraft at Barclays was over the top. On May 28th we had a painful board meeting at Cricklewood with Patrick Hutber at which we agreed to call on Kleinwort Benson for help. They were still the company's financial advisers despite the fact that they had been put out of the picture for some 18 months as I had been getting my advice from Sir Isaac. I left the board meeting with Patrick Hutber and Aaron Wright and called on John Read at Kleinworts to ask him whether they would jointly guarantee our overdraft with Sir Isaac Wolfson. He agreed to consider putting up £250,000 if we got Sir Isaac to put up £500,000. If all had gone well the guarantee could have been sewn up in a couple of days but when Kleinworts phoned Sir Isaac at that moment he was out. It was therefore agreed that I would get in touch with Sir Isaac and fix up an appointment for me and someone from Kleinworts to go and see him some-time next day. I phoned him as planned and put this to him. But he replied: 'You can either come by yourself or not at all.' So I had to agree to seeing him personally—and Kleinworts did not take kindly to being excluded from any negotiations. But in the event it was Charles Hardie, the chairman of Sir Isaac's General Guarantee Corporation, whom I saw and to whom I gave all the Rolls figures and accounts. A few days later I received a message from the partners in Kleinworts saying that they were gravely concerned about the whole posi-tion and that unless I could tell them exactly what Rolls inten-ded to do they would have to announce that they were no longer our financial advisers. The public withdrawal of Klein-worts would have meant instant disaster as they well knew. We had to do something and so Aaron Wright sent them a memo detailing the administration improvements that were being worked on. But it could not reveal much about our financial plans as there was not much to reveal.

There followed several further meetings with Kleinworts, some of which were attended by Sir Isaac, and Kleinworts said they thought the company was in need of a tougher chairman than Reader Harris at that difficult period. They had mentioned to me earlier that Reader Harris should resign at some suitable time. That time had now come. If such a new chairman were appointed and succeeded in knocking Rolls back into shape Kleinworts said they would then consider underwriting some sort of share issue and in that way we could raise the money we needed. If we had disagreed then I was afraid that Kleinworts might still abandon us—with all that it implied. But in any case the scheme seemed feasible so as the first step we agreed to appoint a new chairman. The only remaining question was: who? John Read came up with the name of Claude Miller, a Canadian chartered accountant who was chairman of Francis Sumner, the industrial holding company, and Thomas Blackburn and Co, engineers. Having joined these companies when they were sickly and restored them to health he had gained a formidable reputation as a company doctor. He was asked to join the board but declined to accept outright. Instead he said he would investigate Rolls for a fee of £25,000 payable in advance and then make up his mind. He would do nothing until he had banked his cheque and in any case he could not begin work for two weeks. Time was short but we had to agree.

Further despondency was spread by Reader Harris' report to shareholders which was unveiled on June 10th, giving shareholders three weeks to study it before the annual general meeting—a meeting which loomed menacingly in the background of all our discussions at this period. His report said that the profits to date for 1964 were substantially down and that it was too early to forecast profits for the year. He added that we had high hopes that our new ventures such as RPM and our entry into the automatic field would restore our competitive edge. But he pointed out that these new ventures and a 'temporary' build-up of stocks were straining our ready-cash situation and he warned shareholders that more permanent finance would be needed. The Stock Market's reaction was to lop 10½d off Rolls bringing them down to 13s 4½ and 10½ off E and O making them 16s 1½d.

I was having trouble with E and O in addition to their ever-falling share price as the major shareholders in Rolls. The problem arose with the Bulgarian coach tours. The first one left London's Victoria coach terminal on May 16th and who should be among the 42 passengers but one Michael Hamlyn, a *Sunday Times* reporter? So it was that a week later there appeared in that paper an account of the 2,000-mile drive from Ostend to Golden Sands.

Unfortunately the account was not favourable; the trip had several teething problems. The coach failed to keep what appeared to be an over-tight schedule and, when the party did arrive, the weather was not very good. The following week-end the *Sunday Times* printed Hamlyn's account of the return trip which again had its unfortunate moments—largely because of misunderstandings between the Rumanian and Hungarian tourist authorities. After a telephone call from Budapest from our courier, John Hawkes, we decided, at a cost of £715, to put up our tourists in a Vienna hotel and fly them home by charter plane.

As Hamlyn pointed out, however, many passengers still thought the holiday was marvellous value for money and the following week there were several letters of endorsement in the paper. Lilian Capon, a reader, said the tourists had had a 'wonderful welcome behind the Iron Curtain.... Everyone was overwhelmed, especially when we were presented with a small bouquet of pansies on arrival at the Bulgarian frontier.' She concluded: 'It was worth every penny.' Another reader, G. G. Smith, wrote: 'I am pleased that I went and think that for what we received we had excellent value for our money.'

The main trouble from a practical point of view was that other national tourist agencies were not as well organised as the Bulgarians. It was clear that we could not rely on the coaches arriving at Bulgarian resorts in time to keep to the schedule of the outgoing tourists. And if there was one delay, through a breakdown for instance, the hours lost reverberated down the line.

The faults of that pioneer trip were, therefore, basically minor and easy to rectify. But because it was organised by one of my firms I had to pay the price of detailed scrutiny and adverse criticisms. As a result, I had to make one or two trips to Bulgaria to check if the corrective measures I put in hand were succeeding. I needed to keep a keen eye on the holiday operation since numbers had to be kept up in order to reach the target the government stipulated—which, in turn, would mean that E and O would get the British buying agency. But at the end of May and early June it was time that I could ill afford.

It was because of this renewed involvement in Bulgaria that my chauffeur, John Jenkins was driving across Yugoslavia to meet me on June 19th. The Rolls was involved in an accident in which a seven-year-old boy, Perica Pavlovic, was killed. Jenkins had his passport confiscated and early in July he was given a suspended sentence of 18 months in prison. Meanwhile, I had agreed to compensate the parents of the dead child to the tune of eight million dinars (over £3,800) and on top of this I had the legal fees of one of Yugoslavia's best lawyers.

It was also on June 19th that we announced that we were winding up Bylock and had asked Barclays to apoint a receiver. Shortly afterwards Tallent, who had laid off 50 of their 580 workers at the end of May, said that because washing machines were being stockpiled at Rolls they were having to put some of their people on short-time. And on June 23rd Claude Miller arrived on the scene with the title of financial consultant to the board. Miller, who was wont to say: 'I'm absolutely ruthless,' got to work on three fronts. He started to analyse the whole financial operation, he browbeat the accounts department into getting up-to-date accounts ready—something nobody else had been able to do—and started to analyse the personalities involved at top level.

But the first concrete thing that he did—with the help of Sir Isaac—was to persuade Barclays to continue our over-the-limit overdraft until the end of August. He then stated that £1 million would see us through if we could get it, so I had various talks with Sir Isaac and Felix Neubergh at the Anglo-Portuguese Bank.

I had hoped that Sir Isaac would not let the company slide and would put up the £1 million against stocks or in whatever way appeared best. And on that comforting hope I left for Bulgaria on Saturday June 27th, arriving back in time for the annual general meeting.

Behind the scenes Claude Miller had been trying to arrange a rights issue—one pound of convertible loan stock for every six ordinary shares held—but he hit underwriting problems and Kleinworts declined to put up any money. Miller had also been organising the resignation of Reader Harris and four other directors to be announced at the AGM. The meeting was held, not at the Dorchester as in 1963 but in the works canteen at Cricklewood. The directors who resigned were Rettie, my brothers-in-law Herbie and Malcolm and Arthur Sowley. We and the 50 or so shareholders sat glumly through the proceedings. The only good thing about it all was that the shareholders did not cross-question us on our plans for the future—since the plans were still unformulated. The worst feature was that although the resignations were intended to appear as another piece of streamlining nobody really took them in that light and the fact that we were still uncertain who would take over as chairman did not look well.

Rolls shares fell about 2s 6d to around 10s over the following few days, but it was in E and O shares that the drama lay. They had been the subject of a heavy 'bear' attack—people had been selling E and O shares which they did not have in the hope that they would be able to buy them much more cheaply when the time came for delivering them. While this was going on I was approached by Bernard Rader and Leon Seltzer who said that a syndicate formed to buy E and O shares could well force the price up and cripple the 'bears'; the shares would become very scarce, the syndicate could demand payment and the 'bears' would be forced into buying the shares wherever they could at a high price. I felt that Rolls shares were equally the subject for a big 'bear' attack, of selling short, but with so many shares in issue the 'bears' could always produce shares from somewhere. With E and O, where the number of shares was limited, I felt there was a much better chance of squeezing the 'bears'.

Even so, I was not convinced that a 'bear squeeze' would have any really long-term effect but I eventually agreed. In all there were seven of us in the syndicate. But we were not well organised and bought many more shares than I had expected.

The idea was that our broker would order the Buying-in Department of the Stock Exchange to demand that 33,000 outstanding shares should be delivered on July 3rd—which would have been the biggest buying-in operation in Stock Exchange history. However, when the day came there were only 7,000 outstanding. The rest had been acquired mainly by borrowing shares under the old pals act or by finding shares which we had written off as 'dead' but which had been in somebody's possession since E and O's rubber plantation days. And over the next few days all but a few hundred of those 7,000 shares were delivered. The syndicate eventually lost about £200,000 through buying the slumping shares and I was staggered to be told that I did not have a seventh interest in it, as I had understood, but was expected to pay about £90,000 out of my own pocket—which I was forced to do. Ironically, the size of the buying-in operation, designed to force the share price up, caused a loss of confidence and the shares went down to 9s 3d.

While this was going on, on Friday July 3rd, the day after the annual general meeting, I again went to see Sir Isaac and Felix Neubergh at the Anglo-Portuguese Bank. And, over sandwiches in a private room, it was definitely settled that if I could get board backing for negotiating a loan, Sir Isaac would help by underwriting the rights issue that Miller had been having trouble with. As Sir Isaac did not want anyone to know of his involvement we arranged that he would do the underwriting through some of his myriad contacts abroad. I was to tell everyone that I hoped to get the money abroad, then to spend a few days on the Ariane. By the time I got back, Sir Isaac and Felix Neubergh would have worked out how the secret underwriting could be managed and I would be able to announce how I had acquired the money 'abroad'. I went back to Cricklewood that same afternoon and got the board's agreement to the scheme but over the weekend, while some practical details were being worked out involving people other than Sir Isaac, Felix Neubergh and myself, the plan leaked out and so the foreign ruse became pointless.

For the rest of that week there were talks between Sir Isaac and his associates and Claude Miller, Malcolm Cass and myself. Finally on the following Friday, July 10th—again at the Anglo-Portuguese Bank—it was agreed that General Guarantee would put in £1,100,000 on adequate security of stock. Later they did not, however, regard the available security as sufficient. At this time I lodged £209,719 in a special dividend account at Barclays in order that the 120 per cent final dividend could be paid out on July 24th. To meet this condition I lent the money to Rolls through a nominee company Quistclose Investments and that sum of money became the subject of a long legal tussle. The other main condition was that Rolls should receive a moratorium—an agreement that settlement of bills would not be pressed for—from General Guarantee.

When I left the successful meeting on July 10th I made it clear that I was going to Bulgaria on business and was given until the following Wednesday to decide whether I would become chairman. In the meantime however I had been approached by Norman Williams, an associate of John James, and I went straight from the bank to Paddington and took a train to Bristol. I met John James, explained the potential deal with Sir Isaac and asked him if he would be interested in any similar deal. However the meeting was abortive and I trailed all the way back to London that night, arriving at two in the morning. At about midday I then left for Bulgaria, intending to stay until Wednesday.

On arriving there I discovered that there was no flight back on the Wednesday and that I would have to stay until sometime at the weekend. I accordingly sent a Telex message to London. On the Monday however I received the telephone call from Malcolm Cass saying that I had to make an instant decision about the chairmanship and so I accepted, provided that Claude Miller would become Financial Director. After that I was under the impression that the matter was settled—especially since I received that 'Everything proceeding as discussed' Telex from Malcolm on Wednesday the 15th.

Meanwhile, however, by an unwonted turn of speed the audited accounts for the first six months became available and on the same Wednesday that I was under the impression that all was well Claude Miller was deciding, on the strength of the results, that another £500,000 was urgently needed. Sir Isaac declined to increase the stake he had offered and on the Thursday Claude Miller explained to the Rolls directors that they would become personally responsible for the company's debts unless Rolls went into liquidation. On Friday morning there was a last meeting between Sir Isaac, Jack Jacobs and Aaron Wright which had no effect. By noon they were back at Cricklewood and the Telex message that arrived too late was despatched. After lunch Jack and Irving Jacobs, Leslie Goldbart and Aaron Wright sat discussing the situation and waiting to hear from me. When my deadline expired they decided to go into liquidation.

Since the banks closed at three, the deadline for my reply, it has always been a mystery to me why the decision could not have waited until Monday when I returned. But as it was, by the time I returned there was little anyone could do. It was all over bar the shouting. The only trouble was that the shouting lasted for another six years.

19

NATURALLY, WHEN I RETURNED FROM BULGARIA I HAD desperate talks to try and salvage something. But on the Monday all we could do was to call that Extraordinary Meeting of the board. It was notable mainly for the number of Press men staked out around the factory at Cricklewood, plus the crowds who always assemble to watch, and the crowds who gather to watch the crowds. The directors arrived in ones or twos, creeping in through warehouse doors and back entrances. I decided to walk in through the main door—but not without sending a Rolls-Royce to a side entrance to decoy the newspaper men. At the meeting itself, the atmosphere was bitter and tense. Time after time I tried to find out why Wright and the three musketeers had taken their decision on Friday. I still considered that they could have waited for my return, and several of my co-directors agreed. But the more I pressed the more they dug their heels in and kept repeating that it had been forced upon them. I was also upset to learn that Rolls had paid all its debts to Tallent only a few days before. In any case it was too late to do anything and all we could do was to confirm the Friday's decision to place the company in a creditors' voluntary winding up.

Following this we had a lot of messages and telegrams from people claiming to have all sorts of solutions for our problems. One came from Dr Benjamin Cohen, chairman of Finextra Ltd., investment managers and merchant bankers, who urged us to consider the possibility of his company devising a scheme of arrangement under section 206 of the 1948

Companies Act. This, if successful, would avoid liquidation. Dr Cohen was prepared to undertake the task free of charge if he failed but he wrote that he would expect the shareholders and creditors to be 'gallant and elegant in fixing our remuneration' if he succeeded. But it was Tuesday, July 21st, when I received his letter, by which time it was clear that nothing could be done and the lawyers had more or less taken everything over.

My last real attempt to salvage something came on Monday evening straight after our Cricklewood meeting. I tried to get a moratorium for two years on all debts. Always provided I could get some finance—and Capital were prepared to try and arrange something—this would be the ideal solution. I talked it over with several board members in my flat and we considered that if the big creditors could be persuaded to grant us a moratorium the others would follow. I mentioned this plan to various creditors that night, but not one was willing to help so the scheme fizzled out and, in the end, most creditors did not get a penny.

It was on that same Monday night that one of the most personally upsetting events of the collapse occurred. Colin Jordan, leader of the neo-Nazi British National Socialist Movement, held a tub-thumping meeting in the car park near Aldford House where I had earlier parked my car. He launched into the most vitriolic personal invective against me but, unfortunately for him, several salesmen decided to come round to see me that night to try and cheer me up and happened to be in the car park at the time. They were so incensed that they tried to smash up the meeting and became involved in a scuffle with Jordan's supporters. Police were on hand, however, and dispersed everyone before any bones were broken.

Several of my salesmen, I suppose naturally enough, felt personal animosity towards me and fighting funds were set up to take legal advice. The real reason for any such animosity, however, was that the salesmen—many of whom had been earning £4,000 or £5,000 a year in commission were suddenly out of a job and facing hefty demands from the Inland Revenue for those prosperous years. But it was genuinely comforting for Anne and me that at least some of the salesmen rallied round.

They were not the only ones of course. Jack Hylton was again a wonderful help, inviting us to his villa and asking us to dinner so that we did not feel like social lepers. Freddy Debenham wrote a very kind letter to say that all the directors at Hendon Football Club insisted that I should stay with them. And I had encouraging letters from many people including Max Bygraves, Bernard Delfont, and Lou Levy, who wrote to say that Anne and I could stay with him in case we felt like going to America for a rest. It was nice to know, as Eric Carter, features editor of the *Daily Sketch* wrote to Anne, that I was still regarded by the housewives of Britain as 'almost a friend of the family'. And I was heartened by the comments of Ralph Harris, the general director of The Institute of Economic Affairs. In a letter to *The Times* on Wednesday July 22nd he wrote: 'Mr Bloom has already done more for economic growth in Britain than many of its verbal champions in NEDC (the National Economic Development Council) and elsewhere. His invasion—and widening—of the washing machine market has demonstrated how new enterprise can transform an established industry that had allowed costs and prices to get out of hand.'

The day after this letter appeared Edward Heath, who was President of the Board of Trade, announced that a Board of Trade inquiry would be held into the affairs of Rolls Razor. It was this inquiry and its aftermath that became my main preoccupation for the next six years. At the time, however, I did not think too much about it, having little idea of what it would involve, although my solicitors, D. J. Freeman and Co., did say that I ought to engage a counsel. There was a provisional arrangement that Maurice Finer, QC, should act for me but a day or two later he said that he was unable to do so as he and Sir Henry Benson had been appointed as the inspectors who were going to conduct the inquiry for the Board of Trade.

Every day of the week following my return from Bulgaria there were board meetings at Cricklewood. We decided to appoint chartered accountants W. H. Cork, Gully to examine the Rolls situation so that a statement of affairs could be made to the shareholders as soon as possible and they could vote finally on whether the company should be wound up. From then on we spent all our time assisting the Cork, Gully men to get out the figures which, because of the bomb put under our own accounts department by Claude Miller, were reasonably up to date. Every decision and minute of the board had to be approved by Cork, Gully.

Meanwhile, I personally was battling it out on the E and O front. I had several talks with the men from Capital and towards the end of July I finally agreed to stand down as chairman. In my place they put Douggie Bayle who was cracked up to be a company doctor—which, of course, he was not. I had to divorce myself entirely from the company and I agreed to lend them several sums of money. For instance, I personally put up £72,000 before the end of the year to make sure that everyone who had booked a Bulgarian holiday through E and O Tours did in fact get their holiday. Later on I sold my E and O shares to Douggie Bayle, some for 1s each and others for 2s. Since then there have been various grandiose schemes for restoring E and O to full health but today the shares are still deep in the doldrums.

On Sunday, July 26th, exactly a week after my return from Bulgaria, I went to see Roger Pryer, the advertising man. His agency was in desperate trouble, as were all the agencies to whom Rolls was the staff of life. In many cases they became liable for paying the bills meant for Rolls. Roger Pryer needed a lot of money to prevent his firm from being wound up. He had written to me asking for payment of £92,425 'owed by EM Maintenance' a subsidiary through which I paid agency bills at one time. This sum was made up of £28,940 which I owed him for 1960 and £63,485 which I owed him for the following year. However he had written me a personal letter on January 16th, 1961, confessing that some of his adverts had not been 100 per cent and therefore, he wrote: 'I wish to make my contribution to the future of our two companies and to say to you that the outstanding moneys that are due to us from EM Maintenance can be wiped out as far as I am concerned ... This gesture that I make is purely a personal one to your goodself for I am very conscious of the fact that day by day our friendship has increased and I look forward to working many years with you and for you.'

I had, however, given him a personal guarantee on January 5th, 1963, that I would indemnify him against any failure such as had befallen us. So, knowing how much the agency meant to him I agreed to pay him the full £92,000 which made another large hole in my personal resources. In the event, even that was not enough and, for want of another £20,000 or so, Roger Pryer Creative Advertising folded just the same.

The day after I went to see Roger Pryer, Sir Charles Colston and his associate Aaron Wright left the sunken ship by resigning as directors, leaving a Rolls board comprising of myself, Al Palmer and the three musketeers—the Jacobs brothers and Leslie Goldbart. Instead Colston and Wright put on their other hats and became our largest creditor with a breach of contract claim. On behalf of Tallent they claimed the sum of £866,194 damages for washing machines which they said Rolls had contracted to buy over the next few years.

The following day I was asked to prepare for the coming of the Board of Trade inspectors, and I received a list of documents and books which we should have available for them at Cricklewood on Friday, July 31st. When they arrived they found waiting for them a huge pile of paperwork which covered a large table and it seemed to me that it covered all the information anybody could want. However Sir Henry Benson and Maurice Finer merely said: 'Oh, good. Well that will do for today.' Eventually, such were their powers, they read and investigated virtually every scrap of paper that had any connection with the Rolls Razor organisation. And by the time they completed their investigation a year later Rolls documents took up the whole of one warehouse. At our first meeting that day I was accompanied by my solicitor David Freeman but even with his support I was shaken by what I considered to be the cold and off-hand attitude of the inspectors towards me.

After this first experience and with the pent-up feelings of years exploding as more and more demands were made on John Bloom, I decided to take Anne to America for a brief holiday before I was due to appear before the Board of Trade inspectors at an official hearing. I arranged the flight secretly and asked Lenny Stoegel, the Santa Claus maker, to fix us up with an out-of-the-way hotel. Nobody knew about the trip because for weeks I had not been outside the flat except to visit the office, Cork, Gully, or my solicitors. However, newspapermen have their stocks-in-trade—as we had found before—and when Anne and I arrived at Heathrow airport we found at least a dozen photographers there. We ignored them as best we could and took our seats, but when we arrived at Idlewild airport, New York, it was a different proposition. We were just coming out of the airport buildings and had spotted Lenny Stoegel coming towards us when there was a sudden rush of American photographers and reporters. Their questions were so ludicrously ill-informed that they matched those of the Turkish Press hunting a gang of murderers. We had, they took it, stuffed all our suit-cases with money. Could we tell them how much we had with us? They understood from London that we were expecting the American police to extradite us and therefore that we were going to Brazil where there was no extradition treaty. While all this nonsense was going on Anne and I were fighting towards a car that Lenny had waiting and—to the accompaniment of popping flash bulbs—denying everything that was hurled at us.

We were so shattered that we hardly knew where we were being driven. We were just delighted to get to the small hotel which was our hiding place for our ten-day stay in New York. It was the first time I had been really cut off from business for any length of time and although there were plenty of new problems to worry about I enjoyed the stay. Apart from our over-enthusiastic reception we were never again bothered by the Press. Lenny Stoegel was very sympathetic and the people he introduced to us were very relaxing to be with. It was a revelation to me just how generous and warm-hearted American people could be—and I needed that sort of support. In England I felt I could not venture into the street without being accosted by someone with an axe to grind and, with the collapse of my brainchild and the notable absence of support from people I had considered my friends, I had lost all my usual confidence.

But in New York I became myself again for a while as Anne and I spent the time doing all those normal things we had been unable to do—like going to the cinema, our favourite relaxation.

But this feeling of comparative well-being was very soon shattered when I returned to London and made my first appearance before the Board of Trade inspectors. We came face to face on August 19th in a small bleak room they were using in Abacus House, Gutter Lane—about 500 yards from the Old Bailey. On their side of the table were the two inspectors, and their two chief aides—A. W. Brookland who acted as their secretary and W. Molyneux who headed the staff of 14 chartered accountants and seven assistant accountants examining the Rolls records. Then there was a shorthand writer. On my side of the table there was just myself and my solicitor who on that first day was a fellow called Manning. Before I was sworn in, however, Maurice Finer told him that he would not be allowed to take any notes of any kind except to note down any document that the inspectors wanted and which I might be able to provide for them. Nor was he allowed to interrupt or object to any questions. We were also refused permission to have a transcript of my evidence so that it was impossible to see in the cold light of day whether there were any ambiguities or any errors of fact in what I had said. If there had been I could then have mentioned them to the inspectors at a subsequent meeting.

There were 54 days of such formal hearings, and 53 witnesses. Apart from Rolls directors and employees, these included people from Price Waterhouse and Kleinwort Benson, Toby Hoffman, Hugh Robinson of Fenn and Crosthwaite, national newspaper advertising chiefs Freddy Debenham, Alex McKay, Ronald Perks and Len Slingsby, Patrick Hutber, Claude Miller, Latham and Mathes of Bylock, Roger Pryer, Bertie Veitch, Bernard Rader and Sir Isaac Wolfson. I appeared on 12 days over the next eleven months during which I answered over 8,500 questions fired at me by the inspectors, sometimes alternately in best inquisition style.

There was never any friendliness at any time. 'Good morning'

215

was the extent of the inspectors' sociability. The only refreshment was the one-hour lunch break, except for an occasion when I broke down and was allowed to go in another room for a while and a cup of tea miraculously appeared. As an example of the inspectors attitude towards me there was the occasion in 1965 when they were querying the accounts for 1963. I said to Maurice Finer: 'I do not think the accounts were explained in detail at all.' He replied: 'No, they just grew, I gather, Mr Bloom. It was almost an immaculate conception.' Again dealing with the 1963 accounts Finer said, after I had disputed some of his claims: 'That is another matter on which we take the view that the stock was grossly over-valued, but you do not agree. However, we cannot expect to agree on everything, can we?'

On another occasion I was shown a circular about the position of Rolls sent out to shareholders by Fenn and Crosthwaite. I was then questioned minutely on the source of the information in such circulars and on how much I knew about circulars before they were actually sent out. The exchange with Maurice Finer was as follows:

Finer: 'Did anyone approve the draft? Did they send the draft along and say "Is this all right?"'

Me: 'I think on one occasion, or some parts of it.'

Finer: 'They must have done. You cannot expect us to swallow things which on the face of it are manifest nonsense. They must have got somebody to approve them. Can you imagine Fenn and Crosthwaite putting out a document of the kind I just showed you without at least putting it up to somebody responsible at Rolls Razor for his views, if not for his formal approval?'

Me: 'I think they gave it to all of us for our views at one stage, but never ...'

Finer: 'Of course they did. That was before it was circularised?'

Me: 'No, when it was in draft form.'

Finer: 'When it was in draft form?'

Me: 'In the various parts, but never the whole of this lengthy circular.'

Finer: 'It has taken about ten minutes to get that out of you.'

Me: 'No, not this lengthy thing. They gave us the parts that concerned. You know, "We are selling" ...'

Finer: 'Just slower and quieter. You are not doing what I asked you to do when we started, which is to listen to the question and answer it. I asked you a long time ago what pre-information you were given about the circulars and it has taken me a long time to get to the situation where you tell us you saw the drafts.'

Me: 'No, I did not see the whole....'

Finer: 'We will continue after the adjournment.'

And at that point there was a break.

During that first day we covered in outline the whole of my business career, the personalities involved at Rolls, and then we started on Bylock. Afterwards I felt extremely depressed. I went back to Aldford House and said to Anne: 'I feel as if I'm one of the Great Train Robbers.' Yet one of the most ironic features of the affair is that early in 1970 Maurice Finer, acting for Robert Maxwell, was contesting in the High Court the apparent power of Board of Trade inquiries. He wanted the right to see documents and to cross examine other witnesses.

I had another session with the inspectors two days later on August 21st at which they questioned me on my dealings with Sir Isaac Wolfson, the entry of Capital into the life of Rolls, the Drages deal and the Jackson estate, the camera enterprise, Slough Die-casting and Mercon Metals, the story of E and O and the Bear operation of June and July. After this I was granted a reprieve of several weeks before I needed to appear again.

The next hurdle was the Cork, Gully report which was made to shareholders on the following Thursday morning, August 27th, at an Extraordinary General Meeting in the Kingsway Hall, London. There were about 500 shareholders present when a gloomy and tired Rolls board took the rostrum. I presided and Kenneth Cork of Cork, Gully took 70 minutes to read his 75-page report. There were some 1,200 creditors apart from Barclays Bank who were claiming a total of £455,381. Of these the biggest was Pressed Steel who wanted £434,219, £150,000 of which was disputed. After them the biggest casualties were the advertising people. The publicly-quoted Stowe and Bowden claimed £74,697, Roger Pryer £35,280, Hausman Langford £32,944, and Reid Walker £21,806. In a nutshell, he estimated that Rolls' deficiency at July 31st was £4,065,979. But the figure appeared unnecessarily grim since £209,719 of this represented the shareholders' claim for the declared dividend, £719,271 represented the issued share capital and £1,062,885 were breach of contract claims. This therefore left £2,074,104 for creditors with no security. Kenneth Cork told the meeting that the company had failed basically because it was under-capitalised and criticised the accounts department for failing to provide up-to-date information.

After he had finished there were questions from shareholders and a person called Derek Calo, a member of a shareholders association which had distributed pamphlets before the meeting urging us to bide our time, made a spirited speech for 'just two more months' so that the board could explore every possible avenue in an attempt to save the company. His words found quite a bit of support from the floor and one woman yelled out: 'Some of us still have faith in you, Mr Bloom.' But I was not so optimistic. After repeated pleas from Derek Calo I had to tell him that as the biggest shareholder with some 500,000 shares I would be the first to agree with him if anything could be done. 'But there is nothing that can be done,' I said. 'It is too late. I am very sorry.' So many assets had been dissipated in the chaotic few weeks since July 17th that a revival was out of the question.

When it came to the vote on the board's proposal that Rolls should go into liquidation there was uproar from the floor with people shouting 'We have faith', 'the company can be saved' and so on. In fact the proposal was defeated 74 to 72 on a show of hands but on a proxy vote it was overwhelmingly passed by 1,943,375 to 41,030. At the close of the meeting there was a vote of thanks from the floor and for days afterwards shareholders were writing to me to say that they still had confidence in me and would invest in whatever enterprise I next turned my hand to.

In the afternoon, again at the Kingsway Hall, a creditors'

meeting was held at which I again presided and again Kenneth Cork gave his 70-minute report. There was bitter criticism of the board for their 'colossal failure'. But it was not long before the meeting confirmed the decision of the shareholders by 111 votes to 15, appointed Kenneth Cork as sole liquidator, and formed a creditors' committee. There was the usual small crowd of people waiting as I left the meeting with Len Burt, the Rolls security man, and as he was trying to get through he brushed against Jack Jacobs with whom, as it happened, he was not on the friendliest terms. As far as I could see there had hardly been any physical contact, but a few days later Len Burt received a letter from Jack Jacobs' solicitors demanding an 'unqualified apology' for what was termed an 'unprovoked assault'. Len Burt and I considered this so laughable that he did not bother to reply to the letter.

At that time the Stock Exchange had still not suspended dealings in Rolls shares. They considered that there was no question of people dealing in the dark—it was known that the directors had recommended a winding up—and therefore people were speculating in full knowledge of the risks involved. Even after the Rolls board's recommendation the share had been as high as 1s 6d but by the time of the creditors meeting they had slumped to 4d. After the meeting you could buy a Rolls share for a penny. That was all they were worth. And, psychologically, that was all I was worth, too.

20

AFTER THE FIRST TWO BOARD OF TRADE HEARINGS AND THE meetings in the Kingsway Hall I was back to where I was before my trip to America. In common parlance I was a nervous wreck refusing to leave the flat and quite often refusing to get out of bed. The collapse of Rolls seemed so final and terrible.

Another part of the trial by Board of Trade inquiry was that they told all the directors, former directors and anyone else of any importance in Rolls to whom they might want to talk that we were not allowed to speak to each other under any circumstances. The effect of this was quite ludicrous. There we were, a large number of men who had been working together for years, in fear and trembling in case we happened to clap eyes on each other and in case one of the others ignored the warning and rang us up, thus implicating us in whatever dreadful crime it constituted. I once rang up Arthur Sowley to check on some dates and he was petrified to talk to me.

Not, of course, that many of my former colleagues were worth contacting when the chips were down. The only time that Jack Jacobs—who had started working for Imperial— came to see me, for instance, was to say that the Board of Trade inspectors had been questioning him about the meeting in the Brent Bridge Hotel and the money he received later and to ask me to tell the inspectors that I knew all about it if I were questioned on the subject. This I refused to do. But even so, distance lent enchantment to the view and to me, holed up in our flat, in those first months, contact with former colleagues seemed something to be desired.

I was in moody isolation for about six months—all through the winter—with Anne acting as wife, nurse and amateur psychiatrist. After a few months I felt I might be able to force myself out of the flat and so I got a couple of tickets for my local lending library and in the darkness, just before they were due to close, I used to sneak round the corner to take out a couple of books. As I am a rapid reader these did not take me long to read and so this trip became very frequent.

One of the greatest shocks was that I received no message or visit from either Harvey Langer or Ronnie Pressman who had been my personal assistants. On my 32nd birthday—November 8th, 1963—they had presented me with a large gilt international time clock. It was inscribed: 'From Harvey and Ronnie. In case you need us ... anytime!' Clearly I should not have taken this too seriously. In March, 1965, when I was emerging from my hibernation, I wrote a note to Harvey, brief and to the point. 'Dear Harvey,' I wrote, 'Anne and I haven't got scarlet fever or the plague and would be grateful if you would come round and see us one night! There's no barbed wire round the door!' There was no reply. Harvey and Ronnie, with Ronnie's wife, were at that time busy building up the Carmen Curler Company in Britain. Apparently Mrs Pressman arranged things with the originators—the Carmen Curler Company of Denmark—after the collapse of Rolls. As a matter of fact this was an idea which the Rolls projects division had once investigated.

Another person who let me down, I feel, was Leslie Goldbart who wrote seeking money to indemnify him against losses he sustained as a result of buying 25,000 Rolls shares from me in January, 1964. He was 'very hurt and disappointed' and was having to sell his house in The Bishop's Avenue, the smartest part of Hampstead. I replied that his letter surprised me because it did not accord with the facts as I remembered them. I concluded by saying: 'I am sorry to hear of your present difficulties but although I am not in a position to help you, I do not wish you to regard this as being any indication of lack of friendship towards you.' However the man whom I brought from nothing to put on the board of Rolls has stayed out of my life ever since.

The night club business in which I am now involved dropped into my lap by one of those strange accidents soon after the collapse of Rolls. I did not for a moment suspect that the club life was where my future lay. The story began in 1963 when a certain Norman Jones came to me and asked me to guarantee him an overdraft of £36,000 with Barclays Bank. He wanted to build a club in a cellar beneath a flat next to Baker Street Underground station in London. The prospect seemed a sensible one so Reader Harris and I jointly guaranteed the money and more or less forgot about it as events quickened during 1964. It was the sort of guarantee that businessmen undertake all the time. However, after the collapse Norman Jones told me that the £36,000 had been used up but that the club was only half-finished and the builder was owed another £25,000. The dilemma was: Should I simply write off my share of the £36,000 or should I put in more money so that the club development could continue? My eventual decision, which I reached with Anne, was something of a compromise. We decided that Anne would take over the liabilities in return for shares and would run the whole operation. We had no intention of pouring money into something being run by somebody else.

I was not much of a club-goer and in those hermit months did not want to become involved in anything anyway so I left it all to Anne who had picked up a great deal about the ways of business in the four or so years she had known me. Unfortunately this type of business was totally foreign to Anne who, finding herself in need of help, fastened on to the idea of asking other people to join her in a management committee, all of whom would buy shares. The two main names on the committee were those of Terence Stamp and Jean Shrimpton and the main worker apart from Anne was Eve Taylor, the artists' manager. The plan was to run the club as a discotheque called the 'In Place' where the so-called 'In' people of the show business world would go with their friends. Terry Stamp and Jean

Shrimpton seemed good people to start the ball rolling.

By the time the discotheque was due to open in June, 1965, I was taking much more of a personal interest in it, although the Board of Trade inquiry was still sitting and was as importunate as ever. We had managed to get a late drinks licence which was essential since our potential customers only started looking for the night life when the ordinary people had caught the last train home. The place was on two floors, one called 'The Bottom Floor', which was the more intimate, and the other called 'The Phone Booth' where guests could dial the disc jockey from their table to request a record. I was in America when the big party was held to open the 'In Place' and Anne also stayed away as she did not want it to be known that she was behind it. In the few days that followed, several of the show business people at the opening started turning up and the committee people brought more of their own friends in. The plan seemed to be working well and Anne came over to see me in America. Not long after she arrived, however, we got a phone call from a friend urging us to return to London at once. We were told that members of the public were being turned away if their faces did not suit the show business people who were there as guests of committee members. We went back to find that several personal friends had been unable to get in while we had been away, and that large numbers of show business people themselves were excluded as well if they did not belong to the right coterie. In short, the discotheque was being used as a private club. The 'In Place' had become too In and takings had plunged in a very short space of time. But we had a long way to go to break-even point and we were not running the place just to keep ourselves amused; so Anne disbanded the committee—which, fortunately, was easy since none of them had got round to buying shares. From then on the place began to pick up although we had a setback the following year when nearby residents, annoyed at the noise from the club, successfully objected to our late licence and we found ourselves with a trendy all-night spot which shut its bars at midnight—the Cinderella of London discotheques. To remedy this we rented the night club part of Billy Walker's 'Baked Potato' restaurant in Piccadilly and called it 'Reflections'. It was not making a profit for them and they wanted to let it. We took it because it had a late licence and our customers could either go there if they were late starters or could be taken there from the 'In Place'—later renamed 'The Crazy Horse Saloon'—by car.

This was not my only interest at that time. I was also closely involved with the birth of Radio Caroline through Ronan O'Rahilly, the original whizz-kid of pirate radio. He and Sandie Shaw were both a very great help to me as I started to emerge from the doldrums at the start of 1965. Anne and I met Sandie early in 1964 at a theatre where we had gone to watch Adam Faith in his act. In his dressing room afterwards he introduced us to Sandie whom he reckoned would be a big star. She seemed a pleasant enough girl but Anne and I did not think anything more about her until we suddenly started hearing records of hers on the radio. Soon afterwards we met her several times and became very friendly with her. Anne and she went together on several trips to France. Unlike Adam Faith, Sandie came round to Aldford House (I had taken over the full rent of the flat from Rolls) several times after the collapse.

I remember one occasion when she arrived towards lunch time to find me lying in bed, feeling depressed. She forced me to get up and after I got dressed she announced that we would make ourselves some hamburgers in the kitchen. Unfortunately her knowledge of cooking was less than rudimentary, but she made up for it in enthusiasm. We rummaged round in a cupboard producing tins of meat, vegetables, spices and lots of other things which we thought we might have to use. We then got armfuls of pans, lit all the gas lights in sight and armed ourselves with wooden spoons. The whole operation took about an hour and a half, by which time every surface in the kitchen seemed to be littered with something, most of the cupboards were half empty, the sink was full of dirty pots and there was a slight odour throughout the flat of something singed. After all this the hamburgers we produced looked much more like a stiff stew. We had prodded and patted them to try and make them stick together to at least look like real hamburgers but to no avail. What we had not done was put in some flour to bind everything together. They teach schoolgirls that in the first form. But it never occurred to us.

Ronan O'Rahilly, whom I had met once or twice, popped round from Caroline House to see me early in 1965 and insisted that I should go out for a drink with him. It was one of the first occasions since the crash that I had done this and it was something of a landmark. We went round the corner to Trader Vic's bar at the Hilton hotel and Ronan described to me the Radio Caroline operation which had then been going for about a year. It proved to be incredibly complex with everything apparently geared to disguising the people who were putting up the money.

There were two companies involved, the Ferlin Trust Inc of Panama City and Planet Productions Ltd of Dublin—an unlikely enough combination. Ferlin chartered the ship to Planet and gave Planet the exclusive licence to sell advertising time on the programmes to be broadcast from the ship. Ferlin also manned the ship and was responsible for maintaining it and insuring it although Planet was responsible for footing the bills. Apart from this, Planet each month paid Ferlin ten per cent of the money received from advertising after deducting the commission they had to pay to their agents. Planet, of which Ronan O'Rahilly was a director, had cost a lot of money to launch and the backing had come from John Sheffield the youngest son of Sir Berkeley Sheffield and chairman of Norcros, the holding company.

After waiting a few months for the pirate radio furore to die down, the threats to recede and, most important, the advertising agencies and companies to pluck up their courage, the broadcasts were showing a modest profit of around £400 a week. Before Christmas of course, Planet had chalked up more than £2,500 a week profit and after less than a year of broadcasting the initial outlay had been covered. All the most respected advertising agencies, including J. Walter Thompson and S. H. Benson, were putting their clients on to Caroline, Ronan told me, and over the next few weeks he let me see details of Caroline's costings, advertising revenue and advance bookings. They were receiving contracts at the rate of up to

£15,000 a week. They were advertising everything from *Reveille* to the Royal Lancashire Show as well as carrying the big advertisers like Gillette, Polo, Beechams, Weetabix, cigarettes such as Guards and Richmond, and the Egg Marketing Board.

But although the original plan seemed to be working out Ronan felt there must be some ways that he could expand, some way of making more money out of the venture without it having anything to do with broadcasting as such. For this, he wanted my advice. I immediately thought of direct-selling. Ronan did not even have to pay for the advertising. It all seemed so simple. It was just a question of getting the right product and bulk-buying it. I thought that nylon stockings would be easy to handle and store, cheap to post, especially if we had minimum orders of six pairs—and I imagined that Caroline would have a good teenage girl market to tap. Ronan agreed and went ahead with the project. We offered these stockings through the Caroline Club in a large variety of styles and colours at 35 per cent below shop prices. With every dozen pairs ordered we gave away one pair free, which meant that a Caroline Club member ordering a dozen pairs for her family and friends would get a pair as a quasi-commission. In effect she would be acting as agent for a mail order operation. Simon Dee, who was one of Caroline's half-dozen £35-a-week disc jockeys, recorded the commercial himself for the stupendous sum of £4. The stockings proved a success and were followed by all the other bargain lines, such as T-shirts, which became associated with Radio Caroline.

Another scheme, through which I kept in touch with Charlie Drake, was Ognib (bingo spelled backwards) radio bingo, in which bingo halls and people at home would receive bingo cards by post and a set of numbers would be read out in a quarter-hour daily Ognib programme. The plan was to have more than 100,000 people playing—who would then learn to tune in to Caroline at other times and boost the audience figures for the benefit of advertising revenue. Charlie Drake recorded the commercials, which were being broadcast at the rate of about ten a day on both Caroline North and South, and also acted as the caller on the broadcasts themselves.

Through the summer of 1965 I acted increasingly as Ronan's confidential, and unpaid, adviser. It gave me the outside interest I needed—but with the pressure on me only at a remove. At one stage he asked me to find out if I could arrange for different backers as he was having difficulties with the current arrangement. I had a talk with Douggie Bayle who thought it was worth investigating for E and O and Ronan and I decided to go over first to Lichtenstein to see if we could meet the mysterious people behind Ferlin who were supposed to have an office there. We did find the offices and had inconclusive chats with a Dutchman and a Panamanian who were resident but they appeared to know nothing except about run-of-the-mill matters concerned with the boat itself. We tried to dig for information but failed where many journalists had failed before us. Ferlin seemed to run by magic and Douggie Bayle was not prepared to become involved in an operation in which one half of the people were unknown quantities. So Ronan was left to struggle on as he had been doing.

I was still receiving letters from all over the world from people wanting me to put money or salesmanship into their pet schemes. This went on throughout my time at Rolls but the fact that Rolls had collapsed seemed to make no effect on the number of people wanting me to help them. It may even have increased the number since people felt I must be sitting around at a loose end just waiting for their scheme to drop in my lap. Some of the ideas were worth investigating—such as the Anfreda Bureau's escort service—but many of the people writing in were so cagey about divulging details that I had no idea what they were offering. However I always used to write back and ask for details. One such idea came from a man who wrote from Auckland, New Zealand. It had 'to do with clothing' and would make £6 million a year, but as he only remembered my address out of a newspaper he was not sure I would ever get the letter and so did not want to give the game away on paper. Among the other ideas put up were a revolutionary gaming table, a kitchen for the disabled, a sports car so sensational that it would ruin everyone else's market, imported Japanese dishwashers, a men's magazine, a home videotape recorder and Manx football pools. On top of this someone wanted to put on a documentary play about me called 'A Society Collapses' and had even gone so far as to hold discussions with Peter Hall at the Aldwych Theatre. But legally it was out of the question.

After my summer of release from the Board of Trade inquiry I found it rearing its ugly head again in November when it was announced that the report had been completed and written. It was not published then, however. It was sent to the Director of Public Prosecutions who then had to study all the evidence and decide whether any case should be brought against anyone —which is usually a long process. As soon as this news broke people seriously suggested to me that I should leave the country and take Anne to live in one of the South American countries or in Austria where there were no extradition treaties. They felt that if the police could not bring me to trial they would not bother with anyone else. Personally, I felt it was a little premature to start worrying about trials—and so it proved. In any case a lifetime in Bolivia for the benefit of other people was not my idea of a good business deal.

21

ON BEHALF OF THE DPP THE POLICE PROCEEDED, AS THEY SAY, with their investigations for the next two years. From time to time we heard rumours that some action might be taken, but all these proved unfounded; there were no developments. The last time that we made an enquiry was on the morning of January 29th, 1968, when my solicitors rang New Scotland Yard and were told that there would be no further news for at least two or three weeks. This proved dramatically not to be the case.

That evening I was in my office at the 'Crazy Horse' talking to two fellows from the Anfreda marriage bureau who wanted me to come in with them as a sleeping partner. At about 8.30 I had a telephone call from the girl at the reception desk up on the ground floor saying a Mr Edwards and another gentleman wanted to see me. This of course was Detective Inspector Tom Edwards of the Fraud Squad, who had been more or less running the police investigations after the Board of Trade report. I interrupted my discussions with the Anfreda people and went upstairs to find him with his colleague Detective Inspector Buck. Edwards said: 'Can I see you for a moment, sir, in private?' So I took him down to a minute dungeon-like room which was used as a store. It looked like a very decrepit air-raid shelter and was lit by three fluorescent lights. I closed the door and said: 'Can I help you?' Edwards looked slightly abashed for a moment and coughed. Then he said: 'John Joseph Bloom, it is my duty ...' and so on. He was arresting me on two charges arising from the Board of Trade report.

I was dumbfounded. When Edwards had finished his legalistic marathon he said: 'Right, now that the official things are over, you can make one phone call before we leave for the West End Central.' Anne was on holiday in Spain so I tried to contact David Freeman only to find that he was at the theatre. I therefore had to be content with leaving a message asking him to contact me at the police station the moment he returned. Edwards agreed to keep the news from the Press and we went to the station in a private car, driving in silence past the old Rolls showrooms in Regent Street on the way.

I knew the West End Central since it was by way of being my local station. It was its normal bustling self although my arrest had created an even more animated atmosphere than usual. In fact many people, apart from myself, were in a state of some confusion. I heard several references to 'other arrests' and presumed that I would be joined shortly by all the former Rolls directors—which would at least give me someone to talk to. But the only person who was brought to the station that night was Arthur Sowley. Later my fingerprints were taken, but the constable who took them made an utter mess of the job. Whether he was nervous or simply a novice I do not know but he failed to roll my fingers properly across the paper and nearly every print was smudged. Detective Inspector Buck had to come along in person and took me through the whole performance again. He then noted a few biographical details for the record.

It was 10.30—two hours after my arrest—that David Freeman reached the police station with Michael Sherrard, a barrister who had been involved in various Rolls matters and who, soon afterwards, became a QC. They were both furious about my arrest since the police had told them that morning that there would be no developments. However it appeared that this had been the case when they rang and that the decision to arrest me had come later from a higher authority. I subsequently learned that it had been precipitated by the fact that questions were shortly to come up in the House of Commons

230

about the delay in dealing with my case. Michael Sherrard tried to get me released on bail that night but it was too late to get hold of a magistrate to hear the application. We therefore made all the necessary arrangements for an application the following morning at Bow Street and I stayed the night at West End Central. As Michael Sherrard left he said in a loud voice: 'This will be the first and last night that you will ever spend in custody.'

For the moment, however, I had to make the best of things. I was taken from the charge room and was put in a cell on my own with two men on a murder charge to one side of me. By this time many of my friends had got to know of my plight and sent books in to me. The Press also knew, having been told by New Scotland Yard who obviously had not been informed of Detective Inspector Edwards' assurance to me. They were besieging the station and probably stayed encamped outside all night while I read for a while and then went to sleep. In the morning I was given a cup of tea by a woman whom I had met at a police Christmas party but I declined her offer of grilled sausages. Soon afterwards a policeman came to say that the Press were clamouring to know what I had eaten for breakfast and would I please tell him? I told him and said: 'Why do they want to know? Is this the condemned cell? Is this my last meal?' The policeman shuffled off sheepishly.

At half past nine I and the other assorted prisoners of the night were herded to a Black Maria inside which we each had the doubtful luxury of a cell to ourselves for the trip to Bow Street magistrates court. As we climbed in the driver shouted: 'Any more for Butlins?' And added in a friendly way: 'Not quite a Rolls-Royce is it, Mr Bloom?' It certainly was not. The short trip was very jerky and uncomfortable. It was a pleasure to get out—even if it was only to be hauled before the magistrates.

My application for bail was successful with a personal surety of £75,000 and one from Anne's father for £10,000, with the court taking possession of my passport. Outside, of course, were the inevitable hordes of Press. To shield myself I put on my father-in-law's bowler hat which was a size or two too large

231

and I huddled into the back of his car. This explains the rather Dickensian figure I cut in the morning papers with my coat collar turned up, a bowler resting on my ears and my large sideboards protruding.

This was the picture that Anne saw in Spain when the papers reached there a day later. As I had not had any trouble over bail I had not wanted to spoil her holiday and still had not told her anything about my arrest. I had forgotten that she would be bound to read about it even in Spain. She rang me up immediately after recovering from the shock the news gave her, but I managed to convince her that no useful purpose would be served by her returning as I was not worried about the ultimate result.

Soon afterwards there was a flurry of arrests, and by the time the committal hearing began not only Sowley and I were involved but also Reader Harris, Al Palmer, Herbie Collins and Malcolm Cass. I was named in two indictments. The first one alleged, broadly speaking, that Sowley and I had falsely claimed that Electromatic's assets at the end of 1961 were £100,000 so that the company could be sold to Rolls in accordance with the option they had. In detail the four counts of the indictment accused us of conspiring to defraud Rolls by falsely pretending that Electromatic's assets at December 31st, 1961, were over £100,000; of omitting a purchase tax liability and contingent liability in December, 1961; of putting out a circular with intent to deceive Rolls shareholders which omitted to mention any such purchase tax liability and contingent liability; and of making or concurring in making a false entry in the EM Maintenance minute book.

The second indictment, claimed that, with intent to deceive shareholders, I made or concurred in making what I knew to be a statement of accounts—the Rolls balance sheet for 1963—which was false in certain respects. It also said that I recklessly made statements in a circular dated September 17th, 1963, which were misleading, false or deceptive in order to persuade people to buy shares in Bylock. There were further counts in this indictment involving the other people, but I was only concerned in one more count which alleged that I was knowingly

232

a party to the carrying on of the business of Bylock with intent to defraud creditors.

Like all the defendants I pleaded 'not guilty' to everything when the committal proceedings started on April 24th, 1968, at Victory House in Kingsway. This was not a courtroom but was sometimes used as such when cases involved a number of people and looked as though they would continue for some time. We used to start the day at 10 am and finish at 4 pm. As we settled down to a routine it became clear that the case would take a very long time and a somewhat informal atmosphere developed. This grew to such a stage that the defendants, all lined up at one side of the room, christened the hearing the Victory House Follies. After as few as two days I decided to bring in newspapers and books to read as Michael Sherrard, the other defendants' QCs and David Croom-Johnson, the prosecution QC, went about their business. Eventually, with my compulsory attendance hampering my night club business I took work into court also. At one point I took a large pile of membership cards in with me and Reader Harris and Arthur Sowley helped me to fill them in.

This did not mean that I was taking no interest in the proceedings when I was involved or when witnesses were being questioned. I frequently scribbled on pieces of paper questions that I thought Michael Sherrard might ask. And not only questions but jokes and comments on witnesses. I once gave Michael Sherrard a sheet of paper upon which I had written New British Government to Save the Country. As Prime Minister I put Sir Henry Benson; Minister of War, Sir Oswald Moseley; Board of Trade, Cyril Lord; Minister of Country's Health, (Dr) Douglas Bayle. As Minister of Productivity I had Marie Stopes to which Michael Sherrard added, punningly, 'at nothing'.

At lunch-time I used to meet Jane Goodbody, who was in charge of my personal secretarial affairs, and had a working snack. At first we went to the coffee bar next to Victory House but then we realised that it was being used by the police and the prosecution lawyers so we started to go to another place across the road. In the end, though, we got so used to going to Victory House that our return after every recess was like the first day of a new school term, with everyone greeting each other as long-lost friends. In such a confined space everyone from both sides were on chatting terms with each other. As Tom Edwards said shortly after my arrest: 'We're going to get tired of seeing each other before we've finished.' The only person with whom I was not on speaking terms was Croom-Johnson—but I even managed a few 'hellos' to him by the time the committal hearing finished.

It was January, 1969, before the hearing was complete. There had, of course, been breaks for holidays and illness, but even so, we had been in attendance for 115 days making it the longest committal hearing in the history of British justice. There had been 125 witnesses, 976 exhibits and 1,400 pages of evidence. The case against Al Palmer was dismissed and he was later awarded costs in the High Court. The rest of us were sent for trial to the Old Bailey.

The legal cost would have been astronomical if I had not sorted the whole question out with Michael Sherrard and David Freeman in November of 1968, half way through the hearing. Our negotiations had in fact started before the Victory House affair. So that I would know the money I was going to spend and could budget accordingly, I decided I would prefer to pay lump sums, irrespective of the length of the committal and the trial, rather than pay for the amount of work the legal people actually put in. If I was not committed for trial or if the trial itself was brief this, of course, would be to the advantage of the lawyers, but I was prepared to take that risk. It was therefore agreed that I would pay my solicitors £52,500, Michael Sherrard £27,500 and his junior, Mrs Irene Buckman, £5,000.

I was at ease throughout the Victory House follies largely because of a civil case arising out of the Rolls collapse which had ended before my arrest. In this case, through Quistclose, I was suing Rolls and Barclays Bank for the £209,719 which I had provided in July, 1964, to pay the shareholders' dividend. The dividend was never paid, of course, and Barclays thought they were entitled to keep the money—even though it had been paid into a special account—since Rolls had a £400,000-plus overdraft with them. When the case was considered by Mr Justice Plowman on February 17th, 1967, he ruled that I could not have the money back. I was depressed by this judgment because, coming after the Board of Trade inquiry, it only increased my feeling that the legal system was working against me. However I was persuaded reluctantly that I had a good chance of getting the Plowman decision reversed if the case went to the Court of Appeal. This was indeed so. On December 15th, Lord Justice Harman, Lord Justice Russell and Lord Justice Sachs decided that since Barclays had accepted the money from Rolls on the condition that it was to be used for a specific purpose and knowing that it was borrowed from Quistclose, this implied that if the dividend were not paid the money would go back to the lender. The money was therefore mine. This gave me a new faith in the impartiality of British justice and in a personal sense was the turning point of the legal proceedings.

The turning point as far as the law itself was concerned, came with another civil case in the summer of 1969—after the Victory House Follies but before the trial—which in fact had been postponed to make way for it. In this case, Rolls, through the liquidator, Kenneth Cork, were suing me for £306,904. The claim was based on the Board of Trade report; there had been no independent investigation. Broadly speaking the money was claimed because of alleged breaches of warranty in the contract I had made with Rolls for their purchase of Electromatic. But after a 30-day hearing Mr Justice Fisher threw out four out of the five allegations—that I was liable for alleged breaches in respect of servicing washing machines, advertising, stock and bad debts. He did however find that I was liable for non-disclosure of Electromatic's possible purchase tax liability and that I should therefore pay into court £51,194. Even so the effective result was to tear to shreds the first indictment that I was facing at the Old Bailey. The prosecution could not really hope to succeed with an indictment based on allegations which had been well and truly squashed by a High Court judge.

I got together with Michael Sherrard and David Freeman in the autumn of 1969 as the date of the trial approached. In a lengthy meeting we worked out the pros and cons of the trial and formulated our strategy. Bearing in mind Mr Justice Fisher's judgment, we felt that, on the facts of the case I should win on both indictments if it were being tried on pure law by a judge alone. However a jury was involved at the Old Bailey, a jury who would probably not be able to follow the legal and financial complexities of the case and, because of the large sums of money involved, would probably be prejudiced against me. Yet Michael Sherrard considered that the judge, Judge Bernard Gillis, would leave the case to the jury rather than withdraw it from them. But he advised me that if I pleaded guilty to the two charges in the second indictment, concerning the Bylock circular and the 1963 accounts, then he was confident that the penalty would be largely financial rather than custodial. These charges were largely technical since, although I had to accept ultimate responsibility as managing director of the company, I had played very little part in them. Rather than face a trial which might last two years I agreed to plead guilty. But all the charges on the first indictment I insisted on fighting to the end.

The first Rolls case, for which the Press had been waiting with bated breath, was on the first indictment and so concerned only Sowley and me. It first came to the Old Bailey on September 24th when Croom-Johnson sought leave from Judge Gillis to add a fifth charge to the indictment, in which it was alleged that with intent to defraud we had omitted advertising bills from the Electromatic accounts. I sat at the solicitors' table in the well of the court while Croom-Johnson, in order to tell the judge why the extra charge was being introduced, outlined his case—that by inflating the assets of Electromatic I had acquired 1,140,000 Rolls shares too many thus, allegedly, gaining over £1 million. His application and his case was strongly opposed by Michael Sherrard who recalled that the liquidator had claimed £300,000 on six grounds and had failed in all but one. He said: 'It is an abuse of this court and oppressive to Mr Bloom for the prosecution to invite a jury to say it is satisfied beyond all reasonable doubt that the finding of fact and law by Mr Justice Fisher was wrong. I do not like to use the words

236

"witch hunt", but one of the charges against Mr Bloom seems to say: "You may not be a witch but we have found in your kitchen some twigs which might be made into a broomstick and so we shall charge you with being in illicit possession of them".' He also pointed out the inaccuracy of Croom-Johnson's claim that the shares I had from selling Electromatic were the founding of my fortune. I, of course, already held 1,400,000 Rolls shares at the time of the sale. He also made references to my name being smeared before I came to trial and these references were illustrated dramatically that same day when early editions of the *London Evening Standard*, getting the wrong end of the stick, put up as the front page headline: *Bloom accused of £1 m Fraud*. Michael Sherrard drew the judge's attention to this and both he and the judge appealed to newspapers to take care. The *Evening Standard* changed its headlines for late editions but the effect on potential jurors could only be guessed at. The Press had done it again. Despite the warning, however, the *Daily Telegraph* the following morning had an inside page lead story headlined: *Bloom Accused of Inflating Value of his Company by £1 m*. This, of course, was again totally wrong. What the prosecution alleged was that Electromatic was worth some £43,000 at the material time instead of £100,000—a difference of £57,000, not £1 million.

On the third day of the hearing, September 26th, Judge Gillis ruled that the additional charge could be introduced and so, on the day fixed for the trial proper, October 2nd, I faced a total of eight charges. However the day was a major anti-climax. Crammed into No 1 court were 180 potential jurors to give ample scope to Michael Sherrard's declared intention of having a jury who were as highly intelligent as possible. They filled up the rows behind the dock, overflowed into the benches behind the barristers' seats and there were still some over who had to stand at the back of the court. But all they heard was an application from Croom-Johnson that the case should be delayed for a week. He told the judge that there were 1,280 papers, plus 2,000 pages of documentary exhibits and 600 pages of minutes among the evidence. He, Michael Sherrard and William Grieve, Sowley's QC, had been trying to sift through them to reduce the amount and at the last minute had found they were unable to finish their labours in time. All the QCs pointed out that although a week would be lost it would mean a saving of several weeks later in the trial—which was expected to last four months on the first indictment and seven on the second. After 15 minutes, the judge, mentioning the consequent saving of public money, agreed to a week's adjournment. Sowley and I had our bail renewed and stepped down from the dock without having been asked how we pleaded. The 180 jurors, each able to claim £3 5s allowance, went home.

A week later, on Thursday October 9th, the packed courtroom scene was repeated, except that this time Sowley and I were asked how we pleaded. We pleaded not guilty to all the charges in the first indictment. Then Michael Sherrard caused a stir in the courtroom by asking the second indictment to be read in so far as it affected me. When I pleaded guilty to the Bylock circular and 1963 accounts charges it caused a sensation with reporters rushing out to telephone their papers. Arthur Sowley, who had stood down since he did not wish to plead to the second indictment at that time, was granted bail and simply went home.

Croom-Johnson explained to Judge Gillis that he had been given 'some advance notification' that I might be pleading guilty to two charges and so he had already consulted the DPP, Sir Norman Skelhorne, who was actually in court, and was therefore able to say that the prosecution would accept the pleas and would offer no evidence on the first indictment either against myself or Sowley. The result would mean a saving of between £300,000 and £500,000 in public money. Judge Gillis said : 'I am fully satisfied that it is in the interests of justice that the pleas as tendered should be accepted.' But he added : 'While the court has realised that this will necessarily involve a saving of time and a saving of expense, it must be fully understood that these considerations have played no part in the conclusions to which the court has arrived.' Having studied all the documents in advance and acquainted himself with the case he was fully able to make such a decision without hearing a detailed exposition from Croom-Johnson. The 180 potential jurymen were again sent home.

Nevertheless Croom-Johnson outlined what would have been the prosecution's case and was just getting into his stride at the time of the lunch adjournment. I went down to the cells for the first time and, as arranged, some special food was brought in as a more palatable substitute for the official fodder. However I was told that having pleaded guilty I was now regarded as a convicted person entitled to no such special treatment. It was only after some discussions among Old Bailey officials that I was allowed to have my food as a special privilege. Back in the dock after lunch I listened to Croom-Johnson yet again until he finished his address by reminding the judge of section 188 of the Companies' Act which entitles the court, in the case of someone in my position at Rolls, to disqualify him from being a director or manager of a company.

After Tom Edwards, by that time a Detective Chief Inspector, had given biographical details about me, Michael Sherrard rose to make his plea in mitigation. Tom Edwards had already stressed the amount of strain there had been on me during the committal proceedings and that I had at one time suffered from nervous exhaustion. Michael Sherrard stressed the further strain on someone in my position who, for all public purposes, had to say nothing about the affair until it came to the Old Bailey. He went on: 'I venture to think that when the general public becomes aware of the truth behind the rise and fall of the Rolls Razor empire and John Bloom, suspicion and rumour will be exposed and destroyed and feelings of pity and understanding will take their place.... When the facts as opposed to the rumours are examined and when the man as opposed to the image is understood, it will not only be possible but right in the interests of justice, in the interests of the public, in the interests of Bloom himself, not to impose upon him a sentence of imprisonment.'

He emphasised that I was not one of those 'parasitical company directors who lived off the fat of his company', that the yacht and the plane were mine and were available for the company and that I bore 80 per cent of the costs and expenses of

239

the flat. He also pointed out that if it had not been for Rolls 'thousands of women today would be up to the elbows in soapsuds every Monday'.

Perhaps the most important factor, he said, was that the millions that I had had all disappeared in the crash. 'There are no millions hidden beneath any bed,' he said. 'There are no Swiss banks; there are no safe deposits; there are no assets outside the country.' And as Counsel's time ran out for the day he told Judge Gillis: 'It will be my unhappy task to relate to your Lordship in a little detail the way in which one expert accountant after another, one adviser after another, by what can only be described as monumental neglect, prevented the building of safe financial foundations for the Rolls empire and Bloom's own fortune.' In 1964, he concluded, I had been 'trapped in a morass of incompetence'.

When the hearing was adjourned I was again taken down to the cells. I had expected perhaps to spend the night in Brixton remand prison, which would have meant keeping my own clothes. But, as with lunch, I was now, according to Home Office regulations, regarded as a convicted person and was told I would be spending the night in Wandsworth. After a quick cup of tea I went to the Old Bailey jailer who took charge of effects such as my ring, cuff links and electric shaver, but as a concession I was told I would be allowed to have them all back for my court appearance the next day. After this, in a bit of a daze, I was handcuffed to another man and we clambered with others in one of the green vans which take people to Brixton and then to Wandsworth and in the mornings does the return trip. The fellow to whom I was handcuffed said: 'Aren't you John Bloom?' So I explained the situation and asked about him. He said he'd been 'in a bit of a fight'. I later learned that he was in an affray case and was on a murder charge. But I was glad to learn later that he had been acquitted.

It was about 8.30 when we reached Wandsworth. In an area known, presumably laughingly, as Reception I was put in a cell like a horsebox with a fellow who had just been given three years for armed robbery. I gave him the sausage roll which we had each been given. After waiting some time in the horsebox

I was moved to a room where I had to get out of my civvies and was then supposed to go into an adjoining room for a cleansing bath. But the tiles were so chipped and the whole room so uninviting that I walked straight through into yet another room where I put on my allotted prison clothes—a striped shirt and dungarees. From there it was into the medical centre where everyone tried to be as pleasant as they could. Several of the other prisoners brought me my blankets and other equipment and the warders made jokes such as 'See you soon in the prison laundry'. At a quarter to eleven we were taken out into a brilliantly-lit courtyard that seemed alive with large dogs and I was taken to a wing where there were individual cells. I made my bed and sat on it. The only other things in the room were a small table, a chair, and a venerable wrinkled orange. My reading matter was my prayer book which I was allowed to have with me—although I had been forced to leave several other books at the Old Bailey—and a set of prison regulations defaced by someone with a ribald sense of humour. Somehow, although I was naturally nervous about Judge Gillis' judgment the following day, I went to sleep.

I was wakened at six the next morning and taken down to the horsebox, where this time I was alone, and given a breakfast of tea and a boiled egg. Then I was given back my civvy clothes and told to leave my prison clothes on the seat along with my name. This, I was told, is to make them easy to find when prisoners return to start their sentences! To add to that gloomy information another prisoner, who was due to return to the Old Bailey, told me that the Wandsworth inmates were betting 4 to 1 on that I would be given a prison sentence. But despite all this I was still hopeful as I climbed into the green van.

I was handcuffed to a fellow on a fraud charge. They took the handcuffs off at Brixton where we picked up some more victims and then immediately put on another pair. The ways of the authorities are strange. At the Old Bailey I was chained to my comrade for another hour until it was time to take my place again in the dock—with the public gallery crammed full, and everyone but me, it seemed, feeling clean, well-rested and fresh for the day's events.

After Michael Sherrard had recounted the failings of various former colleagues over the years, he again stressed the psychological turmoil of the years of inquiries—pointing out the intriguing fact that answers given to the Board of Trade inspectors only became usable as evidence under the Companies Act of 1967. He said that if Maurice Finer and Sir Henry Benson had known that my answers of 1964 and 1965 would be used as evidence 'they would not have harried Mr Bloom as they did'. Yet the fact remained that the answers I gave under those circumstances became admissible through an Act which at the time had hardly even been thought of.

Certainly, after my night at Wandsworth, Michael Sherrard was able to assure the judge that if I avoided a jail sentence I would know only too well what I was avoiding. He concluded his plea by quoting the final verse of Coleridge's poem, *The Ancient Mariner*:

> He went like one that hath been stunned,
> And is of sense forlorn.
> A sadder and a wiser man,
> He rose the following morn.

The tension grew noticeably in the court as Judge Gillis started his summing up. He said he was taking into account my youth, lack of commercial training and experience and that I tried, albeit in vain, to surround myself with the best possible advisers. He was also impressed by my attempts to help financially people who had suffered from the Rolls collapse. He therefore fined me £20,000 on the 1963 accounts count and £10,000 over the Bylock circular. I was also barred from holding office in a public company for five years. But there was no prison sentence. I have never felt such a sense of relief. By the time I had recovered, the last few formalities were over and I was led down to the cells to get back my few belongings from the jailer.

I went straight back up to the courtroom where I was greeted by friends and lawyers and then went outside to a car which I had waiting. I was, of course, besieged by the ever-present Press who trailed me to the flat in Hyde Park Square which I had taken when the lease at Aldford House expired. There I met a jubilant Anne who had not dared to attend the trial but who had heard the result over the phone. We posed for endless photographs then went for a walk in Hyde Park with Poncho the chihuahua. It was good to taste the clean air of liberty.

22

MY FINES WERE VIRTUALLY THE SOLE RESULT OF THE WHOLE legal process—which, considering the fact that it took almost six years and cost the taxpayer more than half a million pounds, surely made it a gigantic waste of both time and money.

In March, 1970, my brother-in-law Herbie was fined £5,000 for concurring in a false balance sheet with intent to deceive shareholders, and, on the same charge and at the same time, Arthur Sowley was fined £500. It made me wonder whether the English legal system does not take too much notice of people's means before fining them.

But when the much-awaited trial of Reader Harris and my brother-in-law Malcolm Cass came up, the prosecution case was at last revealed as the flimsy edifice it was. It was on May 29th that an Old Bailey jury found Reader Harris not guilty of concurring in making a statement, with intent to deceive shareholders, in the company's balance sheets which he knew to be false. Earlier in the trial, at the close of the prosecution's case, Mr Justice MacKenna withdrew two charges from the jury: that Reader Harris carried on the business of Bylock between 1963 and 1964 with intent to defraud the company's creditors, and attempted to induce people to subscribe for shares in the company by the reckless making of statements in a circular which were misleading, false or deceptive. A week later Malcolm was acquitted of the two charges against him—relating to the 1963 balance sheet and the Bylock circular. Both Reader

Harris and Malcolm were awarded legal costs.

The important point about this final trial is that they were both cleared of the self-same charges for which I was fined a total of £30,000. The difference between their trial and mine was that theirs was presided over by Mr Justice MacKenna—a man who is very experienced in understanding the complexities of commercial cases. He was sitting in the Old Bailey as a 'Red Judge'—that is, a High Court judge who is hearing a case at an assize court. He really tore into the prosecution's case.

In effect, the judge told the jury that the whole of the prosecution case was based on a false premise. In summing up in Malcolm's case on June 8th and 9th he demonstrated that neither the Bylock circular nor the 1963 balance sheet were misleading, false or deceptive in the first place. Therefore in neither instance could there be any question of anyone intending to mislead shareholders and—the crucial point—the whole question of whether A B or C was guilty of concurring in making them became null and void. The prosecution failed to make first base. The jury could hardly fail to acquit.

One key point which the judge drove home was that the prosecution were not necessarily to be believed merely because they were the prosecution. Referring to a speech by Croom-Johnson, for the prosecution, the judge told the jurors: 'Mr Croom-Johnson explained his conception of the function of counsel for the prosecution, of counsel for the defence and of the judge. And he would have you believe that there is a difference between counsel who prosecutes and counsel who defends—that prosecuting counsel is, as it were, a priest in the temple of justice, impartial, detached and indifferent, while defending counsel strives eagerly for victory. Whether this distinction is right here and, if it is, whether the theory is always observed in practice are doubtful questions which I do not mean to pursue.' However, the judge returned to this theme in almost the last words he addressed to the jury before they went to deliberate their verdict. He said: 'Do not give more weight to Mr Croom-Johnson's arguments on the theory that they have been advanced by somebody who is impartial and detached.'

Mr Justice MacKenna also made some important and interesting observations to the jury on the subject of conflicting evidence. He commented: 'It is no fault of the accused (in this case Malcolm) that there has been this long delay in bringing their case before a jury. Because of that delay many of the witnesses have forgotten the details of conversations and discussions which took place six or seven years ago.' Therefore, he went on, where there was a conflict of evidence, the jury would, he was sure, 'think it right ... to act on the evidence of the accused when he says he remembers, unless you have some convincing reason to doubt its truth. You must not allow the long delay—I would say the shameful long delay—to tell against Mr Cass. That would be very unfair to him.' I wish that this had been the view of the bench right from the beginning of the Rolls Razor courts marathon.

On the charge relating to the Bylock circular, the prosecution claimed the document was misleading, false or deceptive at eleven points. The judge threw, to put it mildly, grave doubt upon the validity of every one of the prosecution's arguments. As an example, in dealing with the prosecution's complaint over the statement that the circular was based on 'internal unaudited accounts'—a phrase which had been the subject of bitter argument since the time of the Board of Trade inquiry—the judge asked the jury: 'Would it have made the slightest difference to any shareholder's mind if the first sentence ... had read "Based on an internal interim account ..."?' The obvious answer to that clearly made nonsense of the prosecution's claim.

More generally, the judge forcibly made the point which Michael Sherrard had made on my behalf before the magistrate and at the Old Bailey but which had never been accepted. Mr Justice MacKenna said: 'Those principally responsible for the drafting of the document (the circular) were Mr Brooks of Kleinwort Benson and Mr Norton, a partner in Norton Rose, Bylock's solicitors. It is recognised that the drafting of such a document is a job for professionals, that is, for merchant bankers and lawyers. They are experts, and they know the requirements in such matters. That is not the sort of knowledge usually possessed by their clients, that is, by companies who employ their services or by those companies' directors.' Surely this point was especially valid in my case; not only did I leave the circular to the experts, I never at any time attended a meeting at which its contents were discussed!

The prosecution case on the 1963 accounts hinged on the allegation that in order to enable Rolls to pay the promised 120 per cent dividend, a false figure of £213,618 appeared on the balance sheet as the value to Rolls of its shares in Bylock and its subsidiaries. The principal point here was that the accounts had been fully approved by Price Waterhouse. I was fined for voting for the adoption of the accounts, but in Malcolm's case, Mr Justice MacKenna left the jury in little doubt as to the way they should look at the matter. He told them: 'It is right to say, as has been suggested so often during this case, that it is the directors of the company who are responsible for the accounts, responsible to the shareholders. If they know that the accounts are wrong, that they do not give a true and fair view of the company's affairs, they cannot shelter behind their own accountants, or the company's auditors, or anybody else. But if the directors believe that the accounts give that true and fair view, they are not to be blamed—at least in a criminal court— if it turned out afterwards that their belief was mistaken. Forming that belief, he, a director, is obviously entitled to give weight, great weight it may be, to the undoubted fact, as in the present case, that the accounts were put before him with the approval of the company's own accountants and its auditors.'

For the prosecution, A. W. Brookland, the Board of Trade inquiry secretary (and one of the partners, with Sir Henry Benson, in the accountancy firm of Cooper Brothers) told the court that if he had been the auditor he would have put the value of Bylock as nil. This piece of evidence was intended to show that the figure which appeared in the accounts was therefore manifestly fraudulent. The judge negatived the effect of this evidence by stressing to the jury that 'Mr Brookland was not the auditor to Rolls Razor in 1964, and his views on this matter are being expressed here for the first time, at least to Mr Cass, in 1970.' The judge went on to explain what he considered to be the flaw in Brookland's assessment of the value of Bylock: 'It

247

has been said against Mr Brookland's approach that he gives no sufficient value to the protection which Bylock gave to Rolls Razor as a source of supply of electric motors. Even though that production fell short of the supplying of the whole of Rolls Razor's requirements, it did protect that company against the risk—the real risk as it seemed to its directors—of supplies being stopped by other manufacturers. If those other manufacturers knew that they could not break Rolls by stopping their supplies because Bylock was there to take their place if necessary, then they would have no inducement to stop them. Ownership of Bylock, it is said, was an insurance against disaster. Insurance costs money, and has a value with the insured person, and to say that no other supplier did stop supplies, except Hoovers, does not meet this argument, or so it seems to me. A policy of insurance is a valuable asset even if no burglar comes. Perhaps that analogy does not put the case strongly enough. It may be a better analogy would be a burglar alarm whose existence is known to the burglars in the district and it keeps them away. Nobody could say the alarm was not worth much because the burglars did not come.'

Finally, on the claim that Rolls was clearly in no position to pay the 120 per cent dividend since it had to borrow from me to do so—a point much used in the prosecution argument against Herbie Collins and others—Mr Justice MacKenna commented: 'This has no bearing whatever on the right to pay the dividend. A company which has earned profits and spent them in some other way is still entitled to pay the dividend, using borrowed money for the purpose.'

From what the judge said it seemed to me absolutely certain that if my own case had come on last, following his comments, I would never have been fined at all. As it was, the epitaph was well written by Peter Gladstone in the *Sunday Telegraph* of June 14th: 'Never has an investigation continued for so long at so much expense to expose so little guilt.'

The only other point worthy of mention is a question which has puzzled me: Why, in view of the allegations against the Jacobs brothers in the Board of Trade report and their positions in the company, were they not lined up with the rest of us to face the charges thrown our way and why were they never even interviewed by the police? Equally, why were Herbert Collins and Malcolm Cass prosecuted? Could it have been primarily because they are my brothers-in-law?

People have commented that it does not matter whether I was fined rightly or wrongly since I had plenty of money. Leaving aside the quality of justice implicit in this theory, it is based on a total misconception about the state of my finances. Although it is true that I had money at the end of 1963 this had more or less evaporated on the crash of Rolls and my expenses since then have been enormous. Here, for instance, are my assets and liabilities on July 17th, 1964, compared with December 31st, 1963:

Assets

December 31st, 1963 £		July 17th, 1964 £
775,468	Rolls ordinary shares of 1s	22,254
2,410,700	E & O ordinary shares of 2s	142,294
1,821,600	E & O unsecured loan notes	—
442,480	Pressed Steel ordinary shares of 5s	1,070
614,888	Bank balances	721,806
10,000	Investments in Quistclose group	10,000
427,790	Other investments at cost	495,328
337,000	Yachts	337,000
—	Aeroplane	15,000
6,839,926	total	1,744,752

Liabilities

202,522	Anglo-Portuguese Bank overdraft	204,454
	Amount due to:	
107,605	Rolls	60,818
60,517	E & O	69,754
—	Unifinance	277,349
92,425	Pryers	97,800
100,000	My sister Noreen	100,000

December 31, 1963		July 17, 1964
£		£
375,346	The Jackson estate	263,494
26,363	Brokers, solicitors and other accounts	31,000
79,000	Tax liabilities	79,000
—	Personal guarantees payable on Rolls failure	130,000
1,043,778	total	1,313,669

In other words, I had £5,796,148 at the start of 1964 which melted away to £431,083 because of the crash.

I later received £227,368 as a result of the Quistclose case but I lost a further £83,000 on E and O shares and £75,000 on other investments. On top of this, between the Rolls crash and my Old Bailey trial, Anne and I had the following major expenditure: £15,000 on accountants; £111,000 on guarantees; £19,500 on abortive business ventures; £96,000 on the criminal case; £13,000 on the Board of Trade inquiry legal costs; £59,000 on other legal matters; £10,000 on insuring the yacht until it was sold; £8,500 on maintaining the yacht; £23,000 on compensating ex-employees for loss of job; £10,000 on business expenses and travel; £2,000 on telephone bills; £3,000 for the Aldford House flat, the lease of which I took over; £10,000 on rent and rates; £5,000 on secretarial expenses; £3,600 on compensating people for losses on shares; £17,500 lost on sundry shares and £20,000 on miscellaneous expenses. From this it is easy to see that my financial position was not all that rosy at the time that I was fined.

However the club business kept growing throughout this period. In January, 1969, Anne and I linked up with G and W Automatics who ran the thriving 800 Club in Leicester Square. In the night club group that was thereby formed I acted as general manager, but just before Christmas of the same year Anne and I decided that we would rather do things on our own and so we unscrambled the arrangement by buying back our shares in the other company and selling back their shares in our company.

Since the beginning of 1970 I have been using a direct mail

campaign to bring night clubs to the working man all over Britain by making membership only £1 a year for all the clubs —which enables them to visit the clubs and benefit from the entertainment without having to spend another penny if they do not want to.

At the time of Malcolm's acquittal, Anne and I, through Sylron Investments, had seven clubs either operating or in the process of being opened—including 'Rasputin's' and, of course, the 'Crazy Horse'. One of the new ones was the '1520 AD' in St Martin's Lane which has an eight-course banquet served by wenches in the style of the court of Henry VIII, with entertainment by wrestlers, minstrels and tumblers. On the upper floor there is a change of period with the Roman Room, where diners can sit on Roman-style couches and watch gladiatorial contests.

As other clubs and discotheques fade for lack of revitalising ideas I examine them to see whether they are worth buying to add to our club complex. This, I feel is where people's increasingly sophisticated leisure tastes are leading. And my future lies in catering for them.